Psychology and Education

Parallel and Interactive Approaches

Psychology and Education

Parallel and Interactive Approaches

Joseph M. Notterman

and

Henry N. Drewry

Princeton University
Princeton, New Jersey

Plenum Press • *New York and London*

Library of Congress Cataloging in Publication Data

Notterman, Joseph M.
    Psychology and education: parallel and interactive approaches / Joseph M. Notter-
man and Henry N. Drewry.
      p.   cm.
    Includes bibliographical references and index.
    ISBN 0-306-44364-3
    1. Educational psychology. 2. Learning, Psychology of. 3. Teaching. I. Drewry, Henry
N., 1924–   II. Title.
LB1051.N65 1993
370.15—dc20   93-1257
                                                  CIP

ISBN 0-306-44364-3

© 1993 Plenum Press, New York
A Division of Plenum Publishing Corporation
233 Spring Street, New York, N.Y. 10013

Printed in the United States of America

For Gabriel, Benjamin, and Arielle, my grandchildren,
and for Rebecca, their grandmother
JMN

For Leonard E. Drewry and Bessie Boyd Drewry, my parents,
both of whom were excellent teachers
HND

Preface

One of us (JMN) first became interested in writing a text in educational psychology when he was asked to teach this course at Princeton University in the mid-1980s. The other (HND) was—during the same period—Director of the Teacher Preparation Program at the same institution; he is now Program Associate at the Mellon Foundation in New York. We both felt that there was a need for a text that challenged the student and that had a decent respect for the historical evolution of different positions in psychology and education. We also agreed philosophically with William James that education is not the child of psychology. The two disciplines are on their best terms with each other when they are just good friends. Thus, although good friends pursue independent paths, they reach out to each other for basic information and advice, as each feels necessary. Hence the title of our book, *Psychology and Education: Parallel and Interactive Approaches*. We hold that psychological principles are of fundamental importance to pedagogical practice, but teaching hardly consists of the mere application of these principles. Teaching is a practice or art that possesses its own understandings.

This lesson was brought home to JMN when he had the good fortune to spend a sabbatical as a senior fellow at the Department of Education's Office of Educational Research and Improvement (OERI). He gained respect for the professionalization of the educators, psychologists, researchers, and staff workers at that office. For his part, HND never lost confidence that educators could concurrently be both good teachers and good scholars. One just has to create the necessary conditions to attract such people and encourage them to do what they want to do—teach and learn! That was his and JMN's position when the two agreed to work together on this book, and remains so today.

We acknowledge with thanks the helpful comments of Stephen L. Benton, Kansas State University; Ron Pedone and Arthur Sheekey, OERI; William Printzmetal, University of California at Berkeley; Daniel N. Robinson, Georgetown University; and Benjamin B. Wolman, Editor-in-Chief, *International Encyclopedia of Psychology, Psychiatry, Psychoanalysis, and Neurology*. We are also appreciative of the suggestions made by two former assistants in the educational psychology course at Princeton, Stephen Winshel and Ute Fisher. Above all, our thanks go out to the many undergraduates who offered solicited (and unsolicited!) comments on the manuscript as it took form over several years. By now, they are far too numerous to mention by name. We must, however, single out Joel Hektner, Princeton Class of 1990, for his laudatory work as our manuscript research assistant during 1989–1990.

We are grateful to Columbia University Press for permission to reproduce for historical background portions of Chapters 3–9, *Forms of Psychological Inquiry* (1985), by Joseph M. Notterman. We are indebted to the staff at Princeton who turned the manuscript into a finished product: Arlene Kronewitter (in charge), Marion Kowalewski, Theresa Mizenko, and Elaine Bacsik. Joseph Pylka, Denise Evans, and Joshua Fost, who were responsible for preparation of the figures, did as professional a job as possible. Mary Chaiken (in charge) and Linda Chamberlain assisted materially with reference searches.

Finally, we wish to express our appreciation to Eliot Werner, executive editor at Plenum Publishing Corporation, and to Robert Freire, production editor, for turning our manuscript into a finished work. Their technical competence, sense of balance, and personal courtesy are a credit to the publishing field.

Contents

I

Preliminary Considerations

What Is Educational Psychology?

The general aims of Part I, Preliminary Considerations, are first, to set definitional limits on what is meant by "educational psychology" (Chapter 1), and second, to consider through some international comparisons the particular values that have influenced education in the United States since the founding of the nation (Chapter 2). In this opening chapter, we briefly and specifically deal with the problems inherent in describing the relations between psychology and education. That there *are* relations, few doubt. The issue comes down to one of consensus—agreement on those paradigms of psychology and of education that are of value to the schoolteacher. Since there are many kinds of psychology, and many types of education, constraints have to be set.

"PSYCHOLOGY IS A SCIENCE, AND TEACHING IS AN ART"—JAMES

It would be so convenient to combine both logic and common sense, and to define our subject matter simply as follows: *Educational psychology* is that specialty of general psychology which is concerned with the identification of principles directly relevant to teaching and learning. And stop right there. However, a significant caveat must be issued: The definition should not be taken to imply that instruction and learning are pure *applications* of psychological theory. William James observed in his highly useful *Talks to Teachers on Psychology*:

> You make a great, a very great mistake, if you think that psychology, being the science of the mind's laws, is something from which you can deduce definite programmes and schemes and methods of instruction for immediate schoolroom use. Psychology is a science, and teaching is an art [skill]; and sciences never generate arts directly out of themselves. An intermediary inventive mind [i.e., the teacher's] must make the application, by using its originality. (1958, pp. 23–24)

James gave these "talks" to the teachers of Cambridge upon the invitation of Harvard's board of overseers. He was by that time (1892) an internationally renowned psychologist. (Although he obtained an M.D. in 1869, he never practiced.) His two-volume *Principles of Psychology* was the most definitive work in the field. Notwithstanding, his views concerning the possible contributions of psychology to education were presented without exaggeration. He said:

> It is only the fundamental conceptions of psychology which are of real value to the teacher; and they . . . are very far from being new. . . . A science only lays down lines within which the rules of the art must fall, laws which the follower of the art must not transgress; but what particular thing he shall positively do within those lines is left exclusively to his own genius . . . [T]eaching must *agree* with the psychology, but need not necessarily be the only kind of teaching that would so agree; for many diverse methods of teaching may equally well agree with psychological laws.
>
> To know psychology, therefore, is absolutely no guarantee that we shall be good teachers. To advance to that result, we must have an additional endowment altogether, a happy tact and ingenuity to tell us what definite things to say and do when the pupil is before us. (pp. 23–24)

Despite his cautionary note concerning "guarantees" (or *sufficiencies*), he implied that a knowledge of psychology was *necessary* to excellence in teaching. He said: "Education, in short, cannot be better described than by calling it *the organization of acquired habits and tendencies to behavior*" (emphasis in original, pp. 36–37). Much of his *Talks* is devoted to a description of the required underlying psychological principles, quite broadly conceived. Indeed, some of his chapter titles could easily be included in the table of contents of a modern psychology textbook: "The Laws of Habit," "The Association of Ideas," "Attention," and "Memory," among others.

Inductive and Deductive Sources of the Teaching Method—Bain

In his *Education as a Science* (1891), Alexander Bain, too, wrote of the need to combine actual experience with theory.He made crystal clear that skill in teaching is not reducible to the utilization of scientific laws:

The Teaching Method is arrived at in various ways. One principal mode is experience of the work; this is the inductive or practical source. Another mode is deduction from the laws of the human mind; this is the deductive or theoretical source. The third and best mode is to combine the two; to rectify empirical teaching by principles, and to qualify deductions from principles by practical experience. (p. 230)

"The Psychologist's Fallacy"

Surely Bain's words are still meaningful a century later. His recommendation helps us to avoid what James termed "the psychologist's fallacy." This is the tendency to develop a hypothesis, and then to confine research only to the hypothesis advanced. If further thought or investigation is thereby excluded, we fall victim to the fallacy of working within a single paradigm, when other more appropriate ones should be explored. By combining theory with experience, we challenge preconceptions of what constitutes "proper" research. This point has been driven home in modern times by Kuhn (*The Structure of Scientific Revolutions*, 1970).

The Proper Concern of Educational Psychology

In a contributed chapter entitled "Content and Boundaries of Educational Psychology" (Mathis, Menges, & McMillan, 1977), the authors addressed the difficulty of defining educational psychology. They concluded that educational psychology is best considered as the *interaction* of basic knowledge (mainly behavioral sciences) × process of education (formal and informal learning) × research methods (theoretical and practical). It is as the suggested interaction (one that is multiplicative, not additive) that educational psychology attains unitary status.

CONSTRAINTS ON WHAT IS ENGAGED IN THE BOOK

We shall comment further on the relations between education and psychology as we go through the book in its entirety. Our present goal is to set reasonable constraints on what we mean to engage. First, we have intentionally sought to be parallelists (i.e., respectful of the identities of each field) in our treatment of education and psychology, at least as a start. We want to control any tendency to engage in masterminding. Where interactions between the two fields are plausible, we are glad to bring together practice with theory. Second, we have deliberately sought to exclude as much as possible accounts of research findings that are irrelevant to our selection of key topics. We do not mean to imply that research is unimportant. To the contrary, we want to emphasize those findings that are relevant to our selection, and thereby avoid blurring these issues by covering matters that are better treated in other works.

PSYCHOLOGICAL THEORY AND EDUCATIONAL FACTORS

It is unquestionably reasonable that for those who teach, included in the grasp of what the process involves should be a sound knowledge about psychological theory and its implications for the teaching–learning process. On this basis, psychology is required as part of the professional education sequence in all college and university teacher-training programs. Our own work includes a broad range of psychological fact and theory, which we believe to be both of immediate and lasting value to the prospective teacher. We have deliberately sought to present diverse aspects of psychology, for we believe that every approach is important, especially when presented in the context of psychology's historical evolution. A glance at the chapter titles comprising Part II of this book, "Psychological Viewpoints and Related Paradigms of Learning," indicates the sequence of psychological topics covered: functionalism, associationism, classical conditioning, behaviorism, gestalt psychology, psychoanalysis, and cognitive psychology. Connections are made, as appropriate to educational matters. These connections are made both in the sense of providing supporting platforms, as well as in indicating concrete examples (Part III).

Consensual experience and the observation of teachers by persons long in the field suggest the following pattern of professional involvement with psychology.

PATTERN OF PROFESSIONAL INVOLVEMENT WITH PSYCHOLOGY

Step 1. Setting psychology aside. In the initial phase of teaching, it is often the case that little or no conscious effort is made to apply psychological theory to one's teaching. The beginning professional views herself or himself to be under considerable pressure, with the result that classroom practices are shaped by a sense of immediacy and survival, and not through any deliberate attempt at psychological understanding. Many decisions made in planning and implementing lessons, and in class management are good and sound, but they are arrived at less by rational consideration of courses taken than by memories of the way one was taught and the kind of teaching one sees among one's new peers, and what seems to be "common sense."

Skillful mentors can assist in relating previous studies of psychology to the beginning activity of a new teacher, but even with expert assistance the theoretical basis for actions does not get the attention it deserves. It should be mentioned that some teachers are quite successful without progressing beyond this stage. There are many excellent teachers in independent schools, and a growing number in public schools, who have never taken psychology. These successes seem to take place most often when the new teacher's image of the way one should teach fits neatly with the student's idea of how he or she should be taught, as is more probably the case in demographically homogeneous private and public schools. Teachers at this level are likely to be most successful when their students' ideas about school are similar to the teacher's own school experience. Such teachers are likely to argue that educational psychology and other education courses are not necessary, and that all one needs is a solid education. They fail to suggest the crucial fact that in such cases, one also needs a cultural experience which is relatively close to that of all or the vast majority of one's students. When important differences exist or when variety exists among one's students, success at this level is difficult to attain unless one can make the uniqueness of learning in the classroom a common denominator (Floden, Buchman, & Schwille, 1987).

Step 2. Drawing upon psychology. A second phase begins for some as early as the middle of the first year. For others it begins later. If by the fourth year it has not begun, it is not likely to occur. In this phase, teachers develop a sense of security that their survival is no longer at stake. Their views expand as to what is possible through their teaching, and at this point they begin to draw on theoretical considerations from their college or university preparation, including a past course in educational psychology, as a basis for classroom activity. For those who are fortunate enough to engage in formal study at this point, if not earlier, it is likely that educational psychology and other educational theory have a major impact on what they teach and how they teach.

Step 3. Keeping abreast of psychological theory. Few successful teachers at or past midcareer appear to devote continued conscious attention to educational psychology. Some have sufficiently internalized findings from psychology or they have developed a sufficiently wide set of experiences on which to draw that, without continued attention to theory, they can call up a variety of appropriate strategies to use in different situations. Beginning teachers observing and admiring these experienced teachers often get the idea that theory is not part of their success, and the experienced teachers are sometimes unwilling or unable to identify earlier study and interest because of the casualness with which education courses are sometimes held. Those experienced teachers who—as Bain suggested—keep abreast of educational research and who continuously reevaluate their practices in light of new information from psychology, make up the small core of truly talented teachers who are not always recognized for their abilities. Unfortunately, because of prestige and/or financial factors, a number are seduced into administration, college work, or into some nonteaching activity within or outside education.

What do these observations and thoughts suggest about educational psychology and the preparation of teachers? They suggest that an undergraduate course or courses in the field are not likely at first to be used by many if not most new teachers, because as novices they are faced with the pressure related to planning and teaching which all beginners encounter. After this initial phase, however, prior undergraduate exposure to psychology can help materially to form the framework in which beginning teachers set their early teaching experiences, and on which they eventually draw for sources of information for professional growth. It further suggests two things: First, the desirability of further study of psychology by teachers after they have passed through the entry phase of the profession, and when they have had classroom experience as part of the perspective from which to consider what they study. For some, graduate study in education (including psychology) might be desirable before taking the first teaching position, but most teachers will gain more from graduate work and will have a better idea of how advanced study serves their needs if they have, as a minimum, one to three years' experience. Second, it suggests the desirability of increased attention on the part of teachers (and in this we include college or university teachers) to the structure and quality of their own teaching, and the extent to which it reflects the influence of psychological theory on educational practices. The foregoing considerations would suggest that they be taken into account by those educators responsible for inservice program development.

THE BOOK'S LIBERAL ARTS VIEWPOINT

Our view of the relations between education and psychology is such as to entertain the idea that not only can each benefit from the other, but that both can profit from drawing upon other disciplines, such as history, logic, philosophy, educational sociology, academic administration, computer science, creative expression, and so on. In this sense, our approach is liberal.

In a similar vein, Ripple (1981) argued in a paper entitled Educational Psychology as a Liberal Art: "that educational psychology has become one of the principal intellectual themes that have shaped and given substance to contemporary civilization. It does this through the substance of its inquiry into how human beings develop and learn" (p. 30). He foresees the time when a course in educational psychology is taken by persons not actively pursuing a career in teaching. For example, one need think only of the "teaching" roles of health-care professionals, nutritionists, clergymen, and a wide variety of supervisors for business and industry to see the possibilities for such an idea.

Such, then, is the structure of our enterprise. This initial chapter sets the tone of our work—a respect for both psychology and education, a welcoming tolerance of contributions from various disciplines and viewpoints, and an avoidance of trivializing the field of educational psychology through the accumulation of more and more factual but unrelated information.

As we write this, our hunch is that at the moment those concerned with teaching are presented with too many isolated facts in psychology and in education. Unfortunately, the harder the attempt is made to pull the facts together, the more artificial the product may become. Dewey's admonition that integrations occur, they are not made, is neglected. We do not think that it is necessary—or even possible—fully to integrate *both* psychology *and* education at the present point in time. The fields need some shaking-out. In psychology, the behaviorist revolution against introspective methodology has given way to the cognitive revolution. In between were the Freudian and the gestaltist schools. Already there are signs that the battle is not over. The strengths of each position shall invariably reemerge, and lead to evolution of a sounder psychology. In education, the public school movement is being criticized for not efficiently serving our democracy, as it originally was supposed to do. Our educational system is mediocre, despite the fact that our democratic institutions demand well-educated citizens. But here, too, we are hopeful; for a democratic society contains within itself the means of correction. In this regard, we cannot overemphasize that neither psychology nor education is isolated from the understandings of other disciplines, at least the ones we have already mentioned, as well as the opinions of the general population. If at times the reader becomes impatient with our wanderings into philosophy, cybernetics, psychoanalysis, sociology, and so on, we urge him or her to remember that many of the major contributions to both psychology and education have been made by persons in other fields. They have done so through their writings, and through their membership on various professional, governmental, and citizen boards or councils.

Hence this book; a collection of diverse ideas and research findings divided into parts and chapters. The assemblage involves exclusion of material as much as inclusion. We have called upon colleagues and students in education, psychology, and other endeavors to help us select the articles, essays, talks, and reports that are most conducive to constructive engagement.

By using various sources and by presenting various points of view grouped into coherent sections, we hope to encourage the kind of intellectual reflections and challenges that qualify as liberal education.

The Quality of United States Schools

An International Comparison with Attention to Values

The general objective of this chapter is to suggest dimensions along which United States schools may be compared with those of other nations. We begin by focusing first upon American schools. But even at the outset, we find it essential to glance briefly at other countries, if only to provide the background minimally necessary for any comparative description. As we become more accustomed to the criteria used in conducting the inquiry, we return to describe more thoroughly how international systems stand in regard to one another. Throughout, the emphasis is, of course, upon psychological considerations.

Right at the start, however, we have to recognize that any comparison of educational systems across nations is fraught with the "peaches versus apples" danger. For example, a comparison made merely along lines of number of years of schooling is a necessary procedure, but one that is hardly sufficient. The reason for the insufficiency is obvious: we cannot make any assumptions as to equal content or similar processes. Even if the same textbooks or their equivalents are used, the modes of instruction might differ. Nonetheless, *some* attempt at comparison must be made, even if only to help us clarify the character of our own system.

MATERIALISTIC VERSUS IDEALISTIC VALUES
AMONG UNITED STATES FRESHMEN

It would be idle to compare the educational systems of different nations without taking into account the societal values of these nations, since the two are closely interrelated. A concrete example is available from a study supported by the American Council on Education and conducted by the University of California at Los Angeles (Dey, Astin, & Korn, 1991). A survey of the aims and attitudes of about 250,000 United States college freshmen was made each year over a 25-year period, yielding a total sample of some 6.25 million. Through these data, efforts were made to examine the dynamic aspects of our society's values. As revealed in Figure 2.1, there has been since 1977 a general tendency for first-year college students to place materialism above idealism in their hierarchy of values, with the trends stabilizing or possibly reversing in 1987. (Here we use the terms *materialism* and *idealism* as colloquial variants of their philosophic meanings.) The stabilizing or reversing effect may well be the joint result of the recession in the United States and the dissolution of the Soviet empire. As indicated in the figure, materialism

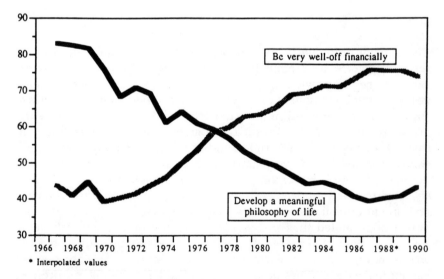

Figure 2.1. Contrasting materialistic–idealistic goals as values of first-year college students from 1966 to 1990. The 25-year trends are beginning to stabilize or even reverse. (From E. L. Dey, A. W. Astin, and W. S. Korn, *The American Freshman: Twenty-Five Year Trends* (1991). Copyright 1991 by the Regents of the University of California. Reprinted by permission of E. L. Dey.)

implies being "financially very well off"; idealism implies developing a "meaningful philosophy of life."

Why the Tendency toward Materialism?

We must inquire as to *why* younger people are generally materialistic. Frequent answers surfacing in the United States (and perhaps true elsewhere) include the following: (1) *Changing job opportunities in lucrative fields.* Freshmen have responded to current and anticipated needs for baccalaureate-level positions possessing increased opportunity for higher salaries, such as business professionals, computer programmers, and some types of engineers, and have reduced their enrollment in disciplines broadly associated with the liberal arts. The student's economic perceptions are not wrong: "first year earnings for recent [college] graduates [in the fields of business, computers, engineering] are often higher than the annual salaries of many *college* faculty" (Astin & Green, 1987, p. 16). Salaries for elementary and secondary teachers lag behind those of their college colleagues, although a widespread need is perceived for able professionals. It is probably safe to assume that the relatively low status of the teaching profession is in large measure responsible. The influence of financial consideration also appears to be reflected in the gradual increase in the percentage of entering freshman (both sexes) expressing an interest in schoolteaching as a career from 4.7% through 1982 to 8.1% in the fall of 1987. This increase, at least in part, probably reflects higher salaries in teaching (Astin & Green, 1987). Dey, Astin, and Korn (1991) provided an update of the teaching-interest phenomenon. First, they indicated that there have been some pronounced changes during the years from 1986 to the present. For example, the percentage of freshmen interested in business careers increased steadily from 11.6% in 1966 to 24.1% in 1986. By 1990, however, the percentage dropped to 18.4%. They wrote: "While the reasons for this turnabout are not clear, it may be that competition for jobs has increased, or that many students are disillusioned by the field of business because of continuing revelations of business scandals" (Dey, Astin, & Korn, 1991, pp. 12–13). Second, they noted that there has been an increase in engagement in teaching careers from a low of 4.7% in 1982 to a solid 9.0% in 1990. They tempered any optimism concerning this increase by observing "interest in teaching careers remains much lower than the level . . . registered in the late 1960s: Interest in secondary teaching careers is only about one-third of the all-time high [from roughly 14% in 1968 to about 4% in 1990], while interest in elementary teaching is about one-half . . . [roughly 9% to 5%]." Third, they remarked that career choices in general engineering and computer science has dropped from a high in 1983 by about 25% for the former, and about 50% for the latter. Along with this, potential career preference for mathematics and statistics has dropped from 4.5% in 1966 to 0.7% in 1990. Although these numbers are small, they remark: "the [approximate] 85% decline in number of freshmen interested in math and statistics is quite alarming" (p. 14). (2) *Decreasing level of students' academic attainment.* United States students are uncomfortable with their academic achievement in high school, and are therefore cautious about enrolling in intellectually challenging or broadening courses in college. Surprising as it may seem, first-year students have offered as an "important" or "very important" reason for going to college the need to improve reading and study skills. The percentage of students in this category has steadily increased: 22.2% in 1971, 35.1% in 1976, 39.7% in 1981, 40.3% in 1986, and 43.0% in 1990. The progressive increase in these data can hardly be dismissed as artifactual. The same cohort has also anticipated an increasing need for some tutoring: 7.8% in 1976, 9.8% in 1981, 11.0% in 1986, and 15.9% in 1990 (Dey, Astin, & Korn, 1991, p. 2). To add to this unhappy situation, "The number of freshmen who 'frequently' or 'occasionally' visited an art gallery or museum in the year prior to entering college . . . has declined by nearly one-quarter (from 69.3 percent in 1968–71 to 53.7 percent in 1987–90)" (p. 9).

In apparent contrast to the foregoing, the same report observed the following:

> At the same time, it is interesting to note that the number of students who belonged to scholastic honor societies actually increased. While this finding seems to run counter to the trend of apparent declines in preparation, it may be that this increase is simply linked to either "grade inflation" or changing standards for admission to honor societies. (p. 2)

Along similar lines, students rationalize their hesitance to enroll in demanding courses by taking advantage of the paradox that those fields *not* requiring courses leading to graduate work and graduate degrees pay *more* at present than those demanding higher training (Astin & Green, 1987, p. 19). Thus, the trend toward materialism is actually reinforced by society. The trend is further reinforced by the temptation, to which some school administrators submit, to reduce academic rigors in order to avoid excessive drop-out rates. (3) *Increasing anxiety about the world's future.* Anxiety about society's future can lead not only to narcissistic concerns for quick material success, but also to conservatism and to conformity. The reason is that anxious persons seek emotional and cognitive control over threatening situations. However, this type of coping can backfire. As noted by Sloan (1980):

> In our scientistic, technologizing ways of thinking we have nearly succeeded in eliminating all that partakes of insight, intuition, wonder, feeling, dreams, and culture, and, thereby have reduced reason to only one of its lesser dimensions: a quantifying, engineering, controlling logic. . . . The truncation of reason in its full sense has resulted in the curious and extreme irony that we are saddled with a rationality that in its monomaniacal drive to control everything, to eradicate all traces of uncertainty, is deeply implicated in all those things that now threaten chaos. (p. 4)

The chaos referred to by Sloan is evidently of a brinkmanship that dominated the nuclear armament escalation, prior to the fall of the USSR. It is still uncertain, however, if the separate republics will be able to control nuclear devices. The man on the street seems to shrug off the reality of the threat. Why is this so? Robert Coles has written in this regard that concern with the need for a nuclear freeze, for example, is largely a leisure class phenomenon. His assumption is that persons lower on the socioeconomic scale (and possessing less schooling) are mainly worried about making ends meet. Their materialistic interest is literally at the gut level and is independent of political system.

However, some complex interactions occur and serve to warn us of oversimplification. For example, the 25-year tendency toward materialism notwithstanding, the percentage of college students attending religious services has not diminished by much. There is a small decline from 88.5% who attended religious services frequently or occasionally in 1968–1971, through 85.4% in 1978–1981, to 82.6% in 1987–1990 (Dey, Astin, & Korn, 1991, p. 10). Evidently the accumulation of wealth is not perceived as being inconsistent with religious practice. Similarly, the fact that college freshmen place a premium upon the accumulation of wealth over the desire for a meaningful philosophy of life has not intruded to a noticeable extent upon concern for America's historic values of egalitarianism, pragmatism, and self-reliance. We shall shortly return to pick up this thread and to see how our educational system was in good measure woven from it.

Finally, Astin and Green (1987) offered this general evaluation of changes in interest in the liberal arts among college students:

> In sum, the data point to sharp and continuing declines in student interest in virtually every field that has traditionally been associated with a liberal arts education. Further, it is important to realize that the aggregate freshmen data—which presumably reflect only tentative choices of college major—are in fact very good predictors of aggregate final choices and behaviors. In other words, the trends in *freshman aspirations* have been followed by similar trends in *bachelor's degrees*. (pp. 15–16, emphasis in original)

We cannot begin to engage these larger issues of liberal arts education, but neither can we ignore them. This chapter can serve only to describe some of the main variables at work in the interaction of educational systems with values.

VALUES AMONG NATIONS, AND HOW
EDUCATION IS AFFECTED

Among the values that interact with education are some that appear to transcend societies and are present in ordinary people without regard to specific culture; for example, an appreciation of the aesthetic *per se*, whatever the beautiful is held to be. Other values are less generic, and seem to have a long history unique to a specific culture. With regard to the United States, Hurn and Burn (1982) have observed:

> There are many structural and organizational differences between American schools and schools in [other countries of] the industrialized world. . . . But these structural differences can only be understood in the context of the different values which justify and support educational practice in America and elsewhere. This is not to say that all or even most organizational or structural differences in American schooling are primarily a reflection of differences in values between America, Europe and Japan . . . . Nor do we wish to imply that values are always static or permanent features of a particular society . . . . We do want to argue, however, that very little of the distinctive character, organization or outcomes of American education can be grasped without prior consideration of long standing value differences between America and the rest of the world. (pp. 9–10)

EGALITARIANISM, PRAGMATISM, AND INDIVIDUALISM:
THE AMERICAN REVOLUTION

The educational system that has emerged in the United States can be traced back to three values espoused during the American Revolution: *egalitarianism, pragmatism,* and *individualism* (or self-reliance) (cf. Hurn & Burn, 1982, p. 11). In turn, these values were imported directly or indirectly from Western Europe (particularly from Scotland), where they had captured the imaginations of the prime movers in the Scottish Enlightenment—John Locke (English), Thomas Paine (English-American), David Hume (Scottish), Thomas Reid (Scottish), to name but a few. Their first- or second-generation students became the leaders of Harvard, Yale, Princeton, Columbia, and the University of Pennsylvania, as well as other early American institutions of higher learning. Why Scotland?

> Scottish history from the time of the Reformation [fifteenth century] until
> early in the eighteenth century is marked by religious factionalism, relentless
> struggles with the English, and a continuing cultural and intellectual cross-
> fertilization with France, a cross-fertilization with roots as old as the thir-
> teenth century. Scotland's Catholics found relief and opportunities on the
> Continent as did members of unfavored Protestant sects. But so too did
> unharried Scotsmen simply eager to expand their horizons or their fortunes.
> (Robinson, 1986a, pp. 171–172)

The close relation between the triad of values cited earlier and the
Enlightenment is made evident by noting Reid's position on the matter.
Simply stated, he was concerned with the reciprocity between a person's
rights and his duties. The one entails and obligates the other. Thereby,
the importance to education of equal opportunity (egalitarianism), concern with consequences as they affect advancement of truth (pragmatism), and respect for individualism (self-reliance) emerge. Such is the
case, because any single member of the triad presupposes the coexistence and influence of the other two members. For example, even as
rights entail obligations, so egalitarianism requires the coexistence of a
concern for consequences and a respect for individualism. We shall see
as we go through this chapter, however, that there are limits to this tidy
description.

Egalitarianism

Although regions of the United States and Canada differ in the
specific application, it is nonetheless true that the United States and
Canadian school systems are constructed on the premise of equal accessibility to all educationally qualified persons. The goal is to offer 8 years
of free elementary school, and 4 years of free high school, without regard to any other factor—religion, race, social status, economic level,
and so on. Indeed, the current trend in these countries is to extend
accessibility in both directions; that is, below first grade and above the
senior year in high school.

But even though free schooling is available in North America, not all
individuals are able to take advantage of it. They need a modicum of
support from a caring person, otherwise they become indifferent to
opportunity. Interestingly, apathy afflicts both rich and poor alike. The
affluent child suffers as the poor child does from a lack of *psychological*
support; financial support is no substitute (Notterman, 1985, May). One
result is an increased rate of drop-out from school in *all* economic classes
(*New York Times*, February 16, 1987, p. 11). Apathy plus a general lower-
ing of academic standards might also help account for the fact that *"the*

average graduate of our schools and colleges today is not as well-educated as the average graduate of 25 or 35 years ago, when a much smaller proportion of our population completed high school and college" (*A Nation at Risk*, 1983, p. 11, emphasis in original). It may well be that even if the proportion had remained the same, the average graduate today might still be relatively less educated. The reason is that there has been in the United States a concomitant increase in the tendency to offer courses more appropriate to merely "getting through" than to broad education.

> The egalitarian approach to education is by now a world-wide phenomenon. . . . The previously enormous gap between the United States and the rest of the industrialized world in the percentage of young people who attend college has been dramatically closed in the years since 1960. College enrollments have more than tripled in the United States since 1960, but they have quadrupled and quintupled in many countries in Europe, and in Japan. Part of this increase reflects the spread of the ideology of equal opportunity from the United States to the rest of the industrial world. (Hurn & Burn, 1982, p. 13)

We can now include major portions of Eastern Europe, the former Soviet bloc. Two other nations (France and Mexico) have extended minimally expensive higher education to their secondary school graduates. However, France and Mexico have encountered difficulty in maintaining an appropriate balance between egalitarianism and educational standards, especially in light of high youth unemployment. The reason is that students in both countries have resisted the notion of regionalization, or having geographically diverse universities select students, and then issue separate diplomas upon graduation. Instead, they wanted to maintain automatic admission and the issuance of a single, national diploma. Evidently they feared that some universities would have higher criteria for admission than others, that a form of functional tracking would emerge, and even that a significant number of students would not be allowed to go to any university, despite high levels of unemployment. The students felt that they would have no chance of bettering their lives. Both countries backed off (*Chronicle of Higher Education*, December 3, 1986, p. 1).

Comparison of Egalitarianism among Nations. Without assuming any qualitative equivalence, Hurn and Burn (1982, p. 61) found it expedient to use number of years of free education (not including college) in comparing *availability* of schooling across still other nations. The former Soviet Union's system of 11 years of combined elementary and secondary school education is considered equivalent to the United States total of 12 years, because students there are required to go to school 6 days per week. The total of combined elementary and secondary school education in West Germany is 13 years, with educational specialists in the

United States therefore giving West German students the equivalent of one year's advanced placement in college. The same holds true for those provinces in Canada that, as in Germany, offer 13 years of schooling. The Japanese attend school for 12 years, but exceed the United States in that their students attend classes about 50 more days per school year (Rohlen, 1985/86). As noted at the outset, however, these figures hardly tell the whole story. It goes without saying that "availability" does not mean compulsory attendance and does not include dropout factors. Moreover, the limitations of mere availability as a measure not only vary from country to country, but also among populations within a country. A study completed in Israel, but with clear implications for other countries, found the following: "the higher the level of disadvantaged students, the lower the level of school attractiveness, the lower the percentage of teachers with B.A. degrees, and the lower the percentage of students who complete high school" (Biniaminov & Glasman, 1982, p. 88). Poole and Low (1982) reported some Australian findings that also would seem to be true internationally:

> Overlaying individual ability, values, and commitment to schooling appear to be factors such as socioeconomic status, school type, and frequency of job discussions with parents. This suggests that a major dimension of the school staying or leaving process is the congruency between individual abilities, values, and expectations and the value climates of home and school. (p. 60)

The same authors pointed to the interaction between gender and dropout:

> Despite higher grades, higher optimism, and conforming attitudes to school values, girls do not construct as lofty images of their own success as do boys. Boys, on the other hand, perceive success for themselves despite lower school achievement levels. This finding suggests a set of sex-linked dimensions of cultural or societal expectations overlaying individual attainments, motivations, and expectations. Boys expect to get on in life, despite school grades. Girls, despite their school grades, do not rate their chances of success too highly. (p. 60)

Interestingly, no mention is made of teenage pregnancy as a distinguishing factor between female and male dropout. An American survey indicated: "More than a fifth of white female dropouts and more than a quarter of minority female dropouts gave pregnancy as a reason for dropping out" (Peng et al., 1983; McDill, Natriello, & Pallas, 1985, p. 418).

Pragmatism and Its Relation to Utilitarianism

The American philosopher most closely identified with pragmatism is William James. Robinson noted that "pragmatism was never intended to be a *crass* utilitarianism, or what contemporary moral philosophers call 'vulgar consequentialism'" [perhaps what we earlier referred to as materialism] (Robinson, 1986b). How, then, are pragmatism and utilitarianism to be distinguished? The question is timely, for there is a current blurring of the two philosophies, one that intrudes upon contemporary research and writing in educational psychology. *Pragmatism* is concerned with searching for *truth*, and does so by way of examining the consequences of an idea or act, as in the laboratory. *Utilitarianism* is concerned with searching for *usefulness*, specified in terms of the common good, but again by way of examining the consequences of an idea or act, as in politics. Neither philosophy is concerned with mere practicality, although the shared communality of active searching and of consequences invites the notion that they are.

Pragmatism is interested in truth; utilitarianism, in usefulness. The two need not correspond. The problem of the researcher in educational psychology is that he must resolve the tensions brought to bear by the forces of truth and of usefulness. Research can center on the abstract or theoretical, and not be concerned with utility. Alternatively, it can be directed toward constructive application, without regard to the establishment of underlying general principles. The resolution of these forces must satisfy all interested parties (and there are many!). It is a difficult but not impossible task. Recognition that there *is* a task facilitates compromise.

John Dewey on the Relations between Pragmatism and Utilitarianism. One of America's most renowned educators, John Dewey (1859–1952), was struck by the interrelation between the search for truth and the search for common well-being. In his view, pragmatic knowledge (in the form of science) and utilitarian morality were diverging from each other.

> Central to Dewey's writing was his concern to overcome the widening gap between scientific knowledge and morality. "Certainly," he wrote, "one of the most genuine problems of modern life is the reconciliation of the scientific view of the universe with the claims of the moral life." The split had arisen, Dewey was convinced, because, on the one hand, ethics had failed to keep pace with the advances of physical science and its technological applications, and, on the other hand, because science often was improperly conceived and practiced. (Sloan, 1980, p. 224)

With regard to the improper conception and practice of science, Dewey drew attention to the following: (1) Science was never entirely independent of the observer's perceptions. (2) Parts of a phenomenon could not be validly examined independently of the whole phenomenon. (3) Knowledge must contain purpose, affect, and value (and not only facts) in order to qualify as understanding. Of course, these much condensed viewpoints concerning science are not particularly original with Dewey; for example, Plato, Descartes, David Hume, Kant, John Stuart Mill—to name but a few—each had something to say about one or another of them. Dewey is in the tradition of educators who, since ancient times, have reminded humanity that knowledge does not necessarily produce morality. We return to Dewey's version of pragmatism and its relation to his progressive education in Chapter 3, Functionalism.

Individualism

One need not search far for the origin of individualism as an expression of American values. The idea is with us right from the founding of the American nation: "We hold these truths to be self-evident, that all men are created equal, that they are endowed by their creator with certain unalienable rights, that among these are life, liberty, and the pursuit of happiness." Known historic and current practice notwithstanding, we take at face value that "all men" implies *everyone*, without regard to sex, race, nationality, religion, and so on. That this inclusion has not been uniformly accepted has complicated and confused our dealings with concepts of egalitarianism and individualism.

We are equal in that each of us has the right and obligation to pursue the search for happiness in his or her own way. Ours is perceived as a highly egalitarian and individualistic society based upon laws that guarantee liberty, at least ideally. These laws are predicated upon mutual respect for each other's individualism. Our political and educational systems take these largely psychological issues into account.

Individualism implies reliance upon one's own abilities and motivations in order to achieve one's goals. We have already noted Thomas Reid's views on the matter—*rights entail duties*. Individualism so construed is neither an invitation to egocentricity nor to hedonism. Duties to others and to society are part of the pact. For that reason, push–pull tension exists between individualism and utilitarianism; a reciprocity between personal good and common good.

The political and educational consequences are

> [that] the high value placed on individualism in Western Hemisphere countries conflicts sharply with the high value placed on collectivism in some countries of the Eastern Hemisphere. Through schools and other centrally directed institutions, modern states undertake to socialize developing citizens to those values which those states consider to be fundamental. (Scheibe, 1977, p. 356)

Japanese versus Eastern Bloc Approaches to Individualism and to Common Good. Of course, the line drawn between private ownership versus collectivism is not at all the same as that between individualism versus utilitarianism, although their equivalence is often assumed. A notable example is that of Japan, a culture in which working for the common good is emphasized, but not at the expense of private ownership.

> The Japanese educational system provides an instructive contrast to both the Soviet and the American. What is perhaps most notable about the Japanese system—and this seems true of Japanese industry as well as Japanese educational institutions—is the amount of cooperative and selfless behavior which is married to a fierce competitive spirit, a combination which seems contradictory to Westerners. In a number of respects, ironically, Japanese school children display the qualities that the Soviet system hopes to encourage in their students. (Hurn & Burn, 1982, pp. 25–26)

According to Hurn and Burn (citing the past Moscow correspondent for *The New York Times*, Hedrick Smith), competition in Eastern bloc schools is encouraged, but—as in Japan—it is supposed to be mainly by groups, and not only by individuals. For example, an outstanding student within a group is expected to help other students who are less bright, and not be content with attaining merely his own personal success. However, the drive for individual attainment generally overrides the collective. The reason is that because of the intense competition for admission to universities, students hardly dare increase the standing of others. Moreover, they are loath to reveal any difference of opinion with theoretical values preached from above. The educational system becomes authoritarian, and the students themselves distrustful. (We have more to say about former Soviet values in Chapter 5.)

Why were the Japanese more successful than the one-time Soviets in combining group loyalty with individual achievement? The explanation most often ventured is that the Japanese have a much more homogeneous population and common culture than did the Soviets, or—for that matter—the United States. (The USSR consisted of 14 republics and numerous racial/ethnic groups. It was almost 2.5 times the size of the United States, and over 60 times the size of Japan.) Thus, the "group" in Japan is more cohesive than in the former USSR. It consists of individuals who more readily can empathize with each other, while still competing.

Some Educational Comparisons of the United States versus Japan. Whether or not based upon homogeneity, the unique capacity possessed by the Japanese to combine cooperation with competitiveness has yielded a society that values both group discipline and individual industriousness. The impact upon education is profound: Despite the fact that the United States spends somewhat more proportionally of its gross national product on education than does Japan (7% vs. 6%), the Japanese have more 4-year-olds attending school (63% vs. 32%), more students graduating from high school (90% vs. 77%) *with the upper half doing better than the average American college graduate*, more daily homework hours during high school (2.0 vs. 0.5), more years of required high school mathematics (3 vs. 1), more years of required high school foreign language (6 vs. 1), and a much lower daily absentee rate ("very low" vs. 9%). (Source for the foregoing comparisons is Rohlen, 1985/86, pp. 30–31.)

However, all is not so cozy. It is a well-documented fact that the competition for entering the university is intense: "Many private universities attract eight or nine candidates per opening, and competition to gain entrance to departments that lead to degrees in medicine regularly reaches a ratio of 20 to 1" (Rohlen, 1985/86, p. 32). It is also well-documented that the Japanese are now concerned about the stress attendant upon such competition.

Interestingly, studies conducted by the American and Japanese governments (released at the start of 1987) suggest that the United States educational system excels in higher education, while the Japanese system excels in elementary and secondary school: "As the two reports make clear . . . each country faces serious problems that are the flip side of its strengths. Japanese political and business leaders worry that . . . the emphasis on conformity . . . is depriving them of much-needed creativity. . . . By contrast, the problems facing American education tend to be those inherent in raising the average achievement of a diverse population" (Fiske, 1987).

SUMMARY

The chapter begins by considering reasons for the tendency to value materialism among undergraduates in the United States. It goes on to discuss values among different nations, and how education is affected. In particular, three values have influenced American education since revolutionary times: egalitarianism, pragmatism, and individualism.

The unique character of education in Japan and what was the USSR are very briefly described, and wherever possible, compared with the educational philosophies and practices of the United States. All told, there are advantages and disadvantages to each country's system. But even as we attend to these comparisons, the American refrain of egalitarianism, pragmatism, and individualism is still heard in the United States after 200 years, and gives every indication of continuing to reach us.

II

Psychological Viewpoints
and Related Paradigms
of Learning

Functionalism

Goal-Directed Activity, Purposivity, Dewey's Pragmatism, and Modern Feedback Theory

There are four objectives to this chapter: first, to define functionalism; second, to comment on "purpose" as a key concept of functionalism; third, to discuss John Dewey's interest in pragmatism; and fourth, to relate purpose to modern feedback theory.

DEFINITION OF FUNCTIONALISM

Functionalism is eclectic. Its interests are so broad that the term resists designation as a "school" falling within sharply defined theoretical or experimental boundaries. There is no single "functionalism," nor was there ever much of a desire among its leaders that there be one. In describing his own version of functionalism, Columbia University's R.S. Woodworth wrote somewhat impatiently that it

> does not aspire to be a school: That is the very thing it does not wish to be. Personally, I have always balked on being told, as we have been told at intervals for as long as I can remember, what our marching orders are—what as psychologists we ought to be doing, and what in the divine order of the sciences psychology must be doing. (Woodworth, 1930, p. 327)

Nonetheless, we still require some overall definition, one that encompasses the broad concerns of functionalism. Functionalism is the study of psychological processes in general, with emphasis upon their adaptive qualities in particular, as manifested in behavior ranging from inner experience to motor activity. Specifically, it includes subject matters as diverse as learning, volition, affect, physiological psychology, developmental psychology, psychophysics—practically everything from nerve cell to neurosis. In short, except for its emphasis upon purposiveness, functionalism is hardly distinguishable from contemporary psychology.

Functionalism was strongly influenced by Charles Darwin's work. Discovery of the propensity of organisms to adapt to the environment led to questions concerning the circumstances under which adaptation occurred. These questions were asked as eagerly by psychologists as they were by biologists. The reason is straightforward. Individual organisms do not survive long enough to produce progeny unless they are first capable of *learning* to contend with the environment, with each other, and with other species. Natural selection includes the organism's ability to learn, or to adapt to circumstances, during the course of its life.

F.S. Keller, one of the founders of programmed instruction, indicated that the functionalists were interested in how purposive movement and feedback conjointly affected adaptation through learning. He did so by way of quoting a remark in H.A. Carr's *Psychology* (1925): "Every movement resulting from a sensory situation inevitably *modifies* that situation, and this change or modification of the sensory situation constitutes a new sensory stimulus which in turn modifies the act that produced it" (emphasis added, 1937, p. 48). Keller went on to say: "This is an important component of the reflex-arc concept, for it stresses the fact that the nature of sensory stimuli depends upon the responses just as much as the nature of the responses depends upon the stimuli—a fact that must be considered in dealing with any sample of stimulus-response activity" (Keller, 1937, p. 48). Keller here anticipated his own work in programmed instruction, which is dependent upon feedback theory, and is discussed later in this book.

William James and Purposivism

William James, one of America's greatest psychologists, held that the ability to adapt to the demands of the world was revealed by the presence of goal-directed behavior. The outward manifestation of goal-directed behavior, in turn, permitted the inference of purpose. And purposiveness was so characteristic a trait of biological organisms that

Harvard's James urged its use as a criterion for distinguishing between living and nonliving entities.

He set the tone in his *Principles of Psychology* (1890):

> If some iron filings be sprinkled on a table and a magnet brought near them they will fly through the air for a certain distance and stick to its surface. A savage seeing the phenomenon explains it as the result of an attraction or love between the magnet and the filings. But let a card cover the poles of the magnet, and the filings will press forever against its surface without its ever occurring to them to pass around its sides and thus come into more direct contact with the object of their love. . . .
>
> If now we pass from such actions as these to those of living things, we notice a striking difference. Romeo wants Juliet as the filings want the magnet; and if no obstacles intervene he moves towards her by as straight a line as they. But Romeo and Juliet, if a wall be built between them, do not remain idiotically pressing their faces against its opposite sides like the magnet and the filings with the card. Romeo soon finds a circuitous way, by scaling the wall or otherwise, of touching Juliet's lips directly. With the filings the path is fixed; whether it reaches the end depends on accidents. With the lover it is the end which is fixed, the path may be modified indefinitely. . . .
>
> The pursuance of future ends and the choice of means for their attainment are thus the mark and criterion of the presence of mentality in a phenomenon. We all use this test to discriminate between an intelligent and a mechanical performance. (James, 1890/1968, pp. 609–610)

James asserted poetically that from the "savage's" personal experience with the affect attendant upon two creatures drawing themselves together, the "savage" projects love between the magnet and the filings. The "civilized" person presumably knows better, and avoids animism by distinguishing between living and nonliving types of matter. James's criterion for establishing this distinction is that of purposiveness. He infers purposiveness from goal-directed behavior. More precisely, he uses observable changes in goal-directed behavior as a criterion for distinguishing between living and nonliving things.

Before examining the validity of James's position, we can sharpen the functionalist meaning of purposivism by reviewing McDougall's elaboration of the concept.

McDougall and Purposivism

The British-born Harvard psychologist William McDougall expanded on James's reasoning by describing seven ways to infer purposiveness from an animal's behavior:

1. Initiation of activity without any obvious external stimulus
2. Persistence of action independently of whatever stimulus may have initiated it

3. Variation in the direction of persistent activity
4. End of activity with goal achievement
5. Readiness of preparation for new activity
6. Improvement in performance through practice
7. The entire organism is involved, not just isolated reflexes. (McDougall, 1923/1968, pp. 615–618)

Within the limits of ordinary experience, James and McDougall are convincing. They distinguish between living and nonliving systems on the basis of the presence of purposiveness in the former, and they suggested criteria by means of which purposiveness may be inferred. Their major criterion is the adjustment of action in such manner as to attain a goal. With the advent of cybernetics, however, the salience of this criterion has diminished.

Cybernetics and Purposivism

Cybernetics deals with self-regulating systems. The word derives from the Greek *kybernetes*, meaning steersman. The logic of James's and McDougall's argument must confront the fact that nonliving systems of the servomechanism variety display changes in goal-directed behavior. A single example suffices to make the point: A "smart" surface-to-air missile can propel itself upon detecting a target, and—once on its way— keep changing its position in accordance with the evasive action taken by the target. It can even "learn" to take advantage of any regularities in the target's evasive path.

Does the hunting behavior of the missile permit us to infer that it possesses "purpose"? The founders of cybernetics attempted to deal with this question about 40 years ago. Norbert Wiener and others implicitly recognized the limitations of the James–McDougall position, and suggested the reason for them. They stated, "The basis of the concept of purpose is the awareness of voluntary activity" (Rosenblueth, Wiener, & Bigelow, 1943, p. 47). Regardless of the merits of their suggestion, we seem to be forced into a metaphysical dispute concerning the nature of consciousness. However, the issues involved will be clarified if we look more carefully at the very concept of "self-regulating system."

The idea of self-regulating systems has been part of the human being's intellectual functioning for ages past. As noted by Ernest Nagel (1955), "Automatic control is not a new thing in the world. Self-regulative mechanisms are an inherent feature of innumerable processes in nature, living and nonliving" (p. 2). For example, the Hindu philosophers conceived of a Harmonious Universe, with the action of each portion influencing all other portions. However, the cosmos cannot be considered harmonious unless each part is capable of being sensitive to changes in each and every other component of the universe. In modern language, we would say that every part of such a universe provides feedback to every other part. Usually this feedback is of the kind termed "negative," because it acts to subtract differences or to reduce discrepancies between activities, thereby bringing the different functions of the universe closer to equilibrium. ("Positive" feedback increases discrepancies. Unless otherwise qualified, "feedback" generally implies negative feedback.)

Dewey and Pragmatism

John Dewey's education philosophy of "learning by doing" is a purposivistic variant of pragmatism and indirectly of feedback theory. It is intellectually tied to functionalism. As noted in Chapter 2, Dewey emphasized the importance of examining ideas and action, and of consequently making individual and social adaptations in the continuing search for truth. In this nontechnical respect—in noting that one's views changed as one experienced their consequences—he was a forerunner of nontechnical feedback theory, as well as a pragmatist.

No consideration of curriculum of American schools after the late nineteenth century would be complete without some reference to John Dewey. His written works, his philosophy of experimentalism, and his Lab School at the University of Chicago reflect the coming together of American intellectual and educational life in the first two decades of the twentieth century. The American-originated philosophy of pragmatism (Chapter 2) provided the basis for Dewey's approach to intellect and learning. Pragmatism developed in opposition to the traditional philosophies of European origin and was popularized by William James. Dewey's experimentalism related pragmatism to intellectual development of the American student. In all his work, Dewey called attention to the integral connection between philosophy and education. In his view, philosophy was useless unless it made a difference in the lives of people. To determine whether they made a difference, theoretical ideas had to be tested in practice. The areas in which pragmatism could be tested included the theory and practice of education. Between 1896 and 1916 he published a series of articles and books focused on the connection of philosophy and education. These works emphasized Dewey's belief that education is essentially social in character, and thus it is necessary to study the social nature of the individual's environment as well as the individual's psychological nature in order to deal appropriately with the individual's education.

> [He held that the] educational process has two sides—one psychological and one sociological—and that neither can be subordinated to the other, or neglected, without evil results following. Of these two sides, the psychological is the basis. The child's own instincts and powers furnish the material and give the starting-point for all education. Save as the efforts of the educator connect with some activity which the child is carrying on of his own initiative independent of the educator, education becomes reduced to a pressure from without. It may, indeed, give certain external results, but cannot truly be called educative. Without insight into the psychological structure and activities of the individual, the educative process will, therefore, be haphazard and arbitrary. If it chances to coincide with the child's activity it will get a leverage; if it does not, it will result in friction, or disintegration, or arrest of the child nature. (Dewey, 1897/1940, p. 4)

Children are seen by Dewey as naturally inclined to action, to communication with others, and to investigation and inquiry. This suggests that the job for teachers is to create an environment that is conducive to constructive self-development, one in which students continuously engage in the changing patterns of problem-solving as the means for developing thinking skills. In this interactive sense, we see that cognitive development depends upon behavioral feedback processes.

Dewey held that thought consisted of five steps: (1) definition of a problem, (2) observation of the conditions related to the problem, (3) formulation of a hypothesis, (4) consideration of the consequences of acting on various alternate hypotheses, and (5) testing to see which of the alternatives best solves the problem. The term *learning by doing* quickly came to be associated with Dewey's educational views. In the curriculum he proposed, students acted on "real life"-type problems. Efforts to solve these problems engaged students in the process of thinking which, for Dewey, was the center of the educational process.

Despite his emphasis upon the relation between *thinking* and *action*, Dewey did not neglect the feedback consequences of *action* upon *emotion*. He categorically stated:

> The emotions are the reflex of actions. To endeavor to stimulate or arouse the emotions apart from their corresponding activities is to introduce an unhealthy and morbid state of mind. If we can only secure right habits of action and thought, with reference to the good, the true, and the beautiful, the emotions will for the most part take care of themselves. (Dewey, 1897/1940, pp. 14–15)

(The student of psychology will quickly note the resemblance of this statement to the James–Lange Theory of Emotion, which also held that emotions were generated by actions.)

Progressive education, as Dewey's views came to be called, was widely accepted in the educational community for many years. It has come under severe attack more recently. However, many who are critical of Dewey's education views, not infrequently use approaches which are in the best tradition of progressive teaching and learning.

FEEDBACK THEORY: EDUCATIONAL AND PHILOSOPHICAL IMPLICATIONS

We turn now to a technical description of feedback theory, in the hope that a fairly precise account will eventually make more productive the educational and philosophical implications of functionalism.

We need to be fairly circumspect in our use of the word *feedback*, because it has become something of a jargony, "you-know-what-I-mean" expression. The techniques and concepts of feedback theory's systems analysis—as employed by economists, educators, environmentalists, social psychologists, clinical psychologists, experimental psychologists, and others—can be quite productive, provided they retain their authentic meanings. As cautioned elsewhere:

> The servo-model as a way of regarding phenomena lends itself to pseudo-explanations, in the sense of labeling. It is difficult to resist the tendency to describe old problems in new terms and to believe that the old problems have thereby been solved. To describe . . . "libido" as negative feedback and "superego" as positive feedback merely adds two more labels to an already overworked jargon. The specific activity of neither the practitioner nor the researcher is changed one iota as a result of the change in labels. (Notterman, 1970, p. 55)

We must remember that the language in which the ideas and analyses of systems theory is expressed remains tied to servomechanism concepts. First, we should consider at what point the logical extension from self-regulating, electromechanical systems becomes a misleading, metamorphical extension to other systems. That is to say, we must determine when the concepts originally derived from electromechanical systems can be used in biological, social, educational, or other systems, without doing violence to their original meaning. Metaphors are an inherent part of science, but unless used properly can make for poor science, as well as poor poetry. Second, we should consider when even the appropriately selected metaphor ceases to retain and to convey the original meaning, and becomes a distortion of the original.

We can undertake these considerations only by gaining a firm grasp of the feedback language from which systems theory was developed. The language referred to is one that describes adaptive processes. We reason here that adaptation, the central concern of functionalism, cannot be fully understood independently of feedback terminology and systems analysis.

Open-Loop Feedback Systems

We begin by distinguishing between open- and closed-loop systems. An open-loop system provides feedback *after* a response; it does not yield feedback concurrently with the response of the system. Thus, it is not capable of self-regulation during the course of any single act. It is synonymous with a "ballistic" response, as exemplified by a frog striking with its tongue at a fly, or a hunter firing a shotgun at a rabbit (or a teacher being completely bound by reading from a lesson plan). Once a response is initiated, no further changes can be made. The action is committed, even if it might be faulty. If the target (student) changes position (comprehension) during the response, neither the frog nor the hunter (nor the teacher) can do anything about it. After a particular act is complete, the system may receive signals indicating a "hit" or "miss" ("correct" or "incorrect"), and modify accordingly the next response. The system is specified as being "open-loop" because of the absence of concurrent feedback during the execution of any single response.

Straightaway we see that it is tempting to consider educational debates bearing upon, for example, the merits of teacher-directed (as above) versus student-centered instruction as being relevant to the open-loop versus closed-loop distinction. However, as is made evident in Chapter 11, Instructional Methods and Nomenclature, either type of instruction can fall into either type of feedback system, depending upon *how* the instruction is offered.

Closed-Loop Feedback Systems

There are two types of closed-loop feedback systems, discontinuous and continuous. The *discontinuous* variety is either entirely "on" or entirely "off." There are no gradations between full output and zero output. A simple physical example is that of a thermostat controlling the temperature of a room. The heating source is "on" or "off," depending upon the setting on the thermostat (input). The system is considered closed rather than open, because the thermostat is continually sensitive to the room's temperature, even though it responds on an all-or-none basis.

If the teacher in the open-loop example were to remain silent until the end of his or her lesson, *but* be constantly attentive to the effect that he or she were having upon the students, then we can extend teacher performance from the earlier open-loop example to the present discontinuous closed-loop case.

Going even farther, the *continuous* closed-loop system is much more sophisticated. It responds proportionately to the momentary difference between desired goal and current state. Thus, it is called *continuous* because gradations of correction are possible. Since the system is almost immediately responsive, it follows that it is sensitive to the first and second and even higher time derivatives of error ("error" is the momentary difference between input and output, or goal and current state of affairs). The first time derivative is "rate"; the second time derivative is "acceleration" (or deceleration). The problem of lag-time in correction, which is troublesome in the discontinuous type, is almost eliminated. Similarly, the tendency to overshoot and undershoot the goal is considerably lessened. Figure 3.1 shows these time derivatives, and describes how such a system operates. "S" designates the momentary visual space between hand and pencil. The figure illustrates the following excerpt from Norbert Wiener's epoch-making book, *Cybernetics*:

> Now suppose that I pick up a lead-pencil . . . our motion proceeds in such a way that we may say roughly that the amount by which the pencil is not yet picked up is decreased at each stage. . . .

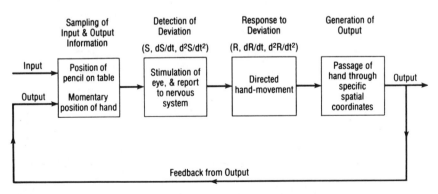

Figure 3.1. Continuous closed-loop system: Wiener's pencil. (From J. M. Notterman, *Forms of Psychological Inquiry* (1985). Copyright 1985 by Columbia University Press. Reprinted by permission of Columbia University Press.)

> To perform an action in such a manner, there must be a report to the nervous system, conscious, or unconscious, of the amount by which we have failed to pick the pencil up at each instant. (Wiener, 1948, p. 14)

Note that the example involves a living system, but this is not a requirement (recall the surface-to-air missile). Further, the pencil need not be in a fixed position on the table. It could move about, as it would were the table on a ship at sea.

Figure 3.2 illustrates both of these features. First, it represents a combined living and nonliving (or man–machine) system. Second, the input changes continuously, unless one were driving on a perfectly straight road.

We should also note that Figure 3.2 illustrates the kinds of behavior involved in learning motor skills, and in perfecting sports activities. Through practice and instruction, the novice learns both to take advantage of whatever regularities there are in the input, and to deal with changes in the spatial conditions of objects in the environment. If only by analogy, we can extend the continuous closed-loop paradigm to include educational systems. Assume that the input is the *desired* educational objective (e.g., as assessed by reading scores and other measures) in a school or district. The error detector and corrector (similar to boxes 2 and 3 in Figure 3.2) is contained in the person of the school principal or district supervisor. He or she observes certain problems and takes appropriate actions to achieve a change in *actual* educational attainment (output). By observing the rates at which the changes occur, the principal or supervisor can more quickly take further corrective steps, as ap-

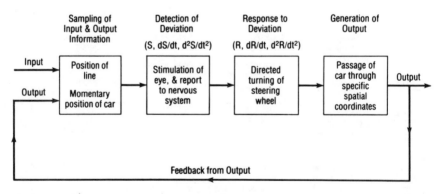

Figure 3.2. Continuous closed-loop system: driving a car. (From J. M. Notterman, *Forms of Psychological Inquiry* (1985). Copyright 1985 by Columbia University Press. Reprinted by permission of Columbia University Press.)

propriate and necessary. Of course, qualitative considerations also apply. For example, reading scores may improve at a good rate, but the principal or supervisor may encourage teachers to slow down the process, because of student anxiety, or teachers "teaching-to-the-test."

Finally, it may contribute toward understanding the functions of the different systems by observing the following: (1) In the open-loop case, both the input and the output are episodic and are independent of each other. There is no direct connection between the two. It is up to the hunter to capitalize upon the occasional synchrony. (2) In the discontinuous closed-loop case, the input is graduated, but the output is not. The latter is of the all-or-none variety. (3) In the continuous closed-loop case, both the input and the output are graduated. The latter is proportional to the former.

Some Reflections Leading to Progressive Education

The keystone of functionalism is its concern with adaptive processes, particularly as manifested in goal-direction. From observation of goal-directed behavior, the investigator infers purpose. Equally important, early functionalists (James and McDougall) used modifications in such behavior as a criterion for distinguishing between living and non-living systems. With the advent of cybernetics, however, scientists were forced to reconsider ancient metaphysical disputes concerning the presence of purposiveness within the universe.

We cannot settle metaphysical issues. We can only note that it is once again no longer obvious that the concept of purpose can be limited to living systems. It will become even more enigmatic a problem in the future, as computers and robots that "learn" become more prevalent.

Scientists tend to become uncomfortable with the idea of purposivity for still another reason. Closed-loop systems invite circular explanations, or a confusion of cause with effect. The quandary is that much of our behavior is of a closed-loop variety, and therefore effects do become causes. Good science demands that we not be so leery of tautologies as to become paralyzed in the laboratory. We must still do all that we can to be deterministic in research concerning purposive behavior. For example, we should not "in our fear of the teleological undertones to the words 'purposivism' and 'functionalism' ignore the evidence that lower forms of life (let alone man himself) can extrapolate in time from the immediate present, based upon cueing information provided by the momentarily changing values of current discriminative stimuli" (Notterman, 1973, p. 130). Organisms can bring the future into the present, as it were, through a combination of current peripheral discriminations, central planning, and motor actions. Consistent with this observation is the evidence that the greater the regularity or coherence in the cueing information available, the greater the likelihood that purposiveness—in the sense of learning to use first and second time-order cues to plan ahead—will be demonstrated (Notterman & Tufano, 1981).

"Awareness" need not necessarily accompany extrapolations or integrations in time from time-derivative information. Awareness may well be the basis for the origin of the concept of "purpose" in the human being's goal-directed behavior. (Recall the remarks of Rosenblueth *et al.*, quoted earlier in the chapter.) Yet awareness is not always necessary for human goal attainment. In routine driving by the well-practiced driver, for example, the quality of awareness is often lost. However, the act of driving is nonetheless purposeful; the driver still has a goal or destination. Furthermore, the individual often modifies his behavior to attain a particular objective, and does so without being aware of the modification or the objective. We return to more striking issues of unconscious motivation and behavior when we consider psychoanalytic theories (Chapters 8 and 9).

Finally, we should bear in mind that the essence of Dewey's progressive education is hardly passé. He argued that the development of thought depends upon actions of a purposeful, problem-solving nature. In turn, the type of problems encountered depends upon the social-environmental conditions in which the organism lives. If the immediate world encountered is one that prizes the utilization of symbols, as in reading, then the child will tend to assume these values. If the world encountered is one of survival, of dog-eat-dog, of drug escape or bravado, then values leading to aggression will be acquired.

In short, even as we "learn-by-doing," Dewey would also argue that we "do-by-learning." It is the latter, additional phrase that pulls together learning and feedback. For if we did not learn through feedback from actions, then what we *do* the next time would remain unaffected by experience. By monitoring feedback, pragmatism—the search for truth or knowledge through examining consequences—is rendered a viable, broadly based educational principle.

SUMMARY

This chapter briefly deals with the basic ideas of functionalism's approach to education, mainly as represented by William James's views on purposivity and John Dewey's views on pragmatism. We seek to bring their contributions up-to-date through describing modern paradigms of feedback theory. We imply that thereby an understanding is reached that may help us better comprehend the axiom "learn-by-doing," and the implications for educational systems and practice.

Associationism

The Experience of Contiguity between Events and Its Molding of Thought, Perception, and Feeling

This chapter discusses philosophical, experimental, and clinical involvement in the topic of association, a topic of fundamental relevance to educational theory and practice. The chapter is cast in a historical mold, not to be especially reverent of history, but to illustrate the kinds of searching questions that initiated and still maintain inquiry into the means whereby knowledge and belief are acquired, and how references and conclusions are reached. Clinical aspects of associationism should be of background interest to all prospective teachers, but especially to those who may be considering "school psychologist" as an ancillary or potential career.

DEFINITIONS OF ASSOCIATION AND ASSOCIATIONISM

The word *association* refers to the spatial and/or temporal contiguity of two or more events. As used here, an "event" is an object, a stimulus, a response, an idea, a feeling—anything that is specifiable, either by measurement or through verbal report. *Associationism* refers to the systematic formulations proposed to describe the psychological consequences attendant upon experiencing the contiguity of events. These formulations fall into three main categories: philosophical, experimental, and clinical. Philosophical concern goes back at least as far as Aristotle and continues to this very day (Murphy & Kovach, 1972; Warren, 1916). Experimental inquiry began with Ebbinghaus and Thorndike almost a hundred years ago, and is still quite timely. Apart from its own unique orientation, abnormal psychology's theory and application weaves in and out of the philosophical and experimental approaches right from their beginnings.

PHILOSOPHICAL ASSOCIATIONISM: DESCARTES, LA METTRIE, LOCKE, JAMES MILL, JOHN STUART MILL, HUME

René Descartes's ideas concerning the reflex arc were important to the development of associationism. His mechanical-hydraulic prototype of the reflex arc, involving vapors going through tubes to connect sensory organs and muscles was associationistic, in the sense that a stimulus automatically evoked a response. One event necessarily followed another event. Descartes's concept of the reflex arc was quite sufficient to account for animal behavior, since animals were considered to be nothing more than biophysical machines. However, the concept had to be expanded in order to account for human behavior. The extension consisted of endowing the human being with a soul that possessed cognitive properties. Through thought, the soul made it possible for the human being to interpret stimuli, render decisions, reach conclusions, and exercise free will in implementing these conclusions. Thus, Descartes pulled together a combination of physiological, religious, and philosophical notions: (1) animals were exclusively machinelike; (2) although some of man's behavior was also reflexive, he was basically rational and capable of free will; (3) such was the case because man possessed a soul.

Was Descartes's position designed to accommodate the opposing secular and clerical pressures of the time? Rosenblith argues convincingly to the contrary; specifically, he maintains that Descartes was genuinely interested in cognition per se, even though he assigned this function to the reverential soul (Rosenblith, 1970). Descartes was truly concerned with those attributes of human behavior which could not be reduced to reflexlike associations. He considered these attributes useful as "tests": "Given machines or automata capable of simulating faithfully various human actions . . . , he formulated 'two very certain tests' that would distinguish man from brute or more precisely identify those aspects of man's nature that could not be reduced to that of an automaton.

The tests relate to (1) the creative use of language and (2) man's enormously varied repertory of actions" (Rosenblith, 1970, p. 231). Both attributes are, of course, quite timely to modern psychology and to education.

La Mettrie was an uncompromising materialist. He rejected the religious overtones to Descartes's explanation of the soul's interaction with the body, but retained the cognitive. He anticipated the Helmholtz doctrine (mind must be reduced to material events) by asserting that complex behavior was not a function of the soul, but was attributable to anatomy and physiology. (Hermann von Helmholtz was a German physicist, anatomist, and physiologist, 1821–1894.) La Mettrie did so by appealing to holistic principles, rather than to elementalistic reductions or associations of any form:

> Since all the faculties of the soul depend to such a degree on the proper organization of the brain and of the whole body . . . apparently they are this organization itself . . . . The soul is therefore but an empty word, *of which no one has any idea*, and which an enlightened man should use only to signify the part in us that thinks. (La Mettrie, 1748/1968, p. 273)

His meaning is probably clearer if the phrase in italics is changed to read "of which no one *can* have any idea."

La Mettrie's transcendental religious views were quite radical for his time. His account of the soul was unconventional, in that he did not conceive of it as a separate entity. He was literally forced into exile because he was not an orthodox soul–body dualist. Tremendous pressure existed (and still does) to conform to strictly interpreted, reified dualisms of one particular sort or another, despite the alternatives offered by other religious or philosophical orientations. La Mettrie's views were considered to be heretical.

Across the English Channel, John Locke's *An Essay Concerning Human Understanding* set the course for the British philosophical movement known as *empiricism*. The following positions were taken as axiomatic. First, all ideas originate directly from sensory experience; they do not arise from pure reason. Second, once ideas are gained by a person, they tend to become associated with each other. Third, thought and knowledge consist of these associations. Thus, education becomes a matter of selecting and establishing associations.

Locke proposed that there are two distinct types of associations, "sympathies" and "antipathies." The former includes associations that are natural; the latter refers to associations that are fortuitously acquired and unnatural. As an example of the first category, we might take "desk-chair." As an example of the second category, we can take Locke's own, retaining the English of 1700:

> Many children imputing the Pain they endured at School to their Books they
> were corrected for, so joyn those *Ideas* together, that a Book becomes their
> Aversion, and they are never reconciled to the study and use of them all their
> Lives after; and thus Reading becomes a torment to them, which otherwise
> possibly they might have made the great Pleasure of their Lives. There are
> Rooms convenient enough, that some Men cannot Study in, and fashions of
> Vessels, which though never so clean and commodious they cannot Drink
> out of, and that by reason of some accidental *Ideas* which are annex'd to
> them, and make them offensive. (Locke, 1700/1968, p. 338)

The relation of the foregoing passage to modern research in aversive conditioning, and to modern views of educational practice is obvious. Not so apparent is the fact that Locke was also hinting at the
psychoanalytic concepts of the preconscious and the unconscious and of
repression and resistance. This is revealed in the paragraph preceding
the quoted passage:

> There is scarce any one that does not observe something that seems odd to
> him, and is in itself really Extravagant in the Opinions, Reasonings, and
> Actions of other Men. The least flaw of this kind, if at all different from his
> own, every one is quick-sighted enough to espie in another, and will by the
> Authority of Reason forwardly condemn, though he be guilty of much great-
> er Unreasonableness of his own Tenets and Conduct, which he never per-
> ceives, and will very hardly, if at all, be convinced of. (Locke, 1700/1968, p.
> 334)

Two further observations need to be made before we pass on to
James Mill. First, it does not seem to have been important to Locke that
sympathies, just as antipathies, were learned and remembered. What a
refreshingly optimistic view of human nature! Locke's vision is not con-
founded by propositions concerning the *innateness* of morally "good" or
"bad" ideas. *All* ideas originated from sensory experience; it is their
connections that were either natural or unnatural, reasonable or unrea-
sonable. Second, it is valuable to remember that Locke was a philosopher, not an experimenter, or a clinician. He based his essay upon observing associations that were already formulated in himself and in
others. He started with an established association, deduced the components through a conjectural analysis, and then argued how the formulated association might possibly have been induced or put together.
Thus, the same person was involved in both the hypothetical deduction
(analysis), and the equally hypothetical induction (synthesis).

The same strategy was used by the other British associationists.
James Mill's view of how ideas become associated with each other, thereby yielding thought, was so dependent upon tight linkages that it became known as "mental mechanics." Mill held that thought consisted of

trains of associated ideas, usually increasing in complexity. Each such train was initiated by a sensation. He wrote:

> Thought succeeds thought; idea follows idea, incessantly. If our senses are awake, we are continually receiving sensations, of the eye, the ear, the touch, and so forth; but not sensations alone. After sensations, ideas are perpetually excited of sensations formerly received; after those ideas, other ideas: and during the whole of our lives, a series of those two states of consciousness, called sensations, and ideas, is constantly going on. (J. Mill, 1829/1968, p. 364)

The example he gives to explain what he means is plain and to the point: "I see a horse: that is a sensation. Immediately I think of his master: that is an idea. The idea of his master makes me think of his office; he is a minister of state: that is another idea. The idea of a minister of state makes me think of public affairs; and I am led into a train of political ideas" (J. Mill, 1829/1968, p. 364). Just at that moment, his thoughts are interrupted by his hearing the call to dinner. "This is a new sensation, followed by the idea of dinner, and of the company with whom I am to partake it. The sight of the company and of the food are other sensations; these suggest ideas without end; other sensations perpetually intervene, suggesting other ideas; and so the process goes on" (p. 364).

Probably Mill was led to his conclusions by working backwards. In examining the first chain of ideas, he may have started out with "Why am I now thinking of politics?" and conjectured analytically to identify in retrospect the links in the chain of associations which had led to the idea of politics. Having identified them, he then presented a synthesis of these components to provide a description of the progression of thought. Needless to say, there was no independent verification at either stage—analysis or synthesis—of this introspective process.

Mill distinguished between two types of associations, synchronous and successive. The former consisted of associations that were established on the basis of spatial contiguity, or "simultaneous existence" in space. For example, "the various objects in my room, the chairs, the tables, the books, have the synchronous order, or order in space" (J. Mill, 1829/1968, p. 364). The objects were all associated because of their proximity to each other. One could look at these commonplace objects in different sequences, the chairs first or the tables first. There was no *inherently mandated*, serial order to the way they were sensed, or to the elapse of time separating the observations. However, successive associations *do* involve serial order and temporal contiguity or "antecedent and consequent existence." For example, "the sight of the flash from the mortar fired at a distance, the hearing of the report" (p. 365). Because the speed of light is much greater than the speed of sound, there is a physically determined basis both to the antecedent and consequent order in which the events are sensed, and to the time separating the two events. Mill also held that of the two types of associations, the successive is more prevalent than the synchronous. The fact is that events in the world, and our relation to them, tend more to keep changing than to remain static. Further, he noted that the strength of both types of associations is influenced by the vividness (i.e., distinctiveness) of the entering component-events, and by how often these events are paired with each other.

Before passing from Mill the Elder to Mill the Younger, we must note James Mill's own uneasiness lest his views concerning the formation of associations be interpreted too rigidly. He carefully observed the following:

> In the successive order of ideas, that which precedes, is sometimes called the suggesting, that which succeeds, the suggested idea; not that any *power* is supposed to reside in the antecedent over the consequent; suggesting, and suggested, mean only antecedent and consequent, with the additional idea, *that such order is not casual, but, to a certain degree, permanent.* (J. Mill, 1829/1968, p. 367, emphasis added)

One can detect in the foregoing passage the beginning of a distinction between nonreflexive association leading to a psychological impression of connectedness, and logical inference leading to a conclusion of causality. Simply put, the fact that we observe one event precede another, does not necessarily imply that the first is the cause of the second. He prepared the way for his son's *A System of Logic*, a work which sets forth rules whereby an inquirer can examine the nature of the relations between regularly correlated events, and can assess the likelihood that a particular antecedent event is indeed the cause of a consequent event.

John Stuart Mill was in accord with his father's distinction between synchronous and successive types of associations. He did not agree with his assertion that complex ideas were reducible to linkages of individual component ideas, trains of which were initiated by sensations. Nor did he agree with David Hume, who held that

> it is a fixed feature of the mind to regard as a *cause* any event which reliably precedes and is always "conjoined" with another event which the mind then takes to be the *effect*. Indeed, the idea of causality is nothing but this constant conjunction between two events narrowly separated in time. (quoted in D.N. Robinson, 1982, p. 19)

Rather, the son believed that complex ideas were generated in a manner analogous to the chemical process whereby water is formed from the combination of hydrogen and oxygen. Even as water has properties that are quite different from its entering elements, so a complex idea possesses characteristics that transcend its entering components. Clearly, J.S. Mill was anticipating the gestalt dictum that "the whole is different from the sum of its parts."

Mill the Younger believed that, once complex ideas are formed, they followed the rules of association, such as synchronicity and succession, laid down by his father. He stated: "It may be remarked, that the general laws of association prevail among these more intricate states of mind, in the same manner as among the simpler ones" (J.S. Mill, 1843/1968, p. 380). The importance of synchronous and successive associations in establishing the psychological impression of relations between events (whether physical or ideational) led J.S. Mill to examine the rules that determine causality. He undertook the task because causality, too, is concerned with the relations between events, but from a logical point of view. Unlike Hume, he tried to separate psychological impressions of connectedness from inferences of causality.

Can a sharp distinction indeed be drawn between the nonreflexive association processes, which yield psychological impressions, and the logical inferences, which indicate causality? The problem was hinted at by Kant. He suggested that the tendency to seek organization among events was a trait *inborn* in human beings. Inborn or not, how much of this trait rests upon impressions, and how much upon logic? The issue can be sharpened if we look more carefully at the fundamental types of association, the synchronous and successive. James Mill's example of the former rested upon the physical proximity of one event to another (his example was the objects in his room). But how "near" is the required nearness of A to B before an association is formed? Clearly, there are limits to the impression of spatial contiguity. These limits are imposed by the amount of intervening space, by the structure and function of A and B themselves, and by the psychological condition of the observer.

The matter of limits notwithstanding, let us accept that spatial contiguity is responsible for Mill's psychological association of chairs with tables. Now suppose he were to have found a nick in the edge of the table he worked on, and a nick in the arm-rest of the chair he sat upon, and that these damages to his furniture were not only spatially contiguous, but were at a common height from the floor. A logical inference he might have drawn is that he had inadvertently jostled his chair against the table. However, other possible explanations exist. For example, his maid may have carelessly used her mop against both the chair and the table, striking each at the same height. Thus, starting with an association based upon spatial contiguity, and then noticing a common factor,

Mill could have drawn the wrong logical inference, and blamed himself for something that another person had done.

In the case of successive associations, the danger of confusion between psychological impression and logical inference is even greater. Using Mill the Elder's own example, it is readily evident that the association between the sight of a specific gun flash, A, and the subsequent hearing of a particular report, B, does not establish that A was indeed the cause of B. The usefulness of seriality between events as a criterion for assuming causality is limited by the number of concurrent antecedent A's that are known (in this case, seen), let alone those that are unknown (or unseen). The notion of seriality is also limited by the length of time elapsing between the events that enter into the sequence; that is, temporal contiguity. If the elapsed time is too great, irrelevant flashes may preempt the observer's attention, and be incorrectly identified as the antecedent event. Thus, the true gun may go unrecognized if other flashes intervene before the actually related consequent sound is heard. Further complications arise from the previously mentioned factors of vividness and frequency of paired events. For example, a larger mortar is more likely to engage our attention because of its brighter flash and louder blast. And a gun that is fired more frequently may be more compelling than one that is fired less often.

J.S. Mill's *A System of Logic* is a remarkable attempt to illuminate the gray area concerning notions of relationship between events that rest upon psychological impressions, and of those that depend upon logical inference. Additionally, his work enables us to understand why even logical inference can be fallible, despite the best efforts of the inquirer. His analysis is as timely today as when it was first published (1843).

He generated several rules or canons whereby logical inferences can be drawn. Among them are procedures now known as the Method of Agreement and the Method of Difference. According to the former, the antecedent of correlational methods, that variable which precedes all instances of a given effect is the causative agent. The logic is illustrated in the accompanying schema:

$$X, Y, Z \rightarrow \text{effect}$$
$$X, Y \quad \rightarrow \text{effect}$$
$$Y, Z \rightarrow \text{effect}$$
$$\text{Therefore, } Y \text{ is the cause}$$

The Method of Agreement is fallible on both experimental and correlational grounds, since the wrong common factor may be identified. There may be another, unknown variable—the "true" cause—that regularly accompanies Y. The method is also fallible on the even prior grounds that no scientist can possibly examine *all* instances leading to a given effect. One or another type of sampling or replication of presumably representative cases must be employed.

In order to illustrate how the Method of Agreement may be involved in educational research, we can raise the question, "What makes for a low drop-out rate in high school?" A hypothetical study is done in which the effects of "good genetics" (X), "caring person" (Y), and "good environment" (Z)—by whatever definitions—are evaluated. We find that the presence of X, Y, Z, or X, Y, or Y, Z in combination leads to a low drop-out rate. Since the common factor is "caring person," we are tempted to attribute the low drop-out rate to variable Y. But for reasons of fallibility given above, we cannot be absolutely certain. The same limitations apply to the Method of Difference, the antecedent to experimental method, where the X, Z combination is considered as a control for Y, either singly or in interaction with X and/or Z.

The logic of the Method of Difference is illustrated as follows:

$$X, Y, Z \rightarrow \text{effect}$$
$$X, \quad Z \rightarrow \text{absence of effect}$$
$$\text{Therefore, } Y \text{ is the cause}$$

The causative agent is that variable which, when present, is followed by the effect; and which, when absent, is not followed by the effect. As with the Method of Agreement, there are two sorts of fallibility inherent in this procedure: (1) Y may be regularly accompanied by some unknown variable, the existence of which is unsuspected; (2) the scientist must draw the line somewhere with regard to the number of times he tests for the presence or absence of the effect, and he may cease replicating too soon.

Must we then give up in despair? Only if we believe that either psychology or logic leads to ultimate truth. If we turn these disciplines into *metaphysics*, then we are using them for purposes beyond their legitimate scope. Despite their fallibility, conclusions of association based upon psychological impressions, and of causality based upon logical inferences, can be correct. It depends upon the acumen and judiciousness of the observer or the experimenter, with the caveat that sometimes even the best are wrong.

British philosophers defined the areas of associationism and of causality and specified the variables and methods of interest, but they did not enter the laboratory. We turn now to those associationists who did, the early experimenters. By firmly grasping the rationale of their research, we establish a baseline, as it were, against which we are better able to evaluate more recent attempts at studying learning and thinking. These attempts include those of largely Soviet investigators (Chapter 5, Russian Dialectical-Materialist Psychology), German scientists (Chapter 7, Gestalt Psychology), and American researchers (Chapter 6, Behaviorism, and Chapter 10, Cognitive Psychology).

EXPERIMENTAL ASSOCIATIONISM: EBBINGHAUS AND THORNDIKE

Psychological research began with Fechner, the combined mystic-mathematician, who almost single-handedly developed the psychophysical methods, techniques for determining the relation between specific stimuli and resulting sensations. The fundamental subject matter studied was "pure" consciousness, and how it was amalgamated from component sensations produced by isolated stimuli. The study of higher mental processes, such as learning and thinking, was deliberately excluded from the fledgling science. It was held that these phenomena were too complex; they went beyond the limits imposed by scientific positivism.

Hermann Ebbinghaus wanted to reach out experimentally toward these complex mental functions, and to do so through the study of verbal learning and remembering. But paradoxically, he used the building-block, Fechnerian version of laboratory methodology to conduct his investigations. Thereby, he set an extraordinary constraint on what might be legitimately construed as comprising his proper subject matter. His elementalistic approach became so pure as to require the use of meaningless nonsense syllables in his examination of the acquisition and retention of verbal associations. As noted by Duane Schultz:

> Ebbinghaus wanted to apply the experimental method to the higher mental processes and decided, probably as a result of the influence of the British associationists, to make the attempt in the field of memory. . . . Ebbinghaus recognized an inherent difficulty in using prose or poetry. Meanings of associations are already attached to words by those who know the language . . . [he therefore] sought material that would be uniformly unassociated, completely homogeneous, and equally unfamiliar—material with which there could be no past associations. (Schultz, 1981, pp. 73–74)

The nonsense syllables he typically employed were of the form consonant-vowel-consonant, such as "VAD." By means of a memory drum, a list of such syllables can be presented sequentially to the subject. A memory drum is a cylinder which rotates about a horizontal axle, with an electric motor supplying the power, and with switches determining the motor's on–off intervals. The syllables are viewed through a frame in consistent, serial order. There is a brief pause between presentations of successive syllables. The task imposed is that of learning to use the first syllable as a cue or stimulus word for the second syllable and to anticipate verbally the second syllable before it is actually shown. The appearance of the second syllable then serves both to provide knowledge of results for correctness of the prior response and to act as a cue for anticipating the next or third syllable. This procedure (formally known as the method of anticipation) is followed until the entire list of perhaps ten or more syllables is viewed and responded to, thereby constituting a single trial. The list is assumed to be fully learned when the subject can anticipate all the syllables in the list without a single error, usually to a criterion of two consecutive trials so as to reduce the likelihood of chance success.

Of course, there are variations of this fundamental technique. Using the method of anticipation, Ebbinghaus even experimented with associative learning and remembering of lines of poetry, and satisfied himself that this type of material, although easier to learn and to remember, followed the same general laws of association as were obtained from nonsense syllables. Properties of poetry that are untapped by the memory drum—such as metaphor and creativity of expression—remained unexamined. His independent variables included: (1) the exposure time of each syllable, (2) the time between syllables, (3) the number of syllables, and (4) the time elapsing between original learning and the test for retention. The type of data gathered, as well as the kinds of issues that emerged, are illustrated in Figure 4.1. The upper panel shows that when either nonsense syllables or familiar names are learned in consistent serial order (e.g., by means of a memory drum), it is more difficult to acquire and to retain the items in the middle of the list than those toward either end. One theory advanced to account for this phenomenon holds that interference with, or inhibition from, each item with respect to the other is maximal in the middle of the list. The lower panel shows that even though the absolute number of errors is greater for nonsense syllables than for names, the *relative* interference (or inhibition) is about the same for both.

Here we must pause for a moment to realize more fully the implications of Ebbinghaus's contribution. Whereas the philosopher-associationists conjectured about the formation of their own trains of *existing* associations, Ebbinghaus studied the formation of *new* associations, and he did so in the laboratory. Thus, a logical argument for explaining the generation of associations did not rest upon the persuasiveness of a

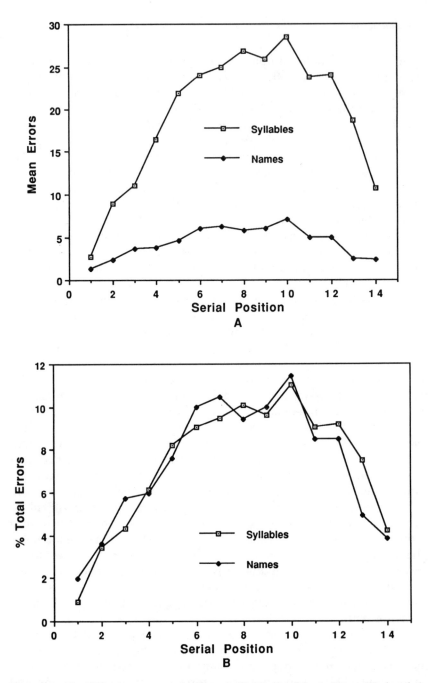

Figure 4.1. The Ebbinghaus approach. (From J. W. Kling and L. A. Riggs, *Woodworth & Schlosberg's Experimental Psychology* (3rd ed.) (1971). Copyright 1971 by Holt, Rinehart & Winston. Reprinted by permission of Holt, Rinehart & Winston.)

single individual. Other investigators could use Ebbinghaus's (or any-one else's) experimental procedures, and determine for themselves whether the data were replicable, and form testable hypotheses concerning explanations of the data.

Whereas Ebbinghaus's tactic of studying the formation of new associations was to use human subjects and nonsense syllables, the educator Edward Lee Thorndike's was to use animal subjects and "puzzle boxes." A puzzle box was a cage into which a hungry animal, most often a cat, was placed. The cat could escape through a door which opened when the animal pulled a lever, or a chain, or a wire loop, singly or in some sequence. Upon obtaining its release, the cat was given a morsel of food, and placed again in the cage for another trial. The time-to-escape per trial was recorded. Figure 4.2 is a representative curve, and originally appeared in Thorndike's dissertation (Thorndike, 1898, cited in Woodworth & Schlosberg, 1954, p. 537).

> Thorndike held that the solution of such a problem by cats and other animals involved the formation of an association between some aspect of the stimulus-situation, such as the wire loop or the wooden lever with the specific movement that led to door-opening. Further, he argued the stimulus-response relation that finally appeared was obviously influenced by the outcome of this movement. The pleasure experienced by the animal in getting out of the box and to the food served to stamp in the connection between stimulus and response that led to the pleasure. By the same token, stimulus-response connections that did not lead to a pleasurable after-effect were not strengthened, and tended to drop out. (Keller & Schoenfeld, 1950, p. 39)

Eventually, Thorndike termed the underlying principle of association the Law of Effect.

But Thorndike was interested in explaining more than just how a cat formed associations. He boldly stated in his dissertation: "our best service has been to show that animal intellection is made up of a lot of specific connections . . . which subserve practical ends directly, and to homologize it with the intellection involved in such human associations as regulate the conduct of a man playing tennis" (Thorndike, 1898, cited in Schultz, 1969, p. 177). He was among the first, along with Pavlov, to argue that animals could be studied in the laboratory in order to illuminate human learning. In this way, he helped establish American behaviorism.

Thorndike's approach stands out for the following additional reasons: (1) His view of stimulus–response connections was one in which stimuli served as *cues*, rather than "goads." His connectionism was a far cry from Cartesian sensory-motor reflexology. (2) His choice of animals, rather than humans, to study associations in puzzle boxes, reflected the

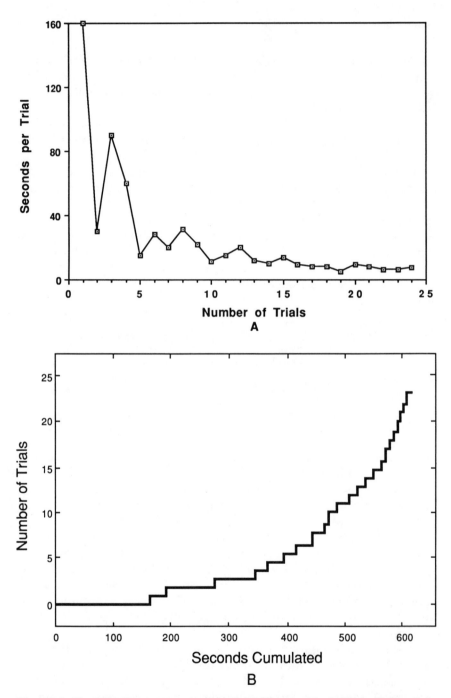

Figure 4.1. The Ebbinghaus approach. (From J. W. Kling and L. A. Riggs, *Woodworth & Schlosberg's Experimental Psychology* (3rd ed.) (1971). Copyright 1971 by Holt, Rinehart & Winston. Reprinted by permission of Holt, Rinehart & Winston.)

influence of Darwin's theory of evolution. (3) His drawing a parallel between animal learning and human intellection was not so much a matter of attributing ideational, cognitive properties to the cat, but rather the other way around; namely, to suggest that much of human behavior did not require deliberate thought. (4) His use of food as a reinforcer for the cat's escape from the puzzle box led to the behavioristic premise that reinforcement could retroactively influence the emission of consequent acts. Figure 4.2 is after that appearing in a classic influential text, and shows the kind of data obtained by Thorndike. It also shows how the data in panel A can be replotted to yield cumulative curves of the Skinnerian-behaviorist variety (panel B). Thorndike's connectionism, less its underlying hedonistic overtones, became fundamental to the philosophy of future American behaviorism, which we consider in a subsequent chapter.

CLINICAL ASSOCIATIONISM: KENT-ROSANOFF, RORSCHACH, JUNG

We include a section on Clinical Associationism mainly to show how philosophical and experimental ideas enter into both routine and unusual associative learning and memory. They do so in the case of the teacher as well as the student. The broadly trained educator should be cognizant of the implications for *both* teachers and students.

Abnormal psychology, like experimental psychology, brought positivism to bear upon the study of associations. The clinician's use of word association tests (such as the Kent-Rosanoff), and of projective tests (such as the Rorschach "ink-blot"), are deterministic extensions of Locke's earlier distinction between natural and unnatural associations. There is a further similarity. As with the British philosophers, clinical-testers deal with *existing* responses, and then work backward analytically to select the psychological variables that might have induced the responses. Both the Kent-Rosanoff and the Rorschach involve the presentation of stimuli to subjects, and then the tester's analysis of the attendant responses or "free" associations to these stimuli. First, a demonstrational word association test (WAT), and later, a projective situation are provided for illustrative purposes.

As is evident from the demonstrational WAT, the analysis is accomplished by comparing the subject's responses with norms gathered from diverse populations. (If the reader is part of a group, he may want to compare his responses with those of others.)

The principle difference between the two types of tests consists of the amount of structure contained in the stimuli. The verbal stimuli of the

WAT are considered to be more structured than the visual stimuli of the Rorschach, and therefore less conducive to sampling a wide range of associations. Nonetheless, the range of associations allowed by verbal stimuli is sufficient to have convinced Jung of the usefulness of this kind of test. He developed one of his own to use for diagnostic purposes, reasoning that departures from conventional norms indicated possible emotional problems. The particular diagnosis made depended upon the *content* of the unique responses, not just their number. Jung was hardly a mental mechanic! He also recorded the time taken to respond to each stimulus-word (i.e., reaction time), and treated long reaction times as evidence indicative of "blocking."

Word association tests (Tables 4.1 and 4.2) are currently used not only by professional clinicians and school psychologists, but also by police and intelligence experts. Charged words, such as the location of a drug outlet, or of a crime and the name of the weapon employed, are included among the routine stimulus words. The content of the responses to these charged words, as well as the time taken to utter them, are evaluated.

Considerable research has gone into standardizing the procedure for giving and for evaluating the Rorschach test. A subject is given ink-blotcards one at a time, and instructed to report what he or she sees in each. Broadly speaking, the quality of coherence (or perception) brought to the sensations evoked by the stimuli depends upon the respondee's characteristic interpersonal relations and mode of organizing the world. Responses are classified according to three major categories: (1) *Location*, or the specific portion of the blot that evokes the response (e.g., whole blot, large detail, small detail). (2) *Determinants*, or the specific stimulus attributes selectively attended to (e.g., color, form, apparent movement, shading). (3) *Content*, or the nature of what is perceived (e.g., humans, animals, objects, processes). Why these particular categories? Some rough examples should help make clear the rationale. Consider "Location": whether the respondee uses the whole blot or only a small detail thereof may indicate how he or she typically organizes life's ambiguous situations. For instance, does he or she try to get at the total picture, or is he or she diverted by minor issues? "Determinant": color is presumed to be related to the ways in which affect influences perception and behavior. The expression "He always sees the darker side of things" conveys the idea. If the "Content" of the responses tends to be *mainly* animals, then it may reflect that the respondee—if an adult—is less than mature in the way he or she relates to other people.

After the responses are classified, the Rorschach expert goes on to consider the interrelations within and among the three major categories

Table 4.1. Demonstrational Word Association Test[a]

Instructions: Below you will see a list of 20 stimulus words. After each word, write the first word that it makes you think of. Start with the first word; look at it; write the word it makes you think of; then go on to the next word. Use only a single word for each response. Do not skip any words. Work rapidly until you have finished all 20 words.

	Stimulus[b]	Response
1.	Table	_____
2.	Dark	_____
3.	Music	_____
4.	Sickness	_____
5.	Man	_____
6.	Deep	_____
7.	Soft	_____
8.	Eating	_____
9.	Mountain	_____
10.	House	_____
11.	Black	_____
12.	Mutton	_____
13.	Comfort	_____
14.	Hand	_____
15.	Short	_____
16.	Fruit	_____
17.	Butterfly	_____
18.	Smooth	_____
19.	Command	_____
20.	Chair	_____

[a] From W.A. Russell and I.J. Jenkins (1954). *The Complete Minnesota Norms for Responses to 100 Words from the Kent-Rosanoff Word Association Test.* ONR Tech. Rep. 11, 1954 (Contract Number N8 ONR-66216). Because they were obtained so long ago, these norms are not strictly valid and serve only for demonstration purposes.
[b] The first 20 stimulus words of the Kent-Rosanoff Word Association Test.

Table 4.2. The Three Most Common Responses to Stimulus Words[a]

Instructions: Using your own sense of discretion as to personal privacy, select any of your associations that are illustrative of Locke's "sympathies" or "antipathies." Select any of your associations that are illustrative of James Mill's "synchronous" or "successive" component events.

Stimulus	Responses
1. Table	Chair, Food, Desk
2. Dark	Light, Night, Room
3. Music	Song(s), Note(s), Sound
4. Sickness	Health, Ill, Death
5. Man	Woman(en), Boy, Girl
6. Deep	Shallow, Dark, Water
7. Soft	Hard, Light, Pillow
8. Eating	Food, Drinking, Sleeping
9. Mountain	Hill(s), High, Snow
10. House	Home, Door, Garage
11. Black	White, Dark, Cat
12. Mutton	Lamb, Sheep, Meat
13. Comfort	Chair, Bed, Ease
14. Hand	Foot(ee), Finger(s), Arm
15. Short	Tall, Long, Fat
16. Fruit	Apple, Vegetable, Orange
17. Butterfly	Moth, Insect, Wing(s)
18. Smooth	Rough, Soft, Hard
19. Command	Order, Army, Obey
20. Chair	Table, Sit, Leg(s)

[a] From W.A. Russell and I.J. Jenkins (1954). *The Complete Minnesota Norms for Responses to 100 Words from the Kent-Rosanoff Word Association Test.* ONR Tech. Rep. 11, 1954 (Contract Number N8 ONR-66216). Because they were obtained so long ago, these norms are not strictly valid and serve only for demonstrational purposes.

Figure 4.3. Panel of modern sculpture designed by Jean Dubuffet. (From the collection of Rebecca and Joseph Notterman.)

of responses. Simply adding up scores is hardly what the Rorschach is about—a holistic, rather than elementalistic, approach is taken.

The principles of projective association apply not only to standardized tests, but extend to works of art that invite a rich variety of interpretations by the viewer. For example, the accompanying photograph of a panel of modern sculpture by Dubuffet (Figure 4.3) can be used to demonstrate the power of projective tests. If two or more people are instructed to look at it with the idea of reporting what they see, and if they write down their responses independently, and then compare them, they will rarely find that their responses are completely identical. Of course, art is meant to be enjoyed for its own sake, without submitting it to psychological scrutiny. But it is also instructive to examine it with the psychologist's eye or ear, as is done in the field of aesthetics.

A CONCLUDING COMMENT

Learning by association is a necessary part of education. The learning may be of the mental mechanics or mental chemistry type. It may be rote or interactive, conscious or unconscious. This is not to deny that other kinds of learning, such as insight, occur. (We shall have more to say about insight-learning in a later chapter.) It is just to assert that the educator should be aware of the rich and broad heritage upon which his pedagogical techniques rest.

Finally, we must not lose sight of the fact that the idea of causality—everyday, educational, and scientific—is influenced by the same parameters that lead to associationistic impressions. There is, to reiterate, a gray area between psychological relatedness and logical inference. In being informed of the philosophical and experimental aspects of associationism, the teacher has a broader and deeper understanding of how ideas, attitudes, and behavior are formulated both in and out of the classroom. He or she is not so prone to accept the conventional wisdom, or the conforming viewpoint, or the quick panacea to the solution of educational problems.

Russian Dialectical-Materialist Psychology

Classical Conditioning and Its Relation to Mentation and Language

By way of preamble necessary to bring the topic to date, we quote the following:

> Momentous events [are] now occurring throughout the former "Marxist" world. [Now that] East and West . . . seek firmer grounds of mutual understanding, it is even more important to recognize certain philosophical and quasi-scientific assumptions that have been sources of division. It is also important for readers to know that Marxism does not *require* a mindless psychology and that Capitalism does not *require* selfishness. (D.N. Robinson, personal communication, 1990)

Russian ideas concerning the proper subject matter of psychology were markedly influenced by social-political events. Indeed, as we shall see, psychology was derived from these events. It did not stand on its own. The psychology of Communist revolutionary (1917) and post-revolutionary times is different from that of prerevolutionary days, and for reasons that were frequently expostulated in terms of Communist doctrine, as well as inherent scientific merit.

Communist doctrine, in turn, rested upon Marx's and Lenin's writings on dialectical materialism. The relation of their theorizing to the field of psychology is often strained, even in the attempted application

61

by Soviet psychologists. But the psychology *per se* is of considerable importance, in that it emphasizes areas that Americans generally have left untouched, or have perceived in entirely different ways.

The foregoing is a salient reminder that even though governments fall or merely change direction, the philosophies that led to particularly creative views of psychology and education, regardless of political setting, tend to linger. We shall see ample evidence of this phenomenon as we go through the contents of this chapter.

The general objective of this chapter is to sketch the major intertwining social-political, philosophical, theoretical, and experimental features of Russian dialectical-materialist psychology. As we shall see, strict attention was given to the economic origin of social and political values, and to the proper inculcation of these values in and out of schools.

DIALECTICAL MATERIALISM: ITS LINK TO RUSSIAN PSYCHOLOGY—HEGEL, MARX, LENIN

"Dialectics" means logical argumentation. Marx utilized Hegelian dialectics, a type which holds that any thesis can be countered by an equally tenable antithesis, and that reasoned consideration of the two opposing points of view will eventually lead to their resolution or synthesis (Georg Wilhelm Friedrich Hegel was a German philosopher, 1770–1831). The synthesis in turn is stated in the form of a new thesis, which leads to its own antithesis, followed by yet another synthesis, and so on. "Materialism" asserts that reality consists of matter; more specifically, matter and its motions.

"Dialectical materialism" is more difficult to define and to grasp than either of its component terms, and there is very little in English that one can consult. The problem is that there are two distinct connotations to its meaning, both of which are fairly foreign to the American. One interpretation is philosophic, the other is economic, even though both views originate in Hegelian dialectics. The *philosophic theory* holds that matter is in a continuous state of transformation. The changes in matter are induced in one of two ways: either (1) by nature—for example, when clouds are turned into rain, and the resulting water affects a tenuous ecological balance, consequently initiating still further changes; or (2) by man—for example, when trees are turned into wooden things, and these articles are used to make or to obtain a variety of other objects. The availability of these objects enables the production or acquisition of still other items, and so the process of material transformation continues.

The *economic* theory affirms that a society containing socioeconomic classes inevitably evolves through political thesis, antithesis, synthesis, new thesis, and so on, toward one without classes. Marx and other Communist writers believed that the economic version of dialectical materialism necessarily followed from the philosophic (Kornilov, 1930; Razran, 1958a,b). (Equally competent capitalist theoreticians disagree and assert that there is no connection. Indeed, the Eastern bloc of nations has apparently been won over to the capitalist view.)

The use of "dialectical materialism" for psychological purposes stems from Marx's argument for tying the economic theory to the philosophic. The line of reasoning is as follows: Whoever owns natural resources (matter) and the means of producing and distributing food and manufactured goods (matter transformed into usable things), directly or indirectly establishes the individual and society's prevailing conception of what is "valuable," or possesses "worth." Through their control of textbooks, television, newspapers, and other forms of communication, those in charge of material can perpetuate or manipulate these values. In short, there is a dynamic interconnection between goods and "value," each category can influence what happens to the other. Private ownership encourages value-concepts which direct production and distribution so as to lead to a selfish, divided society, one that eventually destroys itself. Collective (i.e., state) ownership, however, leads to a cooperative, free society, resting upon the unselfish principle heralded by the slogan "from each according to his ability, to each according to his need."

Because of his emphasis upon the relation between economic theory and the formation of values, Marx was forced to consider issues which were primarily of a *psychological* character. He tried to show that the supporters of private ownership (whether czarist or capitalist) assumed that peasants or workers could be "programmed" like robots to accept reflexively the particular things they *should* cherish. In contradistinction, Marx and other proponents of Communism held that man's behavior was not only reflexive, but also independent. Because of his ability to adapt, his capacity to represent the world ideationally, and his gift for abstract thought, man could *learn* to become both individually purposeful and socially active. It is on these grounds—and not the ones implied by a spontaneous and innate "free will"—that man's behavior can be considered independent. Some of the implications of Communist values for educational approaches are considered in Chapter 2.

In his *Philosophical Notebooks* (published posthumously in 1929-30), Lenin sharpened Marx's distinction between the two opposing views of human nature, reflexive and independent. The reflexive was termed "one-way dialectical materialism"; the independent, "two-way dialectical materialism."

One-way (or one-path) dialectical materialism asserts that an understanding of anatomy and physiology (particulary of the brain and central nervous system) is both necessary and sufficient (hence *one* requirement) for an understanding of human behavior. (Probably the closest American equivalent is neuropsychology.) Mental life is epiphenomenal, and has no independent influence upon action. In its essentials, one-way dialectical materialism is a restatement of the Helmholtz doctrine, which held that mental life was reducible to physiochemical events. Two-way dialectical materialism holds that while a knowledge of the brain's material qualities is necessary for an understanding of human behavior, it is not sufficient: there is a *second* requirement. Mentation (the additional way or path) has its own representative reality (albeit within the constraints mandated by anatomy, physiology, heredity, socioeconomic environment, and past experience), and exerts a perceived autonomous influence on an individual's personal and social behavior. (Probably the closest American equivalent is a mix of conditioning, social psychology, and cognitive psychology.)

Prerevolutionary psychology was dominated by one-way dialectical materialism, mainly in the form of Ivan M. Sechenov's reflexology. Revolutionary psychology tried to come to grips with the political implications of two-way dialectical materialism. K.N. Kornilov's reactology was considered by Soviet authorities and found wanting. Meanwhile, I.P. Pavlov's conditioning research and theory (which preceded and continued through the Russian revolution) was undergoing careful ideological scrutiny, and was eventually decreed to be thoroughly acceptable. Postrevolutionary psychology expanded on conditioning in ways that most Americans are first beginning to comprehend and to relate to their own endeavors. We now look more carefully at each of these stages of Russian psychology, for all have implications for education, regardless of country.

PREREVOLUTIONARY TIMES: SECHENOV, DEWEY'S CRITICISM

As we know, Descartes accounted for animal behavior by means of reflex arcs. He maintained that animals are soul-less, biophysical machines. Human beings, because they have souls, possess the capacity to overcome purely materialistic, input–output reflexes. It is for this reason that man can be held morally responsible for his actions.

Ivan M. Sechenov, a prerevolutionary physiologist, had no place for souls or free will. Unlike Descartes, the *modest* materialist, Sechenov was a *frank* materialist, and he minced no words in presenting his extreme position:

> All psychical acts, without exception . . . are developed by means of reflexes . . . all conscious movements (usually called voluntary), inasmuch as they arise from these acts, are reflex in the strictest sense of the word. The question whether voluntary movements are really based upon stimulation of sensory nerves is thereby answered affirmatively. (Sechenov, 1863/1968, p. 317)

By "psychical activity," Sechenov implied thoughts, ideas, and imagination, phenomena generally assumed to be autonomous. He asserted that psychical activity is based upon neurological residuals (or traces) of what were originally *overt*, physiological reflexes. The development of a wide repertoire of covert, stimulus–response connections or associations is possible only through purely physiological processes, such as facilitation and inhibition. If we eliminate the physiological assumptions (he offered no conclusive data), Sechenov sounds like a latter-day James Mill, the English mental mechanic.

The Russian scientist was well aware that his bold analysis flew in the face of everyday, personal experience. For instance, how can either *voluntary* movement or *autonomous* thought be said to originate from *direct stimulation* of sensory nerves? His position is best understood if we isolate the three premises upon which it rests. They are:

Premise 1. Thought is an optico-acoustic trace of a reflex. In other words, thought consists of visual imagery and hearing one's own internal speech.

Premise 2. The perceived independence (or free-initiation) of "voluntary" movement and "autonomous" thought is illusory. So-called voluntary movement and autonomous thought are really initiated directly by external stimuli that go unnoticed. These stimuli go unnoticed for three reasons: (1) They are weak, and are (in today's language) overshadowed. (2) Because they are weak, these stimuli and their attendant indistinct sensations cannot be discerned as initiating a serial order of events. Hence, a connection between these weak stimuli and the ostensibly voluntary movement or autonomous thought fails to be recognized. (3) The time span between the truly initiating (but weak) stimuli and the consequent movement or thought exceeds (in today's language) short-term memory.

Premise 3. The illusion is maintained through contingencies involving the same thought followed by different acts, or different thoughts followed by the same act. The perceived independence of voluntary movement and of autonomous thought is abetted not only by overshadowing and by the limits of short-term memory, but also by (in today's language) differential reinforcement, as indicated in this illustration. Here is an example:

> I devote my daytime to physiology; but in the evening, while going to bed, it is my habit to think of politics. [Recall that James Mill, too, was taken with politics.] It happens, of course, that among other political matters I *sometimes* think of the Emperor of China [emphasis added, to underscore the third premise]. This [optico]-acoustic trace becomes associated with the various sensations (muscular, tactile, thermic, etc.) which I experience when lying in bed. It may happen, one day, that owing to fatigue or to the absence of work I lie down on my bed in the daytime; and lo! all of a sudden I notice that I am thinking of the Emperor of China. People usually say that there is no particular cause for such a visitation; but we see that in the given case it was called forth by the sensations of lying in bed; and now that I have *written* this example, I shall associate the Emperor of China with more vivid sensations, and he will become my frequent guest. (Sechenov, 1863/1968, p. 317)

It is easy to see why Ivan Sechenov is considered to be the father of "objective" psychology, of which American behaviorism is an offshoot. And why, too, the intellectuals and scientists of revolutionary Russia found his reflexology overly reductionist for a society that demanded independence of action and thought, without which education for individual purposivism and social activism would be impossible.

Interestingly, the American educator-philosopher, John Dewey, wrote what is probably the most devasting criticism of reflexology. He argued that the concepts "sensory" and "motor" are too sharply dichotomous, and do not properly allow for the closed loop, which is characteristic of ongoing behavior. Sensory input and motor output continuously affect each other, and influence the character of the ensuing sensation and action. He also criticized the loose way in which the reflex arc was used as an explanatory concept:

> We ought to be able to see that the ordinary conception of the reflex arc theory, instead of being a case of plain science, is a survival of the metaphysical dualism, first formulated by Plato, according to which the sensation is an ambiguous dweller on the border land of soul and body, the idea (or central process) is purely psychical, and the act (or movement) purely physical. Thus the reflex arc formulation is neither physical (or physiological) nor psychological; it is a mixed materialistic-spiritualistic assumption. (Dewey, 1896/1968, p. 325)

REVOLUTIONARY TIMES: KORNILOV, LOMOV, PAVLOV, SHERRINGTON, BEKHTEREV, KONORSKI, MILLER

The search for transition from a psychology grounded in one-way dialectical materialism to a psychology based upon two-way dialectical materialism was marked by intellectual struggle to maintain a balance between good science and acceptable politics. The writings and research of K.N. Kornilov, head of the prestigious Moscow Institute of Psychology during the 1920s, demonstrate the difficulty of the transition.

In formulating his school of reactology, Kornilov deliberately endeavored to make direct contact with Marxist doctrine. He asserted that while nonreflexive thought and movement were necessary, a true psychology must include the even prior consequences that follow from the production of labor. He pulled together his position in a paper addressed especially to American psychologists. He stated:

> Marxian psychology, along with the biological elements, attaches still greater importance to social agencies and to their influence on man's behavior, . . . from the Marxian standpoint man became a man, the social animal with the most highly developed psychophysiological system, with the gift of speech and thought, only because he began during the process of adaptation to his environment *to prepare* tools for production. Labor and the processes of labor—these are the sources from which sprang the biological changes in the structure of the human organism. Thus labor turned man into a social animal connected with others by complex ties.
>
> Articulate speech grew out of these social relations of labor, and together with this its subjective expression, thinking in words, an indispensible medium for any ideological work.
>
> Thus, everything that is human, everything that distinguishes man from the beasts, is, historically speaking, only the product of labor and, in this way, of social relations. (Kornilov, 1930, pp. 263–269)

In his research, Kornilov tried to show how the Marxist conception of the role of labor could be examined in the laboratory. His underlying assumption was that "the product of physical and mental energy is a constant" (Razran, 1958a). A moment's reflection upon this assumption forces us to a grinding halt. What can his equation possibly mean? Even though most would agree that the mental "energy" involved in writing creatively with a pencil is at least as great as the energy expended in pushing the pencil, is there indeed an inverse relationship between the two, as implied by the equation? If so, how is mental "energy" to be specified?

Many years later, A.R. Luria provided some insight into Kornilov's reasoning and approach:

> He [Kornilov] investigated a series of reactions graded in complexity from simple motor reflexes to associative speech responses. By measuring the latent period and amplitude of the motor response, Kornilov attempted to determine those energy losses which characterize the transition to more complex reactive processes. . . . Although the attempt to measure the energy lost in associative processes was based on a clearly false, mechanistic premise, it had a great effect upon the development of a natural-science approach to the study of certain aspects of human behavior. (Luria, 1969, p. 123)

For example, Kornilov attributed the fact that the reaction time to a complex association (such as to a choice between two or more stimuli) is greater relative to the reaction time of a simple motor reflex, to the greater mental energy expended in the former.

Kornilov's theorizing and procedure for inferring the relative strengths of physical and mental energy (qua *energy*) are no longer taken seriously by psychologists. However, the techniques he developed for recording and measuring simple-to-complex associative processes (changes in reaction time, response topography, and speech patterns) have had lasting influence. At least as important is his continuing effect upon the philosophy of Russian psychology. His emphasis upon the biosocial significance of "processes of labor" is still accepted as dictum in current writings. For example, Lomov (former USSR Academy of Sciences) has declared:

> Soviet psychology believes that the differences between animals and people are primarily qualitative and are determined by a special characteristic of human beings: The main determinants of human life, and of human mind, are work and communication. Abstract thinking, imagination, creativity, indeed human consciousness itself, are products of the development of the human being engaged in the process of work, they are determined by social life, by the structure of society. (Lomov, 1982, p. 582)

While Kornilov was trying to adapt psychology to the Marxist requirements, Pavlov—who was not a party member—was unintentionally and gracefully accomplishing the task.

Pavlov was not a newcomer to the scientific scene. He started his research well before the Russian revolution, and was permitted to go on with it during the revolution. However, it was not until the meeting of the Soviet Academies of Sciences and Medical Sciences held in 1950 that it was officially decided that Pavlov's research on higher nervous activity satisfied the physiological and psychological requirements of two-way dialectical materialism. In order to understand why his work (which in 1904 led to the Nobel Prize in medicine) was eventually found to be in accord with Communist doctrine, we need briefly to review his discovery of conditioning, the laboratory paradigm he used to examine it, and his own interpretation of conditioning's role in human behavior.

Pavlov's main interest as a physiologist was in the digestive system. He had the genius to recognize the experimental utility of the commonplace observation that hungry dogs salivate upon the appearance of their handlers or other external stimuli signaling the forthcoming arrival of food. He was quick to realize that he could examine in the laboratory the transition from a subcortical event (reflexive salivation to food-in-the-mouth), to a cortical event (thus, *"higher* nervous activity," or acquired anticipatory salivation to external signals). Thereby, he could accomplish what Sechenov failed to achieve; namely, the description of psychical activity in a justifiably physiological language.

Simultaneously, and without political motivation, Pavlov made apparent that his conditioning theory and techniques were amenable to the requirements of two-way dialectical materialism, and he did so with perspicacity. He wrote:

> It is quite clear that the activity of even such apparently insignificant organs as the salivary glands penetrates unconsciously into our everyday psychical conditions *through sensations, desires, and thoughts which in turn exert an influence on the work of the glands themselves.* We see no reason why the same should not apply to the other organs of the body. It is, indeed, by means of such impressions that the usual physiological processes of our bodies are guided. (Pavlov, 1902, quoted in Fulton, 1949, p. 537)

At about the same time that Pavlov reported his discovery of salivary conditioning, C.S. Sherrington independently discovered heart-rate conditioning. Sherrington, another Nobel Prize winner in medicine (1932), was doing research on vasomotor reflexes, and was also using dogs as subjects. His procedure involved passing electrical currents through selected nerves. Before energizing his leads, he would carefully check and calibrate his source of voltage, a small transformer called an *inductorium*. Sherrington noted that following each such shock-free check, his recordings indicated a depression in heart rate of his subject. He finally realized that his dogs were responding to a signal of impending shock, the audible hum which often accompanies the passage of current through the wires of a transformer. Even though the animals were not actually shocked during the calibration of the inductorium, they responded because of their anticipation of the shock. Sherrington was fully cognizant of the importance of this phenomenon. He published his findings in the *Proceedings of the Royal Society* (1902), under the title "Experiments on the Value of Vascular and Visceral Factors in the Genesis of Emotion." Unlike Pavlov, he then dropped his interest in conditioning. However, "His prototype, more than Pavlov's perhaps, catches the imagination today. After all, one is not so much concerned in his everyday life, with whether or not his mouth waters. He is more concerned with trauma and preparation for trauma. Quite clearly, Sherrington's work falls into this pattern" (Notterman, 1970, p. 65).

Pavlov's and Sherrington's cases of conditioning are dissimilar in that one involves an appetitive situation and the other an aversive. Nonetheless, a single paradigm is sufficient to describe both. There are two steps to the procedure (the symbol " → " means "is followed by"):

Step 1. Pairing of stimuli

CS	$\rightarrow$	US	$\rightarrow$	UR
conditioned		unconditioned		unconditioned
stimulus		stimulus		response
(signal)		(food or shock)		(reflexive salivation
				or heart-rate change)

Step 2. Emergence of conditioned response, CR

$$CS \rightarrow CR \rightarrow US \rightarrow UR$$

At this point, a cautionary note is in order: The CS does not functionally replace the US, as is implied by the "stimulus substitution" theory. If the CS served only to substitute for the US, then it follows logically that the response to the CS (the CR) would be the same as the response to the US (the UR), which is not the case. Indeed, Pavlov himself commented that: "A further essential difference between the old [inborn] and the new reflexes is that the former are constant and unconditioned, while the latter are subject to fluctuation, and dependent upon many conditions. They, therefore, deserve the name 'conditioned' [originally, conditional]" (Pavlov, 1928/1968, pp. 567–588).

As put by R.S. Woodworth and M.R. Sheehan:

> The "stimulus substitution" theory suggests, incorrectly, that the CS—when conditioning has taken place—produces the actual reflex connected with the US. . . . Closely related to this point is the error in thinking that the CR is the same as the natural reflex. . . . The CR is a *preparatory* response made in advance to the signal of food—a getting ready for the receiving of the food, while the reflex is a *consummatory* response to the food itself. So too with defensive and other kinds of reflex behavior. (Woodworth & Sheehan, 1964, p. 79, emphasis in original)

In point of fact, even the chemical constituents of CR saliva and of UR saliva are different. Similarly, the cardiac CR to a signal indicating that shock is forthcoming, is either a depression or an acceleration depending upon the procedures used, even though the UR to shock is always an acceleration (Notterman, Schoenfeld, & Bersh, 1952).

All told, Pavlov's main contribution to psychology was to show how physiological terminology and technique could be used to describe and to study modifications in physiological function. He successfully integrated aspects of associationism (the pairing of stimuli), reflexology (the importance of inborn reflexes), and of functionalism (the preparatory qualities of the CR). He pointed the way to what is now known in the Eastern bloc as psychophysiology, a discipline that includes much of what is called experimental psychology in the United States and elsewhere.

Pavlov and others working with him were quick to recognize that it was much too cumbersome to depend upon unadorned conditioned reflexes to explain the complexities of behavior. The notion of higher-order or secondary-reinforcing stimuli was an essential development. These were stimuli that attained reinforcing properties in their own right, without depending upon any underlying physiological disbalance. The reasoning has been crisply summarized by Kling and Schrier (1971, p. 660) and is extended to the classroom situation in a manner such as to take into account the interaction effects of socioeconomic background:

> Some events are reinforcing when first presented, while others seem to acquire reinforcing properties only after the organism has certain experiences with them. Events falling into the first category have been called "primary reinforcers" [like food to a hungry dog] while those of the second type have been called "secondary" or "conditioned" reinforcers [like "Good dog!"]. . . .
>
> It is obvious that the reinforcing events which we use in everyday life ordinarily are not primary reinforcers, but rather they are reinforcers which are intimately related to past experiences and closely tied to the cultural milieu of the individual. Indeed, the understanding and appreciation of the secondary reinforcers that are effective in social groups other than our own represents a major problem for teachers and politicians as well as for social scientists: approval and praise in the classroom may be a powerful reinforcing event for the child reared in a middle-class home, but many a teacher has found to her dismay that such is not always the case for children from markedly different backgrounds.

Other behavioral scientists of the revolutionary period were interested in the consequences of an organism's *interaction* with the environment. V.M. Bekhterev studied skeletal muscle conditioning in an aversive situation, using human subjects. He appears to have been the first to examine motor avoidance behavior. Here the US was a shock to the finger, and the UR was finger withdrawal. The two steps in his paradigm are as follows (the symbol "↛" means "is not followed by"):

Step 1. Pairing of stimuli

CS	→	US	→	UR
(light)		(shock)		(finger withdrawal)

Step 2. Emergence of conditioned response

CS	→	CR	↛	US	↛	UR
(light)		(finger withdrawal)		(shock)		(finger withdrawal)

Bekhterev's research is particularly important, since learning to use external stimuli as warning signals to avoid dangerous environmental situations is vital to survival. The finger-withdrawal response in Step 1 is reflexive; it is not in Step 2.

A couple of examples should make clear the educational extensions of Bekhterev's paradigm: (1) *Developmental*. If the CS remains "light" but the US becomes "fire," then the consequence of "learning not to play with fire" becomes obvious. By visual observation, most children learn quickly to avoid fire and other environmental hazards. (2) *Sports*. If the CS is changed to "approaching skater" (or "approaching basketball guard"), and the US becomes "contact," then the acquisition of the CR "withdrawal" is self-apparent. Children learn in active sports when and how to avoid others. The lessons stemming from both types of examples continue through adulthood.

J. Konorski and S. Miller initiated the use of a combination of aversive and appetitive control in motor conditioning. Their paradigm is especially interesting in that the procedure involves motor behavior that is first induced reflexively for a few trials through mildly aversive stimulation. Each such trial is then followed by food reinforcement. They used dogs as subjects.

Step 1. Pairing of stimuli

CS	→	US	→	UR	→	US	→	UR
(placement in cage)		(mild shock to leg)		(leg flexion)		(food)		(eating)

Soon conditioned (or nonreflexive) leg flexion occurs when the dog is placed in the cage. The shock is no longer required to elicit the behavior.

Step 2. Emergence of conditioned response

CS	→	CR	→	US	→	UR
(placement in cage)		(leg flexion)		(food)		(eating)

A simple example indicates how this paradigm has pedagogical utility. In Step 1, call the CS, "students entering the classroom"; the US, "teacher saying 'Sit straight'!"; the UR, "students showing attentive posture"; the US, "teacher saying 'Good'!"; and the UR, "students sensing approval." For most students, the next step, emergence of the CR "attentive posture," quite naturally follows the CS "entering the classroom." Of course, the behavior is not automatic. The teacher must continue to reinforce as necessary, always bearing in mind that the child is subject to other influences.

This type of "push–pull" conditioning is useful when the pure or applied scientist wishes to select a motor response for positive reinforcement, but finds that the response has a low emission rate. Skinner later devised means whereby a selected sample of motor behavior occurred with sufficient frequency (the bar-pressing "free operant") and could be reinforced with food directly, without having first to be elicited reflexively (Skinner, 1938, p. 112).

POSTREVOLUTIONARY TIMES: RAZRAN, ZAPOROZHETS, LURIA, VYGOTSKY

We will now examine specific examples illustrating how and why the research of postrevolutionary psychophysiologists satisfied the doctrine of two-way dialectical materialism. We will see what they actually did in the laboratory to substantiate Pavlov's (1902) claim "that the activity of even such apparently insignificant organs as the salivary glands penetrates unconsciously into our everyday psychical conditions through sensations, desires and thoughts which in turn exert an influence on the work of the glands themselves" (p. 537).

G. Razran described the following experiment, originally reported by Soviet scientists (Razran, 1961, pp. 81–147). A 13-year-old boy was admitted to a surgical ward for an operation involving the salivary glands. Permission was received for the patient to participate as a subject in conditioning research. In one experiment, he was conditioned to secrete saliva to the numerical thought of "10," and to inhibit secretion to "8." Any arithmetic procedure yielding "10" (e.g., 83 minus 73, or $1000 \div 100$) was positively reinforced. The dramatic results of the experiment are depicted in Table 5.2. The columns labeled "Arithmetical Operations Tested," and "Salivary Drops in 30 Sec." tell the story. The data are suggestive of how autonomic responses in general may occur under routine arithmetic education; that is, in the classroom.

In another experiment the same subject was conditioned to salivate to the word khorosho (meaning "good" or "well"), and to inhibit secretion to plokho (meaning "poorly," "badly," "bad"). Generalization to sentences or phrases having the good or bad connotations was then tested. Table 5.1 shows how effectively the "insignificant salivary glands" reflect semantic generalization, and incidentally are quite revealing of the

Table 5.1. Salivation of 13-Year-Old Boy to Various Words and Phrases after He Had Been Conditioned Positively to the Word *Khorosho* [Well, Good] and Negatively to the Word *Plokho* [Poorly, Badly, Bad][a]

Trial no.	Time of experimentation		Words or phrases tested	Test no.	Salivary drops in 30 sec.
	Date	Exact time			
1	6/26/52	11:20'00"	*khorosho*	47	9
2		11:25'15"	*Uchenik prekrasno zanimayet-sya* [The pupil studies excellently.]	1	14
3		11:29'15"	*Deti igrayut khorosho* [The children are playing well.]	1	19
4		11:31'15"	*plokho*	11	2
5		11:32'45"	*khorosho*	48	15
6		11:37'00"	*Sovet-skaya Armiya pobedila* [The Soviet Army was victorious.]	1	23
7		11:42'00"	*Uchenik nagrubil ychitel'-nitse* [The pupil was fresh to the teacher.]	1	0
8		11:45'15"	*khorosho*	49	18
9		11:49'45"	*Pioner pomogayet tovarishchu* [The pioneer helps his comrade.]	1	23
10	7/31/52	10:10'00"	*khorosho*	50	18
11		10:14'00"	*plokho*	12	1
12		10:17'00"	*khorosho*	51	16
13		10:21'00"	*Leningrad—zamechatel'ny gorod* [Leningrad is a wonderful city.]	1	15
14		10:24'30"	*Shkol'nik ne sdal ekzamen* [The pupil failed to take the examination.]	1	2
15		10:26'00"	*khorosho*	52	15
16		10:29'30"	*Brat obizhayet sestru* [Brother is insulting sister.]	1	1
17	8/1/52	11:20'00"	*khorosho*	54	12
18		11:25'30"	*Rybaky poymali mnogo ryby* [The fisherman caught many fish.]	1	18
19		11:31'30"	*Sovet-skaya konstitutsiya—samaya demokraticheskaya* [The Soviet Constitution is the most democratic (of all).]	1	17

Table 5.1. (*continued*)

Trial no.	Time of experimentation		Words or phrases tested	Test no.	Salivary drops in 30 sec.
	Date	Exact time			
20		11:36′30″	*Fashisty razrushili mnogo gorodov* [The Fascists destroyed many cities.]	1	2
21		11:40′30″	*Uchenik razbil steklo* [The pupil broke the glass.]	1	2
22		11:41′30″	*Sovet-sky narod lyubit svoyu Rodinu* [The Soviet people love their Motherland.]	1	17
23		11:45′30″	*Moy drug tyazhelo zabolel* [My friend is seriously ill.]	1	2
24		11:47′30″	*Vrazheskaya armiya byla razbita i unichtozhena* [The enemy army was defeated and annihilated.]	1	24
25		11:51′30″	*Uchenik sdal ekzamen na posredstvenno* [The pupil passed the examination with a mediocre grade.]	1	10

[a] From G. Razran (1961). The observable unconscious and the inferable conscious in current Soviet psychophysiology. *Psychological Review, 68*, 81–147. Copyright 1961 by the American Psychological Association. Reprinted by permission of the American Psychological Association.

kinds of values inculcated by the former Soviet society, and relates to Chapter 2.

A major challenge for Soviet scientists was to elucidate upon what Lomov referred to as the "qualitative" difference between animals and people (see p. 68). One strategy is to examine the interaction between exteroceptive (mainly visual) and kinesthetic governance of motor behavior, an inquiry which began with Sechenov's reflexology, continued through Kornilov's reactology, and has been sustained in several modes of conditioning. The issue of which type of cue is more salient on a developmental basis to which type of species, is important because—as noted shortly—it may explain the more adaptable behavior of the human being. Investigators at the Leningrad laboratory found that for the ape, kinesthetic cues dominate visual cues, and do so even for the mature adult. Their conclusion rests mainly upon experiments done with a

Table 5.2. Salivation of 13-Year-Old Boy to Different Arithmetical Operations after He Had Been Conditioned Positively to "10" and Negatively to "8"[a]

| Trial no. | Time of experimentation | | Arithmetical operations tested | Test no. | Salivary drops in 30 sec. |
	Date	Exact time			
1	8/12/52	11:10'00"	83−73	1	15
2		11:40'00"	5+5	1	16
3		11:18'30"	20−12	1	2
4		11:20'30"	1000÷100	1	18
5		11:24'30"	5×2	1	19
6		11:28'00"	56÷7	1	2
7		11:32'00"	24−14	1	19
8	8/14/52	13:15'00"	19−9	1	7
9		13:19'00"	8+2	1	19
10		13:22'30"	48÷6	1	3
11		13:23'30"	4×2	1	2
12		13:24'00"	80÷8	1	17
13		13:27'30"	112−102	1	11
14		13:29'30"	4+4	1	3
15		13:31'30"	470÷47	1	11
16	8/14/52	13:33'00"	99−91	1	3
17		13:35'00"	80÷8	2	21
18		13:38'00"	88÷11	1	3
19		13:40'30"	35−25	1	25

[a]From G. Razran (1961). The observable unconscious and the inferable conscious in current Soviet psychophysiology. *Psychological Review, 68,* 81–147. Copyright 1961 by the American Psychological Association. Reprinted by permission of the American Psychological Association.

single chimpanzee, Rafael (Ladygina-Kots & Dembovskii, 1969). (More will be said about the Russian research with primates when we consider gestalt psychology, since they interpreted their experiments as constituting a refutation of Kohler's work.) A.V. Zaporozhets reported a similar tendency for kinesthetic dominance in human beings, but only up to about 4.5 years of age (see Figure 5.1) (Zaporozhets, 1960). From that point on, human beings rely much more upon visual stimuli, especially those involved in initial familiarization with (i.e., orientation toward) objects in the environment. Eventually, even imitation-learning can occur by means of vision alone, a fact of vital importance to the design of educational systems. Taken together, the propensities for visual orientation and imitation learning constitute a crucial step forward in behavioral adaptation and biological evolution. Zaporozhets also indicated that visual-motor skills can gradually become so routine as to require little attention to concurrent feedback during their execution. Such is the

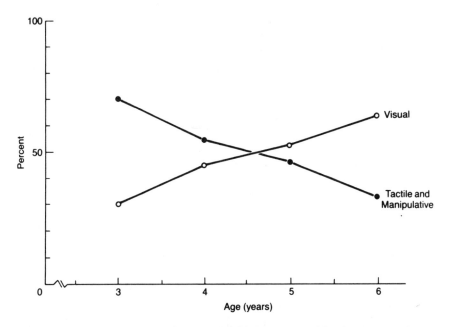

Figure 5.1. Orientative activity of preschool children upon initial familiarization with new objects, expressed as percentage. Data shown are reduced from Zaporozhets (1960), Table 3. (From J. M. Notterman, *Forms of Psychological Inquiry* (1985). Copyright 1985 by Columbia University Press. Reprinted by permission of Columbia University Press.)

case because human beings can learn rapidly (even through verbal instructions) to utilize initiating cues that trigger off a whole train of motor behavior. In today's terms, we call such behavior "motor programs," actions that reveal the functional organization of entire segments of limb or body movements.

A.R. Luria explored further the "qualitative" distinctions of man by examining the developmental interactions between the human being's observation of the environment and the emergence of language and thought (Luria, 1969). He discovered that for children learning how to talk, the *initial* form of paired-associative speech is as follows: If the stimulus-word was an object (a noun, such as "dog"), then the response-word consisted of an action (a verb, such as "bark"). This stage was followed by object–object associations (e.g., "dog"–"cat"). The latter associations are mainly acquired in school. The importance of this finding exists in the fact that—right from the start—the developing human organism learns how to talk in a manner that reflects an active interrelation between him and the environment. The *particular* environment, in turn, influences the kinds of language and thought that ensue, a psychological fact of enormous social-political significance.

From these initial, primitive, paired-word associations, the child begins to attach meaning (or semantic content) to words. At first, these meanings are bound to the physical attributes of the objects or actions from which they stem. Thus, the dog–cat association might lead to the limited, *designative* concept of "four-legs" or "furry." Eventually, the child generalizes to broader concepts. Thus, increasing exposure to the dog–cat type of association, but with other creatures, leads eventually to the more sophisticated concept "animal." The concept "animal" is semantically distinguished from "nonanimal" increasingly through numerous, finer, more subtle discriminations, perhaps abetted by a course in biology. The process continues evolving in adolescence, and perhaps even beyond.

Luria held that verbal behavior and thought (including consciousness) could not be equated with each other. Each has its own set of rules. It is a materialistic error to equate thought with internal verbal behavior, or implicit speech. Luria and his associates demonstrated that thought can occur without implicit speech, or visual images, or grammatical rules, or logical rules—although the *development* of thought is never completely independent of them.

Finally, a close friend and colleague of Luria's, L.S. Vygotsky, argued that any theory of mind should take into account three basic propositions: (1) That the human's mentation must be understood in light of its social, and not only its individual, origins and history. "Thus, his focus was on such issues as how the thinking and memory processes of a twentieth-century Soviet engineer might differ from those of an eighteenth-century Russian peasant or a preliterate Uzbek herdsman" (Wertsch, 1988, p. 84). (2) That individual behavior derived from social behavior, not the other way around. (3) "[T]hat higher mental functioning is mediated by socioculturally evolved tools and signs. Human language plays a central role in this regard" (Wertsch, 1988, p. 85). Along these lines, Scribner and Cole (1981) noted earlier that Vygotsky went an important step further than Marx in his conception of the dialectical-materialist approach to psychological understanding. Whereas Marx emphasized the importance of the kinds of *tools* a person used in contributing to the formation of his consciousness (e.g., a peasant using a hoe vs. a farmer using a tractor), Vygotsky extended the analysis to include *signs* as well as tools. "By 'signs' he referred to socially created symbol systems such as language, writing, and number systems, which emerge over the course of history and vary from one society to another" (p. 8).

SUMMARY

Many of us conclude our studies in behavioral science with a conception of classical conditioning that is a caricature of its true nature. Oddly, we Americans tend to view classical conditioning within the constraints of one-way dialectical materialism. We perceive Pavlovian conditioning to be some sort of rigid, elementalistic, switchlike approach to psychological inquiry. It is not. We tend to be unfamiliar with the rich contributions of the Eastern bloc scientists in fields that *we* separate into cognitive psychology, neuropsychology, psycholinguistics, educational psychology, and so on. The Russian investigators considered—for historical and political reasons—such research to be part and parcel of a two-way dialectical-materialist approach to "psychophysiology." We overreact to the narrowness conjured up by this word. Politics aside, there is increasing convergence between Russian psychophysiology and American general experimental psychology.

Behaviorism

Instrumental Conditioning and Programmed Instruction

The main objectives of this chapter are first, to understand B.F. Skinner's principal contribution to behaviorism, namely the study of operant conditioning; and second, to see how his underlying ideas led to programmed instruction.

SKINNER'S "SOCIAL ENVIRONMENTS"

But we must do so in the context of Skinner's views of "social environments," otherwise his technology appears to overwhelm his philosophy, especially insofar as educational matters are concerned. He wrote in an article that was completed the evening before he died:

> Modeling [showing], telling [advising], and teaching are the functions of the social environments called cultures. Different cultures emerge from different contingencies of variation and selection and differ in the extent to which they help their members solve their problems. Members who solve them are more likely to survive, and with them survive the practices of the culture. In other words, cultures evolve. . . . The fact that a culture prepares a group only for a world that resembles the world in which the culture evolved is the source of our present concern for the future of a habitable earth. (Skinner, 1990, p. 1207)

He asserted on a more optimistic note, that behavior analysis can be helpful "by making it possible to design better environments—personal environments that would solve existing problems and larger environments or cultures in which there would be fewer problems" (Skinner, 1990, p. 1210; see, for example, his *Walden Two*).

ORIGIN AND PHILOSOPHY OF BEHAVIORISM

Behaviorism grew mainly out of functionalism, and partly out of classical conditioning. Unlike functionalism, it sought to avoid appeals to purposivity and to mental states as explanations of behavior. J.B. Watson asserted that psychology should deal only with observable facts. "By 'fact' he implied any event that lent itself to counting or measuring operations, and to independent verification of these operations by other observers" (Notterman, 1985, p. 100). He did not exclude the examination of implicit and glandular responses (hence the relation to classical conditioning), for they met the criteria both of measurement and of verification.

Twenty-five years after Watson's publication of his famous manifesto, "Psychology as the Behaviorist Views It" (*Psychological Review*, 1913), Skinner published his research volume, *The Behavior of Organisms: An Experimental Analysis* (1938). "By 1966, it had gone through seven printings. . . . A 1975 survey found that he was correctly identified by 82 percent of a college sample, heading a list of the top twenty American scientists of *all* fields" (Notterman, 1985, p. 98, emphasis added).

In his research, Skinner was narrower than Watson in specifying a behavioral fact. He restricted the sample of psychological facts to movements (actually, the *effect* of movements), and the environment in which these movements occurred. He designed for laboratory use what has come to be known as the "Skinner Box." He examined bar-pressing with rats (later, keypecking with pigeons) in a field he named operant conditioning. *Definitions*: The key feature of operant or instrumental conditioning is that the organism has to *operate* (take some action) upon the environment (for the rat, the bar) prior to obtaining reinforcement. Thus, the response is *instrumental* to the appearance of reinforcement. Positive reinforcement increases the likelihood that the act which produced it will be repeated. Although the reinforcement is contingent upon the response, this aspect is only necessary, it is not sufficient. To be sufficient, the organism must meet other contingencies or requirements established by the experimenter, such as a predetermined schedule of when the reinforcement will or will not actually be obtained.

Note that Skinner's radical behaviorism does not assign an explanatory role to "purpose." He held "that a scientific analysis of operant behavior precludes the necessity for dealing with the layman's conceptual schema of 'purpose'" (Notterman, 1985, p. 103). He maintained that "purpose" was merely a retrospective verbal account of behavior already acquired, the behavior lying dormant until appropriate cues and motivation occasioned its release. The behavior had been established by the consequences of its prior production. By "consequences" he implied history of reinforcement. According to Skinner, the inference of purpose is unnecessary, if we just stick with the observed facts of the organism's behavior and attendant reinforcement. Unlike Dewey, the pragmatic philosopher, who did not hesitate to use the idea of purpose, Skinner, the pure scientist, rejected it.

Instead of treating free will and purpose as behaviors originating in reinforcement contingencies, today's person *labels* these behaviors, neglects the *fact* of the labeling, and then attributes causal properties to the labels themselves. It is these labels that then become homunculi—phony causal agents of behavior. Skinner's most cogent statement of his position appears in *Beyond Freedom and Dignity* (1971). In his piercing review of this work, Noam Chomsky declared:

> In support of his belief that science will demonstrate that behavior is entirely a function of antecedent events, Skinner notes that physics advanced only when it "stopped personifying things" and attributing to them "wills, impulses, feelings, purposes," and so on (p. 8). Therefore, he concludes, the science of behavior will progress only when it stops personifying people and avoids reference to "internal states." No doubt physics advanced by rejecting the view that a rock's wish to fall is a factor in its "behavior," because in fact a rock has no such wish. For Skinner's argument to have any force, he must show that people have wills, impulses, feeling, purposes, and the like no more than rocks do. If people do differ from rocks in this respect, then a science of human behavior will have to take account of this fact. (Chomsky, 1971, p. 19)

Skinner did not find such criticisms to be devastating. He still maintained: "So long as we cling to the view that a person is an initiating doer, actor, or causer of behavior, we shall probably continue to neglect the conditions which must be changed if we are to solve our problems" (Skinner, 1981, p. 504).

For Skinner, then, a scientifically valid regard for human welfare demands a behavioristic approach; otherwise we fall victim to current forms of primitivistic reification or labeling.

Relation of the Debate to Russian Dialectical-Materialist Psychology

The debate between Skinner and Chomsky is reminiscent of the opposing positions taken by the prerevolutionary and postrevolutionary Russians. In both instances, the basic conflict lies in what the antagonists would accept as a causal agent.

For Skinner, causes of behavior cannot be attributed to thought or free will or purpose. These nouns must be reduced to verbs, and the verbs to reinforcement contingencies—to the *consequences* of stimulus–response correlations. In this sense, Skinnerian behaviorism subscribes to Sechenov's analysis of mentation; namely, that autonomous thought, free will, and purpose are illusions (epiphenomena) and cannot be immediate causes of behavior. For Chomsky, causes of behavior *must* be attributed to thought, free will, and purpose. The attribution is crucial, because he works within a philosophical frame of reference, one that requires that he be cognitive, volitional, and purposive. Thus, Chomsky is drawn to a semblance of the position held by two-way dialectical materialism, but for philosophical rather than psychological reasons.

The issue of identifying the "true" determinants of behavior cannot be resolved by disputes between psychologist and philosopher, since each is bound to be "right," according to the rules that he goes by. As students of psychology, we should consider the issue as being between psychologist and psychologist, without becoming so proprietary as to believe we have an exclusive interest in, and understanding of, the matter.

So, as psychologists, let us confront the question: Are autonomy of thought, free will, and purposivity incompatible with the principle of determinism, or even with Skinnerian behaviorism? It is possible to answer "No, not necessarily." The behaving organism *does* make choices, and—if human—he can report the experience he has preliminary to the act of choosing. Perhaps what we call free will *is* this experience. Of course, once the choice has been made, it is theoretically possible to search out the antecedent events or reinforcement contingencies that inevitably led to the decision, and thus to disregard the private experience of choosing. However, we generally cannot identify the necessary and sufficient prior circumstances that preceded a choice. Thus, the more proximate *experience* of choosing is reified (or made a thing of) and is identified as the cause. In this sense, thought, free will, and purpose are indeed epiphenomena.

But we must go one step further, as did the two-way dialectical materialists. We must consider the possibility that our tendency to use nouns and higher abstractions to describe known and unknown reinforcement contingencies is essential to human behavior. Without this tendency, internal thought and communication with others would be virtually impossible. The foregoing is practically a restatement of the two-way dialectical materialist position that "mentation has its own representative reality . . . and exerts a perceived autonomous influence on an individual's personal and social behavior" (Chapter 5).

A Finer Statement of the Problem

The foregoing analysis is echoed in biographer Leon Edel's discussion of Henry James's novel, *The Ambassadors:*

> In this novel he comes to the question of determinism. He doesn't ask, "What is life?" He accepts life. The question he asks is how much of life one can live within the restraints of civilization. One may not be technically a free man; one may be a slave of instincts, drives, conditionings. One is formed by heredity and environment, but one has the *imagination of freedom*, or, as James calls it, "the illusion of freedom." In his old age, James was prepared to live by that illusion. (Edel, 1977–1978, p. 62, emphasis in original)

RELATIONS AMONG OPERANT CONDITIONING, EDUCATION, AND PROGRAMMED INSTRUCTION

In a lecture at the Royal Society in London (1964), Skinner noted:

> The application of operant conditioning to education is simple and direct. Teaching is the arrangement of contingencies of reinforcement under which students learn. . . . A teaching machine is simply any device [he included computers; see Skinner, 1984, p. 948] which arranges contingencies of reinforcement. . . . In this sense the apparatuses developed for the experimental analysis of behavior [operant conditioning] were the first teaching machines. (Skinner, 1968, pp. 64–65)

Skinner's paradigm of programmed instruction and its application to the classroom were foreseen by the educator-psychologist, E.L. Thorndike, over 50 years earlier: "If, by a miracle of mechanical ingenuity, a book could be so arranged that only to him who had done what was directed on page one would page two become visible, and so on, much that now requires personal instruction could be managed by print" (Holland & Skinner, 1965, p. 190; see also original work published by Skinner in *Teachers College Record, 65,* No. 2, 1963). (Parenthetically, Thorndike, as did Skinner, perceived the advantages of using animals as subjects in order to illuminate human learning. We have already commented upon his use of cats in puzzle boxes in Chapter 4.) However, as

Skinner observed, "Thorndike never realized the potentialities of his early work on learning because he turned [mistakenly] to the measurement of mental abilities and to matched-group comparisons of teaching practices" (Holland & Skinner, 1965, p. 190). In similar fashion, Skinner dismissed the possibility that the Socratic method was a forerunner of programmed instruction, even though there was a superficial resemblance. He stated:

> A good program [in manner analogous to the Socratic method] does lead the student step by step, each step is within his range, and he usually understands it before moving on; but programming is much more than this. What it is, and how it is related to teaching machines, can be made clear only by returning to the experimental analysis of behavior which gave rise to the movement. (Skinner, 1968, p. 61)

Let us go along with Skinner's argument that in order to appreciate the contribution of programming to educational psychology, we must first thoroughly understand the bar-pressing laboratory paradigm upon which programmed instruction is based. Toward that end, it will be helpful if we know in advance of our discussion of bar-pressing that Skinner distinguished among four different aspects of teaching programs (cf. Skinner, 1968, pp. 65–79). Although nominally separate, their characteristics could be combined in various ways to form a single program. Each of the four has its origins in the behavioral phenomena studied in bar-pressing research, and is thereby related to programmed instruction. These phenomena are: (1) the development of new behavior through *chaining*; (2) the establishment of external control of new behavior through *discrimination*; (3) the alteration of temporal, spatial, or intensive response properties through *shaping*; and (4) the maintenance of behavior through *intermittent reinforcement*. (See Notterman & Mintz, 1965, for a detailed research account of all four of these phenomena, focusing upon force of response.) They are now described in terms relevant to the laboratory, after which we extrapolate from the laboratory to the classroom (Figure 6.1).

Laboratory Example: The Skinner Box

A typical laboratory exercise involves a light-on, light-off discrimination, with the rat required to learn to press the lever (i.e., bar) only when the panel light (just above the lever) is lit. The links in the chain of behavior that are conditioned in this situation are as follows: The panel light comes on (cue, or discriminative stimulus, S^D; refer to the expression in the section under "Chaining"). This information signals the rat to press the bar all the way down (about 1/4 inch excursion) with one of its

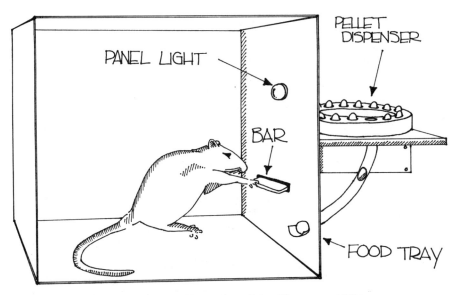

Figure 6.1. Typical Skinner box. (After Notterman, 1970.)

forepaws (bar-pressing response, R). When the lever is completely de-pressed, it closes an external switch. This is accompanied by a click (another S^D). The sound signals the rat to approach the food tray located at the side of the bar (tray approach, t.a., another R). A pellet of food, automatically dispensed when the switch is closed, is obtained. The idea is to provide circumstances such that the animal is reinforced only when the light is on, and then only when it presses hard enough to overcome the slight elasticity of a spring inside the switch, thereby moving the lever all the way down, closing the switch, and producing the click.

Extrapolation from Laboratory to Classroom: Chaining, Discrimination, Shaping, Intermittent Reinforcement

It is clear from the foregoing description that operant conditioning proceeds in small links. It is not at all apparent from the description, that the response *furthest* removed from the reinforcing pellet (i.e., the bar press) is the one that is the last attached or acquired. It is also not clear for the person who is unfamiliar with the animal laboratory, how Skin-ner and his colleagues extrapolated from the laboratory to the class-room, and the four major qualities of teaching-programs: chaining (probably the most important), discrimination, shaping, and intermittent reinforcement. A few observations are in order to help clarify both of the ambiguities.

1. *Chaining.* The chain of behavior required to obtain a pellet is established with the two major responses (tray approach and bar pressing) being conditioned from right-to-left, and not in the sequence left-to-right, as appears in the expression below. (The symbol "→" means "is followed by.")

$$S^D_{(light-on)} \rightarrow R_{(b-p)} \rightarrow S^D_{(click)} \rightarrow R_{(t.a.)} \rightarrow pellet$$

The animal is *first* trained to approach the food tray only upon hearing the click. This often requires separate training, in that the switch (actually, the bar), is initially tripped by the experimenter from outside the cage, as he or she sees the animal randomly come near the tray. The experimenter reinforces the "$S^D_{(click)} \rightarrow R_{(t.a.)}$" link with a pellet, automatically dispensed when the switch is closed. The bar-pressing response is attached to the click-approach link, if and when the animal happens to press the bar far enough down to produce the click and receive the pellet or reinforcement. Finally, the animal must learn that the bar-pressing and click-approach links are effective only when the panel light is on.

As a very crude analogy, think of a toddler being taught to put his or her hand into a cookie jar, one with a screwed-on top. When the child approaches the jar, the parent unscrews the top, thereby providing an auditory signal (cue or S^D) similar to the click in the expression, that the cookie is available. The child's subsequent act of putting his or her hand into the jar is equivalent to the tray-approach R. The cookie is analogous to pellet. To continue with the rough comparison, assume that the parent capitalizes on the cookie-jar response in trying to teach the child to put toys away on the shelf (attaching a new response, as in bar pressing). He or she encourages the child to do so by being the one to first place the toys away (modeling or showing), and waiting for the child to imitate. (Other techniques are used with rats when necessary.) Eventually the child accommodates the parent. The father or mother then unscrews the cookie jar as he or she says "Good!" The toddler hears the cover come off, goes after the cookie, and reinforces himself or herself for putting the toys away. Once the ensuing chain of behavior has been established, the parent can begin to run it off by saying, "Please put the toys away" (equivalent to the external, panel-light cue). Also, the parent more and more comes to rely upon "Good!" as a secondary reinforcer, and not upon cookies, to reinforce the behavior.

The untrained observer watching a conditioned organism (human or other) can be fooled into assuming that the links in a correctly performed chain of behavior were learned in sequence A–Z, rather than—as in the bar-pressing situation—retroactively from Z to A.

But neither sequence is entirely correct when applied to the classroom. What *is* generally correct, however, is the axiom that the teacher proceeds from the known to the unknown, with the caveat that the known can be located variously, anywhere in the sequence of past links in a chain.

To illustrate, Keller and Schoenfeld (1950) opened their chapter on chaining with this quote from James Mill (the passage is from Mill's "Analysis of the Phenomena of the Human Mind," 1829):

> In learning [the Lord's Prayer] we repeat it; that is we pronounce the words in successive order, from the *beginning* to the *end*. The order of the sensations is successive. When we proceed to repeat the passage, the ideas of the words also arise in succession, the preceding always suggesting the succeeding, and no other. *Our* suggests *Father*, *Father* suggests *which*, *which* suggests *art*; and so on, to the end. How remarkable this is the case, any one may convince himself by trying to repeat backwards, even a passage with which he is as familiar as the Lord's Prayer. (p. 197)

Of course, the reason that it is difficult to recite the Lord's Prayer backward is because that is neither the succession in which the words are learned, nor become meaningful. More specifically, in teaching this or another prayer or poem to a young child, the parent or teacher will *not* proceed in the manner indicated by James Mill, because the child will occasionally have trouble recalling a word in *different* parts of the chain. For this reason, the teacher will not demand repetitious, serial learning, but will deliberately leave out a word, and invite a group response. Thus, "Our ('class'?) which art in ('class'?), and so on. These blanks will be changed to other blanks ("Our father which ('class'?) as necessary to ensure meaningful learning.

The overriding point is that the parent or teacher need not begin acquisition with a key word toward the end of the required prayer or poem, as would be the case if he or she were to extrapolate directly from the bar-pressing situation to the verbal passage situation. There are various strategies, depending upon the subject matter, the stage of learning, and the student—a fact that is generally true about programmed instruction.

2. *Discrimination*. Each discriminative stimulus not only serves to introduce the next link in a chain, but also serves to reinforce the immediate segment of behavior that produced the S^D. Thus, each S^D has a reinforcing, as well as a cueing function. In the classroom, this means that either the teacher, through a comment such as "You're doing fine!"

or the machine (including computers), through indicating that the student made the correct choice or wrote the correct answer, is providing reinforcement for the previous response, as well as setting the stage for the next one.

3. *Shaping.* Shaping entails the reinforcement of emitted responses that approach a particular standard of proficiency, and withholding reinforcement when the response is too crude. Through reinforcement of responses that approximate the desired one, skilled performance is gradually attained. The influence of shaping upon spatial, temporal, and intensive aspects of response is more readily observable in the education/training of visual-motor skills (shop, sculpture, rehabilitation, athletics, typing) than in courses more obviously dependent upon language or symbols. However, Skinnerian behaviorists hold that the same basic types of shaping are essential to the development of reading, writing, arithmetic, and other such cognitive skills. For example, they assert that the child's learning neatly to copy individual letters and numbers initially depends upon the effective reinforcement of selected properties of *observable responses*, the presence of assumed cognitive processes notwithstanding. Exhortation alone does not do the trick.

4. *Intermittent reinforcement.* Intermittent reinforcement (or not reinforcing after each response) was originally studied with rats as subjects to see how it affects the strength of an operant response. In general, intermittent reinforcement increased the persistence of bar-pressing behavior. It would, therefore, appear to be useful in maintaining newly learned subject matter. However, it has the same side effects in the classroom situation as in the laboratory; namely, it induces anxiety, emotionality, and aggression. As Skinner put it:

> We could, of course, resort to the techniques of scheduling [of reinforcement] already developed in the study of other organisms, but in the present state of our knowledge of educational practices scheduling appears to be most effectively arranged through the design of the material to be learned [rather than by a schedule directly imposed by the teacher]. By making each successive step as small as possible, the frequency of reinforcement can be raised to a maximum [because the student is right most of the time], while the possibly aversive consequence of being wrong are reduced to a minimum. (Skinner, 1968, p. 21)

Table 6.1 contains a program developed by Skinner and his associates for the instruction of high-school physics. "[A teaching] machine presents one item at a time. The student completes the item and then uncovers the corresponding word or phrase shown at the right" (Skinner, 1968, p. 45). By going over it, the reader can observe for himself or herself the processes of chaining, discrimination, shaping, and intermittent reinforcement.

Table 6.1. Part of a Program in High-School Physics[a]

	Sentence to be completed	Word to be supplied
1.	The important parts of a flashlight are the battery and the bulb. When we "turn on" a flashlight, we close a switch which connects the battery with the _____.	bulb
2.	When we turn on a flashlight, an electric current flows through the fine wire in the _____ and causes it to grow hot.	bulb
3.	When the hot wire glows brightly, we say that it gives off or sends out heat and _____.	light
4.	The fine wire in the bulb is called a filament. The bulb "lights up" when the filament is heated by the passage of a(n) _____ current.	electric
5.	When a weak battery produces little current, the fine wire, or _____, does not get very hot.	filament
6.	A filament which is *less* hot sends out or gives off _____ light.	less
7.	"Emit" means "send out." The amount of light sent out, or "emitted," by a filament depends on how _____ the filament is.	hot
8.	The higher the temperature of the filament the _____ the light emitted by it.	brighter, stronger
9.	If a flashlight battery is weak, the _____ in the bulb may still glow, but with only a dull red color.	filament
10.	The light from a very hot filament is colored yellow or white. The light from a filament which is not very hot is colored _____.	red
11.	A blacksmith or other metal worker sometimes makes sure that a bar of iron is heated to a "cherry red" before hammering it into shape. He uses the _____ of the light emitted by the bar to tell how hot it is.	color
12.	Both the color and the amount of light depend on the _____ of the emitting filament or bar.	temperature
13.	An object which emits light because it is hot is called incandescent. A flashlight bulb is an incandescent source of _____.	light
14.	A neon tube emits light but remains cool. It is, therefore, not an incandescent _____ of light.	source
15.	A candle flame is hot. It is a(n) _____ source of light.	incandescent
16.	The hot wick of a candle gives off small pieces or particles of carbon which burn in the flame. Before or while burning, the hot particles send out, or _____, light.	emit
17.	A long candlewick produces a flame in which oxygen does not reach all the carbon particles. Without oxygen the particles cannot burn. Particles which do not burn rise above the flame as _____.	smoke
18.	We can show that there are particles of carbon in a candle flame, even when it is not smoking, by holding a piece of metal in the flame. The metal cools some of the particles before they	

(continued)

Table 6.1. (*continued*)

Sentence to be completed	Word to be supplied
burn, and the unburned carbon _____ collect on the metal as soot.	particles
19. The particles of carbon in soot or smoke no longer emit light because they are _____ than when they were in the flame.	cooler, colder
20. The reddish part of a candle flame has the same color as the filament in a flashlight with a weak battery. We might guess that the yellow or white parts of a candle flame are _____ than the reddish part.	hotter
21. "Putting out" an incandescent electric light means turning off the current so that the filament grows too _____ to emit light.	cold, cool
22. Setting fire to the wick of an oil lamp is called _____ the lamp.	lighting
23. The sun is our principal _____ of light, as well as of heat.	source
24. The sun is not only very bright but very hot. It is a powerful _____ source of light.	incandescent
25. Light is a form of energy. In "emitting light" an object changes, or "converts," one form of _____ into another.	energy
26. The electric energy supplied by the battery in a flashlight is converted to _____ and _____.	heat, light; light, heat
27. If we leave a flashlight on, all energy stored in the battery will finally be changed or _____ into heat and light.	converted
28. The light from a candle flame comes from the _____ released by chemical changes as the candle burns.	energy
29. A nearly "dead" battery may make a flashlight bulb warm to the touch, but the filament may still not be hot enough to emit light–in other words, the filament will not be _____ at that temperature.	incandescent
30. Objects, such as a filament, carbon particles, or iron bars, become incandescent when heated to about 800 degrees Celsius. At that temperature they begin to _____.	emit light
31. When raised to any temperature above 800 degrees Celsius, an object such as an iron bar will emit light. Although the bar may melt or vaporize, its particles will be _____ no matter how hot they get.	incandescent
32. About 800 degrees Celsius is the lower limit of the temperature at which particles emit light. There is no upper limit of the _____ at which emission of light occurs.	temperature
33. Sunlight is _____ by very hot gases near the surface of the sun.	emitted
34. Complex changes similar to an atomic explosion generate the great heat which explains the _____ of light by the sun.	emission
35. Below about _____ degrees Celsius an object is not an incandescent source of light.	800

a From B.F. Skinner, *The Technology of Teaching* (1961). Copyright 1992 by the B.F. Skinner Foundation. Reprinted by permission of the B.F. Skinner Foundation.

A word of caution: The production of programs is by no means cut and dried. It appears that Skinner and his colleagues, as did William James (Chapter 1), also had to fall back upon the presence in teaching of something more than science or technology: "Further research will presumably discover other, possibly more effective techniques. Meanwhile, it must be admitted that a considerable measure of art is needed in composing a successful program" (Skinner, 1968, p. 49).

Read only as much of the program as is necessary to get the idea, and interests you. Not everyone cares for programmed instruction!

Assessment of Programmed Instruction

In the abstract, it can be said that programmed instruction attempts to maximize what a good teacher tries to do in the conventional school situation: (1) Establish objectives. (2) Work consistently and carefully toward those objectives. (3) Proceed in small steps from the known to the unknown, but not *so* small as to become boring. (4) Take individual differences into account. (5) Encourage a positive attitude toward study and learning; certainly avoid scolding, exhorting, or embarrassing students.

Evaluations as to the effectiveness of programmed instruction are mixed. Those who are adherents to behaviorism are obviously more sympathetic to programmed instruction than those who are not. The latter include psychologists who assert that behaviorism does not do full justice to human properties such as thought and feeling. They hold that in the behaviorist's efforts to avoid the use of phony causal agents as explanations of behavior, he or she may have come to treat human beings as machines. Education becomes a matter of a teaching machine, teaching a *human* "machine."

In fairness, however, such a position does not do justice to Skinner's expressed position:

> The student is more than a receiver of information. He must take some kind of action. The traditional view is that he must "associate." The stream of information flowing from teacher to student contains pairs of items which, being close together or otherwise related, become connected in the student's mind. This is the old doctrine of the association of ideas, now strengthened by a scientific, if uncritical, appeal to conditioned reflexes: two things occurring together in experience somehow become connected so that one of them later reminds the student of the other. The teacher has little control over the process except to make sure that things occur together often and that the student pays attention to them—for example, by making the experiences vivid, or, as we say, memorable. Some devices [mistakenly] called teaching machines are simply ways of presenting things together in ways which at-

tract attention. The student listens to recorded speech, for example, while looking at pictures. The theory is that he will associate these auditory and visual presentations.

But the action demanded of the student is not some sort of mental association of contiguous experiences. It is more objective and, fortunately, more controllable than that. To acquire behavior, *the student must engage in behavior* (emphasis in original). This has long been known. The principle is implied in any philosophy of "learning by doing." But it is not enough simply to acknowledge its validity. Teaching machines provide the conditions needed to apply the principle effectively. (Holland & Skinner, 1965, p. 46. See also original work published by Skinner in *Harvard Educational Review, 31,* No. 4, 1961.)

A more recent explanation of programmed instruction, one offered in the context of a critique of cognitive psychology, is available in Skinner (1984, pp. 947–954). He held that cognitive psychology is not so much a "revolt" as it is a "retreat" to prebehavioristic pseudo-explanations. Further, he held that current computer-aided instruction (claimed by cognitive psychologists as being new) is nothing more than an extension (not a breakthrough) of earlier teaching machines and programmed instruction.

Interestingly, there is one type of programmed instruction that has been enthusiastically received by a goodly sample of those who have been critical of Skinner's version. We refer to F.S. Keller's Personalized System of Instruction (PSI).

Keller's Personalized System of Instruction

It is paradoxical that Keller introduced PSI by means of an article entitled "Goodbye, Teacher." In point of fact, Keller's is the most successful of the different types of programmed instruction, mainly because it frees the teacher to say "Hello!" He noted about his system: "Advance within the program depends on something more than the appearance of a confirming word or the presentation of a new frame; *it involves a personal interaction between a student and his peer, or his better, in what may be a lively verbal [or mixed written and verbal] interchange, of interest and importance to each participant*" (Keller, 1968, p. 84). PSI involves combining the best of two approaches: Verbal interaction with a teacher or peer, plus the student's utilization of a program. It is a flexible combination.

Wittrock is quite lavish in his praise of PSI:

The single most significant conclusion to be reached from research on innovatory teaching methods in *higher education* is that the Keller Plan is clearly superior to other methods with which it has been compared. Indeed, the Keller Plan has been so consistently found superior that it must rank as the method with the greatest research support in the history of research on teaching. (Dunkin & Barnes, 1986, p. 759, emphasis added)

However, as far as secondary schools are concerned, the positive findings characteristic of colleges and universities are not clearly replicable. Instead, results obtained from PSI and other types of programmed instruction are quite similar to those of conventional approaches (Bangert, Kulik, & Kulik, 1983). The reasons for the disparity between college and secondary school are said to include the fact that college students are more carefully selected and are more highly self-motivated.

On the other hand, a couple of insightful qualifications to the foregoing assessment of the relations between PSI and conventional teaching in secondary schools have been offered by Kulik, Schwalb, and Kulik (1982). Their article indicated:

First, programmed instruction boosted student achievement more in its *recent* implementations than in *early* applications (emphasis added). Second, programmed instruction added more to student learning in social science than in science and mathematics classes. These findings may have practical implications for the future use of programmed instruction in secondary schools.

The first finding—that programmed instruction produced stronger effects in recent applications—is apparently not a chance result. . . . Three separate meta-analyses showed that studies of the early sixties found little superiority of programmed over conventional instruction and that recent studies found results more favorable to programmed instruction. . . . It seems . . . to us that the art or science of programming has improved in recent years and that recent studies used better programs than the older studies.

There are also some reasons for expecting subject matter differences in the effectiveness of instructional innovations . . . One fact to consider is that programmed and conventional instruction may be more similar in the "hard" sciences than in the "soft" sciences. Conventional instruction in the "hard" sciences may already incorporate such features of programmed instruction as explicit objectives, small steps, and active student response. . . . [It may also be the case] . . . that social science teachers are simply very discerning in their use of programmed instructions. They may develop better programs and use them more appropriately than do other science teachers. (pp. 137–138)

It would seem that since PSI qualifies as a more "recent" type of programmed instruction (and therefore, an "improved" variety), and since PSI can readily accommodate to soft-science subject matters, its future in the secondary school system is promising. Perhaps especially so, since it is strongly interpersonal (interactive) in nature, and therefore satisfies the social needs of the adolescent more than does the traditional variety.

This possibility was driven home by an unannounced visit to a class

Table 6.2. Energy Time Line: Example of Programmed Instruction, PSI-Type[a]

Finish the "Energy Time Line"

Instructions: Research and patience will help you to fill in the blank spaces provided for you on this "Energy Time Line." Read each sentence carefully for clues. Some dates are statements and do not have anything for you to fill in.

1776	In England, James Watt puts tow engines to work in factories and starts an energy revolution. The energy he used to run his engines was _____.
1783	Two men fly in a balloon at _____ (give place). The energy used is _____.
1785–90	Most people burn wood for heating and cooking and travel by horse or on foot.
1800	In Italy, _____ invents the battery and gives his name to the volt. The energy he produces is _____.
1804	An Englishman, Richard _____, puts James Watt's engine on wheels and rails. He is the father of the railroad locomotive.
1807	Robert Fulton doesn't build the very first _____ but he makes the one people first pay to ride on.
1815–20	Wood continues to supply most household energy needs. Coal begins to do more in factories and railroad engines.
1821	First attempt to develop and market natural gas near Fredonia, NY.
1829	An American named _____ and an Englishman named _____ each invent a generator. Who was first? _____. The energy produced was _____.
1837	Americans put new inventions to work. First comes McCormick's _____, then the steam shovel by _____ and then the telegraph by _____.
1845–55	Railroads expand rapidly, hauling freight and passengers brave enough to stand the jolts and to risk hot cinders that often fly from the engine into their cars. England is first and America is second in railroad locomotive production.
1859	_____ is the first man to strike oil in Pennsylvania, beginning the petroleum industry.
1860	Lenoir of France invents the _____ engine.
1870	An explosion inside a cylinder paves the way for the later invention of the automobile. An oil strike hastens the discovery of the fuel that will run it.
1880	Coal and wood still furnish most of the energy in homes. Coal-fired "iron horses" (railroads) and real horses continue to take most people places. Although the electric bulb has been invented, most people still use kerosene or gaslights to read by.
1884	In England, Charles Parsons perfects the steam _____ and advances the development of electrical energy.
1886	Karl _____ builds the first successful automobile.
1892	The oil-burning engine is invented by _____. Eventually, this engine will replace steam engines.
1895	The power of Niagara Falls is harnessed to make _____.
1903	The engine in the Wright brothers' plane is powered by _____.

Table 6.2. (*continued*)

1905	Albert Einstein develops a theory for measuring energy and prepares the way for the _____ age.
1910	Ford makes the first mass-produced auto called Model _____.
1920	By the end of this period, many new homes have coal furnaces in the basement and more and more cars appear in garages.
1926	Robert Goddard tests a _____ in New England.
1936	Hoover Dam on the Colorado River is built to generate _____ power.
1940	_____, a fiber made from oil, coal, and water, makes its first public appearance.
1942	In Chicago, Enrico Fermi sets off the first _____ chain reaction.
1945	Many homes convert from coal to natural gas for heating. Most families own at least one car and some have two.
1952	Mr. Strickhart is born on the same day Eisenhower is elected president.
1952	Bell scientists raise hope for our energy future with the _____ battery.
1957	The U.S. gets its first big _____ electric power plant at Shippingport, PA.
1960	Demands for energy grow. America gets more people, more homes, more factories and businesses, more cars, more trucks, more planes. Demand grows faster than supply.
1970	Congress passes the _____ Air Act.
1973	OPEC nations _____ and create an energy crisis.
1980s	Americans continue to look for ways to _____ the energy we have and find new sources.

[a]Used at Franklin High School, Somerset, New Jersey. From R. Strickhart, unpublished classroom material. Reprinted by permission of R. Strickhart.

in environmental science in Franklin Township, New Jersey. The teacher (Robert Strickhart) informed the group of about 12 students that they were going to go to the library. He distributed duplicated copies of "Energy Time Line" (see Table 6.2). Note that the items combined both "hard science" and "soft science." He asked the class to complete the blanks by consulting the appropriate references. Those that finished sooner than others could work on a science report due the next week. After the students left for the library, the visitor inquired if his use of programmed instruction was routine. The teacher replied: "I mix it. Sometimes I give them a program, sometimes I lecture, and sometimes we talk." We then went to the library. The students were sitting at adjoining tables, working cheerfully and industriously. The necessary references were on nearby shelves. The teacher excused himself from chatting with the visitor saying, "Let me circulate a bit."

In short, the flexible manner with which the program was written, together with the flexible way with which it was implemented left little doubt that it was of the type known as Personalized System of Instruction. Other interactive systems, such as ACT* (Adaptive Control of Thought, star), have been developed by J.R. Anderson and others. They emphasize the use of the computer as an interactive, "intelligent tutor." Of course, a balance needs to be struck between the computer and the teacher as means of interaction with the student.

Read only as much of Table 6.2 as is necessary to get the idea of the program, and interests you.

Note on Behavior Modification in the Classroom

It is only appropriate that we briefly mention another application of behavioristic principles to education, before closing the chapter. "Behavior modification" is the broad utilization of findings from studies in operant conditioning, toward the end of establishing socially acceptable behavior in human beings. With regard to education, behavior modification concerns ways to study and improve "student conduct, teacher performance, academic quality and productivity, and various social and emotional behaviors. Behavior modification has been contributing toward making educational systems more effective and satisfying to students and school personnel" (Sulzer-Azaroff, 1981, p. 68). A simple example involving "selecting the target behavior" affords a feeling for the approach. Sulzer-Azaroff cites such an instance:

> In one case, a request for consultation [obtaining advice from S-A] derived from the staff of a curriculum research and development program. Two teachers who had in the past encountered only cooperative high-school students found themselves attempting to field test their newly developed curriculum materials in an elementary-school setting. Though apparently very popular with the students, they experienced serious difficulties as the youngsters roamed around the room, spoke without permission loudly enough to interfere with other students' work, and in general were making things unpleasant for the teachers. A few days observation [of the target behavior] suggested that the teachers were giving the major portion of their attention to students while they were being disruptive. It was suggested that the teachers attend instead to students while they were engaged in nondisruptive behavior. Thereby, appropriate rather than inappropriate behavior would be reinforced.
>
> In another case, the teacher gave "points" (secondary reinforcers) for improved academic work. The points could be accumulated, and exchanged for primary reinforcers, including extra activity. (Sulzer-Azaroff, 1981, p. 68)

Finally, we return to the sense of unease with which we opened the chapter; namely, that the scientific essence of philosophy of behaviorism (specifically, its objection to explanatory use of "purpose" and "mind") might be lost in its technical language. To gain perspective, without necessarily agreement, we return to Skinner's last article:

> In face-to-face contact with another person, references to an initiating self are unavoidable. There is a "you," and there is an "I." I see what "you" do and hear what "you" say and you see what "I" do and hear what "I" say. We do not see the histories of selection responsible for what is done and therefore infer an internal origination, but the successful use of the vernacular in the practice of psychology offers no support for its use in a scientific analysis of behavior for a mind or self. . . . In short, [non-behavioristic] psychologists have unwittingly been analyzing contingencies of reinforcement, the very contingencies responsible for the behavior mistakenly attributed to an internal originator. (Skinner, 1990, p. 1209)

SUMMARY

In this chapter, we pushed the behaviorist argument for the utility of programmed instruction as far as we think it reasonable to go. We began with Skinner's philosophy of psychology. The chapter then analyzed the bar-pressing paradigm in detail, and showed how it bears upon programmed instruction, a pedagogical approach first suggested by Thorndike. Evidence is cited to indicate that Keller's version of programmed instruction is unusually successful, probably because personal interaction occurs between student and teacher, as implemented by the program. Thus, the personalized system of instruction does what a good teacher would normally have done in the classroom anyway, but uses modern technology to provide selection by consequences through reinforcement, thereby enhancing the process. This same might be said about Anderson's ACT*. However, although it can be enormously helpful, modern technology *per se* is neither necessary nor sufficient. The good teacher remains at the core of education.

Gestalt Psychology
Perceptual Illusions and Insight-Thinking

This chapter has four objectives: first, to provide an overview of gestalt psychology's stand against elementalism; second, to consider the meaning and implications of the gestaltist model of the brain's structure and function; third, to comment on the evidence offered for and against the existence of insight-thinking and representational processes in humans and apes; fourth, to survey the highlights of gestalt psychology's influence upon educational theory, personality theory, and social psychology.

GESTALT PSYCHOLOGY'S STAND AGAINST ELEMENTALISM: KOHLER

The unique feature of gestalt psychology, one that gives this school its special character, is its complete rejection of atomistic approaches to an understanding of behavior. Gestaltists hold that elementalism is the primary hazard of scientific method, philosophy, and art. One can become so careful in trying to specify variables and techniques as to lose the integrity of whatever he or she is investigating, communicating, or creating. A dilemma arises because human endeavor *without* specification of terms or techniques is confused and imprecise. Yet with excessive attention to terms or techniques, human endeavor becomes stilted, and only those issues for which concepts and methodologies already exist are treated. We no longer create, we just reproduce.

By now, reactions to the problems presented by elementalism are not new to us. We have seen how attempts to reduce mental phenomena to physiological events failed. We have seen how the mental mechanics of James Mill gave way to the mental chemistry of John Stuart Mill. We have seen how the reflexology of one-way dialectical materialism was forced to yield to the psychophysiology and higher-order conditioning of two-way dialectical materialism.

The only school, other than gestalt psychology, that did not have to overcome an initial predisposition toward elementalism is American functionalism, the school associated with Thorndike and Dewey. But the two schools are vastly different: Gestalt psychology's *exclusive* interest is to search out holistic phenomena which are especially illustrative of the fact that levels of organization cannot necessarily be equated with their entering components. Functionalism does not dispute the existence of these phenomena, although it reserves the right to question the gestaltist interpretation of them. Functionalism has broader interests than gestalt psychology. It is not so much against what gestalt psychology does as it is against any school's tendency toward giving what Woodworth long ago dubbed "marching orders." Thus, functionalism could absorb Ebbinghaus's nonsense syllable technique and Thorndike's puzzle box procedure, and continue to find meaningful use for them. Gestalt psychology, however, abandoned these experimental paradigms as being too unnatural. Watson and Pavlov were also dismissed for having modeled their views too closely upon stimulus–response reflexology. In the gestaltists' eyes the conditioners moved too quickly from observation of the rich and qualitatively different varieties of learning and perception to a restrictive quantitative analysis. Wolfgang Kohler drew the distinction this way:

> Unfortunately, human interests tend to be so narrow that preoccupation with only the quantitative phase of research leads to . . . trouble. People who suffer from this ailment will soon fail to recognize problems which do not lend themselves at once to quantitative investigation. And yet, at the time such problems may be more essential and, in a deeper meaning of the word, scientific, than many purely quantitative questions. (Kohler, 1929, p. 47)

One can agree with Kohler and even say "Bravo!" but refrain from committing the error of becoming too narrowly confined to qualitative problems of a *special* sort. Perhaps, in this respect, gestalt psychology has been overzealous and has been so since its very beginnings.

Apart from Kohler, the year 1910 marked the arrival at the University of Frankfurt of two other new assistant professors, Max Wertheimer and Kurt Koffka. Collectively, they were well-grounded in philosophy, physics, physiology, and mathematics. Each had his own theoretical and research concerns, but they developed a common, fervent mistrust of elementalism, regardless of the form of psychological inquiry in which it was manifested. Together, they founded gestalt psychology.

Every student of psychology is familar with the counterelementalistic battle cry, "The whole is greater than the sum of its parts." However, this slogan is an erroneous version of the gestaltists' actual position. As noted by C.C. Pratt in his introduction to Kohler (1969):

> One phrase frequently associated with the unique properties of organized wholes was actually not used by the Gestalt psychologists, but nevertheless gave them no end of trouble: *The whole is more than the sum of its parts.* Many American psychologists were inclined to regard that statement as the quintessence of absurdity. Kohler often said that he wished his critics would remember that what he really said was that the whole is *different* from the sum of the parts. (p. 10)

Kohler's statement pertains to the nature of reality. By asserting that the whole possesses its own inherent reality, the gestaltists made direct contact with the Kantian view that human beings possess an innate tendency to organize events. This tendency is of importance to perception and to problem solving which depends upon perception, and thereby to our grasp of the educational process. We consider perception first. The gestaltists argued that reality is based upon perception, and that perception depended upon the bringing of an overriding coherence or organization to sensations, and to the stimuli evoking them. We are generally familiar with this argument insofar as it is illustrated by visual phenomena, but much less so when it comes to touch. In Katz's *The World of Touch*, he quotes Titchener concerning the perceptual organization of uniquely comprised "touch blends":

> Wetness is a complex of pressure and temperature. It is possible, under experimental conditions, to evoke the perception of wetness from perfectly dry things—flour, lycopodium powder, cotton wool, discs of metal; and it is possible, on the other hand, to wet the skin with water and to evoke the perception of a dry pressure or a dry temperature. (1989, p. 37)

Katz also emphasized how vital it was to education that the developing child learn the importance of organizing the sensations attendant upon moving the hand in active touch, rather than in passively detecting tactual stimuli. Obviously, this idea is related to Dewey's "we learn by doing." The *idea* of perceptual organization (but not necessarily the tactual phenomena just described) is also related to the occurrence of visual apparent movement, a subject to which we now turn.

Apparent Movement and Psychophysical Isomorphism: Wertheimer

Max Wertheimer pursued the attack against elementalism through his research on apparent movement (or phenomenal, as distinct from real, movement; hence, "phi"). The problem that he examined (with Koffka and Kohler often serving as subjects) is one with which we all have at least a passing acquaintance through our going to the cinema. A motion picture film is composed of successive frames or stills that are passed rapidly through a beam of light, with the images focused on a screen. Without giving it a second thought, we perceive *continuous* motion of the actors, actresses, and scenes across the screen, even though we are in fact seeing a series of *discrete* pictures, with each still being progressively different from the preceding one.

The motion picture camera had not yet been perfected, but the stroboscope and tachistoscope were available to Wertheimer. He used these instruments to study parametrically the specific temporal and spatial conditions necessary to generate the illusion of real movement from sequentially presented, *stationary* lights and objects. The "whole" was the organization by the viewer of apparent motion from what were separate, static events. Successive, stationary events were pulled together by the viewer and perceived as continuous, or real, movement.

Wertheimer's experiments resulted in the rejection of the then prevailing explanation of the perception of movement; namely, that the phenomenon depended upon sequential stimulation of visual receptors by an object moving across the retina, and through the retina, the visual cortex. As noted by I.M. Spigel:

> It is both tempting and convenient to give as a necessary condition for the perception of movement the successive stimulation of adjacent retinal loci. But any position which demands continuous displacement over a portion of the retinal mosaic as the necessary condition for movement perception is, to say the least, complicated by the existence of the phenomena of apparent movement. In the case of *phi* movement, for example, the appearance of continuous movement may be produced simply by the successive stimulation of discrete retinal loci, in the absence of continuous displacement of the stimulus upon the retina. (Spigel, 1965, pp. 1–2)

Quite quickly, others identified a variety of visual, auditory, and tactual phenomena of a gestaltist character. Of the visual, a number did not require movement, and so have lent themselves to reproduction as figures in standard textbooks. (The Sander and the Muller-Lyer illusions are particularly compelling, and are shown in Figure 7.1.) Collectively, they demanded something more than a wire model of the brain's neurological connections, and a brick-and-mortar idea of perception.

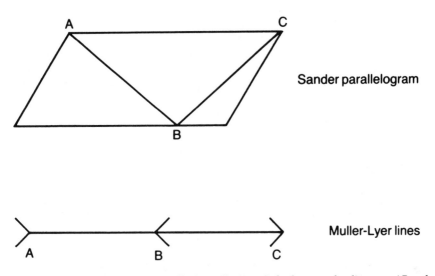

Figure 7.1. The Sander and the Muller-Lyer illusions. In both cases, the distances AB and BC are equal. (From J. M. Notterman, *Forms of Psychological Inquiry* (1985). Copyright 1985 by Columbia University Press. Reprinted by permission of Columbia University Press.)

Thus, Wertheimer and his colleagues went a considerable step beyond that of the poet. They held that reality, and perhaps beauty too, are *not* in the eye of the beholder, but merely *begin* there. What we conceive as being "true" depends upon the organization we bring to sensations. The particular form of organization, in turn, depends upon our momentary motivation and attention, upon our sensory organs, and—most important of all—upon the physics and processes of the brain. They urged that the linear-wire construct be replaced with a solid-conductor model taken from field physics, a discipline dealing with the way electrical charges distribute themselves or pass through masses. (Kohler had studied field physics under the eminent Max Planck.) Thereby not only phi, but other more cognitive organizational phenomena could be explained. The purported connection to cognition is this: How we solve problems, learn, and generally become educated, depends upon what we perceive. What we perceive depends upon how we organize sensations. Theories of how we organize sensations depend upon whether we emphasize that sensory information passes through nerves in a simple, go/no-go fashion, or whether we assert that the same information is conducted through a mass or solid in a complex, eddylike manner. By analogy, the brain serves as a mass conductor, with (*at least*) afferent (input) and efferent (output) nerves serving as "wires."

Kohler's research strategy was to concentrate on those cases of perception—e.g., apparent movement and other "illusions"—which he asserted could not be explained in terms of linear-wire models of the brain. He then offered interpretations in the language of field physics, and thereby implied that the brain—and of necessity, perception as well—followed the rules of field physics.

It is essential for the educator to understand that any appeal to a *particular* view of how the brain works is fraught with danger. Apart from the perils of reductionism, and the false sense of explanatory security thereby attained, the plain fact is that the brain is a remarkably versatile organ. Almost any psychological theory (past, present, and probably future) can fall back upon the brain's functions for support.

Even Kohler himself recognized limitations to his argument. He issued the following disclaimer:

> Unfortunately, we cannot yet give such perceptual observations as apparent motion or optical illusions a clear interpretation in terms of brain currents. This is not possible for simple technical reasons. In order to proceed in such directions, one would have to obtain records of the whole distribution of the cortical currents within the brain, of interactions between several such currents, and so forth. With present techniques one cannot take such records. Naturally, one electrode attached to the head or the brain over the active region does not give us information on how the given brain currents behave in the tissue as a whole. (Kohler, 1929, p. 118)

However, even if advancing technology were to approach the ideal set forth by Kohler, it is by no means obvious that his attachment of importance to the relation between field physics and perception is all inclusive. It is probably safer to assume that depending upon circumstances, the brain functions either as a linear-wire system, a network-wire system, or a mass conductor, and that each of the three types of structure and function is of importance to perception.

As we shall see, gestaltist interpretations of perception surface again in our considerations of psychoanalysis and cognitive psychology; indeed, wherever the tension between elementalism and holism comes under scrutiny.

INSIGHT-THINKING AND REPRESENTATIONAL PROCESSES IN APES

Kohler believed that "the whole is different from the sum of its parts" applied just as readily to thought, particularly to problem-solving of the insight type, as it did to perception. His reason for asserting that there was a resemblance becomes clearer if we substitute the word "solution" for the word "whole," thus, "the *solution* is different from the sum of its parts." The "aha" phenomenon is experienced when we are able to transcend the properties of the individual components that enter into and constitute a problem, and are *suddenly* able to organize the solution.

We require still another step to understand the gestaltist's argument for relating thinking to perceiving, and Kohler helps us to take this step. In what may well have been his last formal lecture, "What Is Thinking?" he discussed different usages of the term: (1) "an inspection of memories" [e.g., I was thinking of our recent vacation]; (2) "a synonym for having an intention" [e.g., I think I will go to lunch]. Of these first two types, he stated: "In both cases, the thinking involved is no particular achievement. It just refers to having mental contents, *in the absence of corresponding perceptual realities or actions* (Kohler, 1969, p. 133, emphasis added). (Note that Kohler did not bat an eyelash in taking it for granted that we are capable of *mentally representing* our perceptions of, and interactions with, the outside environment.) Kohler then discussed the third and most important usage of the term: (3) "when thinking does become an achievement, that is, when it is productive. This happens when it changes our mental environment by solving problems which this environment offers. Now this is, of course, an entirely different story. . . . It is with thinking in this sense, with productive thinking, that I will . . . deal" (pp. 133–134). In other words, although all three types of thinking involve representational processes, the productive (or creative) type is the only one in which mental representations are changed during and by the very solutions they generate.

The importance of productive thinking to education was emphasized by Wertheimer in his last book, *Productive Thinking* (1945). According to Woodworth and Sheehan (1964), Wertheimer held that: "A *teacher* can so present problems as to favor insight and can foster in his pupils a genuine problem-solving attitude" (emphasis in original, p. 235). Woodworth and Sheehan (1964) selected an excellent example of the kind of approach Wertheimer had in mind. It involved first teaching children how to find the area of a rectangle by dividing it into rows containing a constant number of squares, counting up the number of such rows, and multiplying the one by the other. The children were then presented with a parallelogram, and requested to compute its area based upon what they already knew about computing the area of a rectangle. "Many older children as well as adults, gave the 'associationist' type of answer: 'I haven't learned that yet' or 'I used to know that but I've forgotten.' But some, even of the younger children, reached a 'fine, genuine, original' space solution" (pp. 236–237). They did so by recognizing that the two ends of the parallelogram could be cut-away, so as to leave a rectangle. The two newly formed right triangles could then be joined to form a separate rectangle, which in turn could be added to the major one.

Wertheimer "concluded that school teachers tend to depend too much on repetitious drill in the application of authoritarian rules, and that in this way children are 'educated' to depend on rules rather than on their own intelligence. [He] charged that the associationist and connectionist psychology, applied to education, supports the traditional emphasis on drill, and that only the Gestalt psychology offers any hope of improvement." "'Repetition is useful, but continuous use of mechanical repetition also has harmful effects. It is dangerous because it easily induces habits of sheer mechanized action, blindness, tendencies to perform slavishly instead of thinking, instead of facing a problem freely (Wertheimer, 1945, p. 12)'" (Woodworth & Sheehan, 1964, p. 237).

While it is true that early forms of associationism and connectionism fit Wertheimer's description, modern programmed learning—especially of the Keller, teacher-oriented, PSI variety—does not. We see here further evidence of the tension between elementalism and holism. It is a tension which can serve as a constructive force for improvement in education.

"Insight" is a special aspect of productive thinking. We infer insight if a problem is suddenly solved in the absence of changes in the *outside* world, and in the absence of overt trial-and-error approaches. Further, we infer that a change has occurred in the mental representation of the problem, and that the insight-solution to the problem will remain indefinitely with the organism.

In 1913, Kohler was given an opportunity to extend his research interests actively from the area of perceiving to the area of insight-thinking. The Prussian Academy of Sciences had named him director of the Anthropoid Station on the island of Tenerife in the Canaries, off the northwest coast of Africa. Because of World War I, Kohler stayed much longer than he had expected—a total of more than 6 years. His enforced sojourn gave him sufficient time for research, reflection, and writing to lead to his book, *The Mentality of Apes*. In this volume, he described his experiments with problem-solving, using chimpanzees and other anthropoid apes as subjects. Of course, his research with nonhuman primates has a Darwinian rationale. First, apes are closer to us biologically than are cats or rats. Second, Kohler believed that he was dealing with insight (or productive thought), and not merely with conditioning or chaining. The two major classes of problems he studied are well known.

In one type, the animals had boxes of different sizes available to them. They were either to select one large box, or to assemble the right combination of smaller boxes and stack them, in order to climb up and reach a suspended banana. The chimpanzees displayed marked individual differences in their ability to solve the problem. Sultan, the smartest of his apes, did so quite readily. Rana, "a chimpanzee of particularly restricted intellectual gifts," was unable to do so, even after repeatedly watching Sultan (Kohler, 1969, p. 157).

In the second type of problem, the chimpanzees had a number of hollow bamboo sticks of different widths available to them. Each stick by itself was too short for the apes to reach a banana lying outside the experimental cage. They were required to select two sticks and, by inserting one into the wider opening of the other, make a single pole long enough to pull in the fruit. Sultan spent an hour in complete failure. He first tried using a single stick alone. He then tried pushing one stick with another toward the banana, but without joining the two. Finally, he arrived at the solution all at once. While squatting on a box, Sultan joined the two bamboo sticks, ran immediately to the bars of the cage, and reached out for the banana. Rana, however, never solved the problem.

Based upon the performance of his sample of chimpanzees, ranging in ability from Sultan to Rana, Kohler interpreted their behavior as indicating that at least the more gifted apes were quite capable of insight-thinking.

Soviet Refutation (or Is It?) of Insight-Thinking Apes

Kohler's work with insight-thinking in apes posed a serious challenge to the two-way dialectical-materialist tenet that only human beings possess productive or creative representational processes. For the Soviets, animal behavior, including that of higher apes, was to be understood entirely in terms of elementary conditioning phenomena, wherein productive thought has no autonomy and plays no part.

The experiments of Pavlov's student, E.G. Vatsuro, are directly germane to insight-thinking. He worked in Leningrad for 9 years with a male chimpanzee named Rafael. Even before Vatsuro began this research (1937), biologists on the scene had already determined that Rafael could not solve the standing-on-a-box (or stacking-of-boxes) problem. The biologists found that "after unsuccessful attempts to obtain the reward from a height of two boxes, Rafael grabbed a third box and put it on his head!" (Ladygina-Kots & Dembovski, 1969, p. 64). Vatsuro accepted their results, and their methodology.

As to the joined-stick problem, Vatsuro hypothesized that Kohler's chimpanzees did not really "solve" a problem that was new to them, let alone show insight. The situation was not novel, because the act of reaching out for an object with a branch to obtain a fruit is commonplace in their natural habitat, and readily generalizes to a stick in the laboratory. It is only in this sense that the chimpanzee can use a "tool"; the animal cannot fashion one, as superficially appears to be the case in the joining of two sticks. Vatsuro claimed that the joined-stick solution did not demonstrate either insight or tool-making, because of an artifact in Kohler's research design. Specifically, the visual-motor field to which the chimpanzees were exposed was severely restricted. Vatsuro believed he proved his point by having two phases to his own experiment. The phases differed in the extent to which the visual-motor field was limited.

Phase 1. During the first phase, Vatsuro gave Rafael two bamboo sticks of different diameters. By joining them, the ape could reach through the bars of the cage and obtain a banana. It took two days for Rafael to succeed in the task, but he did not retain the solution. On the third day, the chimpanzee again tried to reach the banana with just one stick; only occasionally, when unsuccessful with the one stick, would he join the two, and pull in the banana.

Phase 2. After 10 days, Rafael was again given two sticks, one of which was modified as shown in Figure 7.2. The wider of the two sticks was altered to have a junction of three *side* openings, in addition to the "natural" hole at the end of the stick. The latter opening was the only

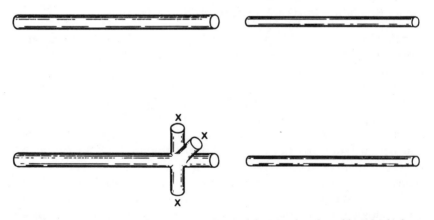

Figure 7.2. Kohler's (top) and Vatsuro's versions of the joined-stick problem. In the latter case, insertion of the narrow stick into the side-openings (x) was not effective in making a single long stick. (From J. M. Notterman, *Forms of Psychological Inquiry* (1985). Copyright 1985 by Columbia University Press. Reprinted by permission of Columbia University Press.)

one which, when chosen, was effective in lengthening the narrower stick. Rafael tried numerous combinations, until he stumbled on the correct strategy for joining the two components. But after doing so, he did not attempt to reach the banana.

An analysis of Vatsuro's experiment first appeared in Polish, in Y.N. Dembovskii's *The Psychology of Apes*, published in the Soviet Union in 1963. According to Cole and Maltzman (1969, p. 41), Chapter 5 of Dembovskii's book is included in Ladygina-Kots and Dembovskii's *The Psychology of Primates* (1969). In the same retrospective account, Dembovskii's book is cited but not referenced. A translation of Vatsuro's observations follows:

> (1) The correct solution did not occur immediately; (2) repetition of the experiment did not evoke immediate reproduction of the previous solution; (3) Rafael joined the sticks even in the absence of the reward; (4) originally the sticks were joined without effectively lengthening the tool as a whole; (5) in the process of repeating the experiments, the animal, as a rule, repeated all the previous errors. All this does not indicate an intellectual solution of the task. The manipulation of the sticks cannot be considered a part of the whole process of food acquisition since it has its own stimulation. It may occur with the same success both with and without a reward. There is no doubt that the aim of manipulating the sticks is not to lengthen the stick. The ape's frequent errors even after the solution of the task indicate the absence of his comprehension of the situation. (Ladygina-Kots & Dembovskii, 1969, p. 63)

It is interesting to conjecture whether the multiple-opening, joined-stick problem could have been solved by Sultan, Kohler's brightest ape. Perhaps Vatsuro's Rafael was more like Rana, one of Kohler's less-gifted chimpanzees, than like Sultan. Striking individual differences in visual-motor organization exist among human beings (Notterman, Tufano, & Hrapsky, 1982). They may also exist in chimpanzees.

Regarding Language in Apes

Research into whether chimpanzees are capable of a human type of thinking such as insight invariably raises the question of whether chimpanzees can be taught a human type of nonverbal language. Presumably this follows, because if the apes could be taught to communicate semantically with their experimenters, it would buttress the argument that they were capable of abstract or representational thinking.

The Soviets demonstrated in the 1940s and early 1950s that apes could be taught to use sign-language (finger and arm signals) to *designate* different foods (Ladygina-Kots & Dembovskii, 1969). Their findings implied, however, that semantic or syntactic gestural language were beyond the ape's capacity. After surveying the results of his own extensive research at Columbia University, experiments in which the chimpanzees were trained to use hand signs to put "words" together, Terrace came to the same conclusion as the Russians: chimpanzees are not capable of putting together a sentence, or of following grammatical rules. The previously reported, apparently successful efforts (including his own) accomplished nothing more than having trained the apes to emit conditioned chains of behavior (Terrace, Petitto, Sanders, & Bever, 1979).

Regarding Cognition in Apes

Can chimpanzees or other higher apes think productively or creatively, as asserted by Kohler, notwithstanding their apparent inability to generate syntactic language? Overall, do chimpanzees possess cognition and consciousness even remotely resembling that of the human being? A special issue of the journal *The Behavioral and Brain Sciences* was devoted to this second broader question (Harnad, 1978). There were almost as many answers given as there were author-commentators. Although he was not among the contributors, W.A. Mason elsewhere provided the crispest reply to date. He wrote:

> Attributes such as "richness of associations," "reflective thought," "symbolization," "images," and the like, so often cited as differentiating man from ape, remain elusive and ill defined in the human case and can hardly provide a firm basis for interspecies comparisons. To foreclose the issue now is to say, in effect, that the ape utterly lacks abilities and functions that have yet to be adequately described in ourselves. (Mason, 1976, p. 291)

Koffka, and Back to Human Psychology

Of the three co-founders of gestalt psychology, Kurt Koffka was the most daring in attempting to apply gestalt principles to problems of human behavior. He argued that the organizational rules of gestalt psychology, as established in perception, are fundamental to an understanding of most other aspects of human behavior, including personality and social psychology. In a word, the way we perceive is basic to *all* behavior.

The steps leading to his position are suggested by Woodworth and Sheehan's somewhat hesitant interpretation of Koffka's *Principles of Gestalt Psychology* (1935). The first step is one with which the reader is already familiar. We do not ordinarily respond directly to stimuli, but to our perception of them, that is, to the way we organize sensations. Koffka drew a general distinction between the perceived (or—his term—"behavioral") environment versus the real (or physical) environment. The second step is this: the way we perceive stimuli depends upon field physics and their attendant organizational principles, as explored here in the discussion of the brain as a mass conductor of sensory information. Third, the child's unfolding idea of self versus not-self depends upon the perception of qualitative differences between *outside* or public exteroceptive stimuli (mainly visual and auditory) and *inside*, or private, interoceptive stimuli (including tactual, proprioceptive, and internal sensations). Fourth, the distinction between one's self, other such selves, and the environment is always in a state of flux or tension. The reason is: "The physical situation may be deceptive or at least difficult to grasp, our senses have their limits, and our desires may blind us to the real facts. Persons as well as things are not always what they seem" (Woodworth & Sheehan, 1964, p. 230).

In summary, the point is that we become what we are on a personal basis, and act the way we do on an interpersonal basis, because of the way we perceive. And the way we perceive, in turn, is governed by the rules of gestaltist, organizational principles.

GESTALT PSYCHOLOGY'S SPECIFIC CONTRIBUTIONS TO EDUCATION

Can gestalt psychology lay claim to a specific approach to instruction? Yes and no. Gestaltists have certainly drawn attention to the holistic nature of perception, and to the unusual character of insight. The prospective teacher can benefit from these reminders. This achievement is no small matter. But it does not necessarily follow that if a teacher is concerned about how his or her students perceive themselves, others, and the world about them, that the self-same teacher is a "gestaltist." The same point applies to an interest in and encouragement of insight. It is quite possible, for example, for a student to attain insight while using a programmed text in book or computer form. It is even more likely to occur if the teacher actively seeks to facilitate insight through his or her guidance or questions.

Maria Montessori added to the contribution of gestaltist views to human psychology through her emphasis upon the importance of purposive hand movement and the utilization of language by the developing child. She objected to parental admonishment such as "Don't touch!" and asserted that the child stores speech and "uses it according to the need of the moment" (Montessori, 1984, p. 83). Her work is considered "gestaltist," because it draws attention to *privately* purposive problem solving and to *creative* language production, both of which imply that "the whole is different from the sum of its parts," and thereby insight.

As has been noted about every other aspect of psychology we have thus far considered, no truth is exclusive of other truths. This observation extends to gestalt psychology.

SUMMARY AND THE FUTURE TASK
OF GESTALT PSYCHOLOGY

Gestalt psychology has had the salutary effect of restraining educators, behavioral scientists, and therapists from oversimplifying their subject matter. By itself, that is a major contribution. As noted in the opening to this chapter, however, the gestaltists are not alone in their battle against an overly zealous elementalism.

But the gestalt school has accomplished more than a rejuvenation of mental chemistry. Investigators have demonstrated previously unsuspected holistic phenomena within perception and cognition, and have established important theoretical connections among perception, productive thought, and education (Kohler and Wertheimer). Gestalt relations between perception on the one hand, and emotion, motivation, and purposivity on the other, undoubtedly also exist, as implied by Koffka. These relations have not yet been as well-formulated as those between perceiving and cognition.

In general, the future task of gestalt psychology continues to be what it was when the three new assistant professors arrived at the University of Frankfurt in 1910. Namely, the challenge is to maintain the integrity of a phenomenon by avoiding elementalism and reductionism. As we shall see, the same challenge has surfaced in modern-day cognitive psychology.

8

Freudian Psychoanalysis
Therapy as Reeducation

The point of view is maintained in this chapter that psychoanalysis is a reeducational process. In that sense, the teacher and the therapist share common goals and should be alert to the potential for mutual enlightenment regarding professional understandings. To facilitate this exchange, the chapter has the following objectives: First, to provide a brief overview of the major constructs, principles, and therapeutic phenomena of Freudian psychoanalysis; second, to illustrate how the Freudian concepts and techniques are related to the variables of conventional psychology, especially those relevant to educational psychology. We emphasize at the outset that our interest in psychoanalysis is as educators, not as therapists.

Are we straining credibility in asserting a relationship between psychoanalysis and education? In his twenty-eighth lecture, the last of a series delivered at the University of Vienna during 1915–1917, Freud stated: "The labour of overcoming the resistance is the essential achievement of the analytic treatment; the patient has to accomplish it and the physician makes it possible for him to do this by suggestions which are in the nature of *education*. It has been truly said therefore, that psychoanalytic treatment is a kind of *re-education*" (Freud, 1957, p. 459, emphasis in original). Further, the American Academy of Psychoanalysis included in its 1987 meeting a panel discussion on the Art of Psychoanalysis as a Technology of Instruction (Notterman, 1987, January).

It is no exaggeration to suggest that Freud considered the psycho-analyst to be a master teacher. As we shall see when we deal briefly with repression and resistance at various points in the chapter, the uncovering of and education about objectionable psychosexual material is at the core of the psychoanalytic process, and requires the skill of a gifted educator–therapist.

THE UNIQUENESS OF PSYCHOANALYTIC THEORY

Sigmund Freud's psychoanalytic theory differed from all other forms of psychological inquiry then prevalent in this one crucial respect: the psychoanalytic movement had its beginnings in the therapist's office with attempts to help neurotics. As Freud pondered the problems of his patients, he formulated his theory. As he met with success or failure, he modified his theory. As he became more confident of his conceptions, he extended his theory, even to the point of application to "normal" persons, as in his *Psychopathology of Everyday Life*. Of course, neither teachers nor students are exempt from that application. Indeed, both parties are often unwilling observers of the darker side of human nature, including aggression, and sexual abuse or sexual passivity. Teachers need to understand various theoretical viewpoints. However, such an understanding is not an invitation to act as therapists. Remedial engagement must be left to trained individuals. It *is* an invitation to become enlightened, and thereby to become more realistic and compassionate.

The reasonably well-read individual who is curious about the sources of human behavior will sooner or later encounter ideas that are attributable to Freud. Although some knowledge on the reader's part of Freud's writings can therefore be taken for granted, we will review them briefly so that we might have a common point of departure. We reserve for the next chapter various criticisms of Freudian psychoanalysis. Our task now is to secure a knowledge of the basic psychoanalytic propositions, and to do so briefly, without bias or preconception. We begin our survey of psychoanalysis with definitions of Freud's major theoretical constructs, bearing in mind that they were originally formulated in late Victorian, Viennese society, just after the turn of the century.

Freud's Constructs

There are two categories of concepts in Freudian theory. The first describes levels of consciousness or awareness, the second, functional components of personality. For our purposes, personality is defined as an individual's characteristic modes of dealing with himself or herself, with the world, and with the people in it.

Levels of Consciousness. For Freud, there are three levels of consciousness—the conscious, the preconscious, and the unconscious. They are to be viewed as lying along a continuum of awareness. The *conscious* is that part of personality of which the individual is ordinarily aware. It includes his or her thoughts and feelings, especially those that he or she assumes to provide the basis of activities. The individual can readily communicate these thoughts and feelings to others, as deemed necessary or desirable. The *preconscious* is that part of personality of which the individual is not aware at the moment. However, he or she can bring preconscious thoughts and feelings into awareness without great difficulty. The *unconscious* is that part of personality of which the individual is unaware, and which generally cannot be brought into awareness without assistance. Its contents either have never been conscious, or have been repressed—pushed back from awareness.

Functional Components of Personality. An individual's personality is comprised of three functional elements: the id, the ego, and the superego. The *id* consists of primitive asocial urges that demand immediate gratification. (According to the *Random House Unabridged Dictionary*, the word "id" is a special use of the Latin *id*, meaning "it"; in turn, a translation of the Greek *es*, meaning "primal urge.") The id is entirely unconscious. The *ego* mediates between the id's demands for immediate gratification and the requirements of reality. (The word "ego" is derived from the Latin *ego*, meaning "I.") The ego is partly conscious, partly preconscious, and partly unconsciousness. The *superego* exerts pressure on the ego to curb the desires of the id and to feel guilty about gratification. It is generated from the rules initially laid down by the parents, and later by society in general. Schools obviously play a special role, from kindergarten on up. The superego is partly conscious, partly preconscious, but largely unconscious. It is because the superego is largely unconscious that it is not quite synonomous with the colloquial view of conscience. In the everyday conception of conscience, we have a little voice within us telling us what to do and what not to do. The superego does not provide such instruction, because of its mainly unconscious character. For example, if one is too conservative or rigid about certain demands of the id, one probably cannot implicitly or explicitly verbalize why; in fact, it is likely that one is unaware of that condition.

Freud believed that anxiety stemmed from the pressure brought upon the ego by the id, the superego, and the external world of reality. He wrote:

> The proverb tells us that one cannot serve two masters. The poor ego has a still harder time of it; it has to serve three harsh masters, and has to do its best to reconcile the demands and claims of all three. These demands are always divergent and often seem quite incompatible; no wonder that the ego so frequently gives way under its task. The three tyrants are the external world, the superego, and the id. . . . The ego . . . feels itself hemmed in on three sides and threatened by three kinds of danger, towards which it reacts by developing anxiety when it is too hard pressed. (Freud, 1932, p. 103)

Although Freud eventually elaborated upon his explanation of the sources of anxiety (for example, by indicating that the ego's perception of what is going on in the real world changes, because the ego itself keeps changing in response to imbalances from the opposing forces of the "tyrants"), the quoted statement remained central to his theory.

Freud's Principles

There are two major principles that account for the development of personality. They are the pleasure principle and the reality principle. Each is implemented by its respective means of operation, the primary process and the secondary process. For practical purposes, the respective principles and processes may be considered equivalent.

Pleasure Principle. This law begins to take effect during infancy, when the id is virtually in entire command. It describes the early circumstances that lead to immediate physiological satisfaction. Pleasures, such as nourishment and cuddling, are brought to the infant. Aversive stimuli are removed or kept away. In its essentials, the pleasure principle is derived from a hedonistic, homeostatic model of stimulation, the steady or "normal" state of which is nonirritation, or even contentment. The principle operates by means of the *primary process, and continues doing so into adult life, a crucial fact which is often overlooked.* The realization that the primary process operates in adulthood vastly increases our understanding of human nature, in and out of the classroom. The primary process is quite arational; it draws no distinction between true and fantasized events, and is oblivious to the actual serial ordering of events in space or time. For the ordinary, law-abiding person, the primary process dominates mainly during dreaming (certainly not in class or on the street), when the pleasures sought in fantasy are expressed symbolically as wishes seeking fullfillment (latent content), and when events in time and space are rearranged, condensed, distorted, and even disguised (manifest content)—all to accommodate the underlying pleasure principle. However, the accommodation occurs within constraints imposed by the reality principle.

Reality Principle. This law describes how the ego evolves as a consequence of the pressures brought upon the individual by the id, by the superego, and especially by the real world. The human being must learn to interact with his or her natural and cultural worlds in such a manner as to be more than a passive recipient of pleasures, and to do so in a manner that is amenable to society's conventions. To reach this state, the infant must first distinguish between mental representations or memory images of objects in the real world, and his or her immediate sensory experience of them. Therein lies a crucial difference between the id and the ego: "The basic distinction between the id and the ego is that the former knows only the subjective reality of the mind whereas the latter distinguishes between things in the mind and things in the external world" (Hall & Lindzey, 1957, p. 34).

The reality principle governs the individual's growing awareness of the difference between mental imagery and sensory experience. It counters the pleasure principle to allow the person *actively* to seek returns in the real world, and even to plan ahead or to postpone gratification into the future. The reality principle operates upon the ego through the *secondary process.*

> By means of the secondary process, the ego formulates a plan for the satisfaction of the [particular] need and then tests this plan, usually by some kind of action, in order to see whether or not it will work. . . . In order to perform its role efficiently the ego has control over all of the cognitive and intellectual functions; the higher mental processes are placed at the service of the secondary process. (Hall & Lindzey, 1957, p. 34)

It is apparent that formal and informal education are dependent upon the secondary process. Note that although the ego *uses* cognition, the ego and cognitive processes are not equivalent. Freud's "I" is not to be confused with Descartes's "I" in "I think, therefore I am." To get the proper perspective, we need but recall Freud's comment concerning the ego's triad of masters. We need also recall that the pleasure principle influences the classroom situation, because it continues being present during adolescence and adulthood; indeed, during the entire life span. It goes without saying that the blurring of fantasy and reality is abetted by drugs and peer pressure that bring illusory contentment, and diminish the capacity to distinguish right from wrong.

Psychosexual Stages of Development
and Freud's Scolding of Educators

Although the theory of psychosexual stages of development is important to Freudian doctrine in its own right, it also serves to illustrate the relation between the pleasure and reality principles. What Freud tried to do in formulating his hypotheses was to indicate where tensions between the two principles and their respective processes might arise as a consequence of changing conditions, and where removal of these tensions might take place.

If a person undergoes sequential changes in the source of sexual stimulation in a normal way (with the connotations of sexual being *extremely* broad), "the person becomes transformed from a pleasure-seeking, narcissistic infant into a reality-oriented, socialized adult" (Hall & Lindzey, 1957, p. 55). According to Freud, the newborn infant can be stimulated and will have a pleasurable sensation more or less amorphously in any area of his or her anatomy. This first stage is called the diffuse stage of psychosexual development. Touching the skin, brushing the hair, touching the toe or finger or stomach, just plain cuddling are pleasurable to the infant. Quickly, however, the major site of pleasure becomes the mouth, the lips, the buccal cavity. In this stage, the child is busy suckling and presumably derives most of his or her pleasure from oral contact. There is a transition at the end of 8 months (these time periods are not very specific) to the anal zone as the principal site of erogenous stimulation. The anal area remains the chief pleasure zone up until the age of about 2 or 3 years. This span of time corresponds to the toilet-training period in an individual's life. The type of pleasure involved is first an expulsion of feces, and then, as toilet training becomes effective, retention. Some time between the second and fourth years, the anal phase gradually gives way to the phallic (or early genital) phase. Here the child finds his or her main source of pleasure in the stimulation of the genital area. Because of the child's obvious physiological unreadiness, and the social pressure conveyed by the repressive admonishments of parent, surrogate parent, and other authoritarian figures, this phase gives way eventually to the latent phase. Although immature sexuality may be present in this stage, it remains dormant. It is during this latent stage of psychosexual development that the well-known Oedipus complex comes to the fore, with the boy being in love with his mother and repressing thoughts about the relationship; similarly, the girl is in love with her father. This attachment is accompanied to greater or lesser extent by hatred or fear of the parent of the same sex. These dynamics are complicated enough in the routine family situation. They become even more so when there *is* no family nucleus.

Finally, the child becomes an adolescent, reaches puberty (genital stage), resolves the Oedipal conflict through identifying with the parent of the same sex, and ordinarily makes a heterosexual adjustment, such that his or her pleasure comes from and with a member of the opposite sex.

Freud held that if the human being goes through these stages of psychosexual development in a normal manner, no neurosis is possible. (Neo-Freudians disputed his emphasis upon the exclusively sexual origin of neurosis. We shall consider a sample of their views in the next chapter.) A neurosis develops when the individual becomes arrested or fixated at some particular stage of psychosexual development. This is not to imply, however, that the person may not reach heterosexuality and establish a lasting relationship with a member of the opposite sex. This can occur, and does occur, but with the neurotic individual unknowingly deriving an inordinate amount of satisfaction from some previous stage of psychosexual development. For example, Wolman (1989) defines the oral character as being:

> An individual with permanent and consistent patterns of functioning which reflect fixation on the oral stage as a result of abundant or more frequently, insufficient oral satisfaction. In the former case, the individual develops optimistic but overdependent attitudes; in the latter, depressive and aggressive tendencies may develop. In both cases, narcissistic supplies are demanded from external sources. The individuals are self-centered and characterized as selfish or "takers." They may be compulsive eaters, drinkers, smokers, or talkers. (p. 55)

The anal character is defined by the same authority as being:

> A person with permanent and consistent patterns of overt and covert behavior reflecting issues that were important during the period of learning to control bowel movements. There is a fixation at the anal level due to the child's being unable to reconcile the wish for anal pleasure with the demands of society. The conflict might be resolved by the child's finding pleasure in anal expulsion, which results in such traits as extreme generosity, conceit, suspicion, and ambition, or in anal retention, resulting in such traits as obstinacy, defiance, parsimony and/or avarice, orderliness, and compulsive behavior. (p. 54)

Elsewhere, the same source indicates that sadistic aggression may originate in the oral, or anal, or phallic stages, and be accordingly expressed.

According to Freud, such an individual would be "neurotic" in the sense that some of his or her energy is expended in what are essentially immature ways of coping with the environment and with other persons. To be sure, we are all "childish" to greater or lesser degree in this regard, sometimes viciously so.

Freud anticipated (accurately, as it turned out) considerable hostility

by teachers to his notions of psychosexual development and fixations. He somewhat sarcastically commented:

> Experience must have taught educators that the task of moulding the sexual will of the next generation can only be carried out by beginning to impose their influence very early, and intervening in the sexual life of children before puberty, instead of waiting till the storm bursts. Consequently almost all infantile sexual activities are forbidden or made disagreeable to the child; the ideal has been to make the child's life asexual, and in course of time it has come to this that it is really believed to be asexual . . . the sexual activity of children is overlooked—no small achievement, by the way—while science contents itself with otherwise explaining it away. . . . The children alone take no part in this convention; they assert their animal nature naively enough and demonstrate persistently that they have yet to learn their "purity." (Freud, 1957, p. 321)

Therapeutic Phenomena

Freud was indebted to his early colleague, Joseph Breuer, for the idea of using the technique of free association, as a means whereby the contents of the unconscious could be revealed. Breuer was treating patients suffering from hysteria; that is, a paralysis or a memory loss without neurological basis. Breuer routinely took case histories, with particular attention given to when the symptoms first were noted. He found that in many instances, the symptoms disappeared after the patient recounted the details of the circumstances surrounding the onset of the ailment. Breuer called this phenomenon *catharsis*, a "talking-out" or "purging." Unfortunately, catharsis afforded only temporary relief. Nonetheless, Freud was sufficiently impressed to elaborate upon his colleague's finding. He encouraged in his patients not only recollections associated with the origin of symptoms, but associations of *any* sort that came to mind. He found that his patients would, without deliberate instruction, recount childhood memories, including even those of their early dreams, to which, in turn, they would again volunteer associations. Freud's conviction grew stronger that the associations were not random, but existed for a reason. There was a cause behind each association. Further, he became certain that special importance should be attached to the contents of the patients' dreams, as well as to their associations to those contents. Between the two—the dreams and the associations to them—dream interpretation became possible. Thereby, he saw facets of their personalities that not only would otherwise have remained obscured, but which he considered to be essential to comprehending their problems, and thereby assisting reeducation.

The "royal road to the unconscious," as Freud called dream interpretation, can be found if the patient who has had the dream, and the analyst going over the dream plus its associations with him or her, can recognize the latent content, after examining the manifest or symbolic content. The reason why one can get at the unconscious through dream analysis is that, during sleep, the ego relaxes.

Figure 8.1 suggests why, at least in the Freudian system, dream interpretation is so important. It represents a crude way of tying together the functional components underlying psychoanalysis, and the behavior of the individual. To review, the id is largely unconscious and makes demands upon the person for immediate gratification. The ego filters these demands in terms of the dictates or requirements of a perceptually changing reality. The superego puts pressure on the ego in a direction opposite to that of the id, as suggested by the arbitrary use of plus and minus signs in the figure. In the dream itself, the dictates of reality are partially discounted by the ego. Thereby the demands of the id and superego are able to come out to a greater extent. By looking at the demands of the largely unconscious id and superego, as revealed in dreams, the therapist can obtain a view of the dynamics of the patient's unconscious. These dynamics include repression, resistance, and transference.

The following definitions transmit the full Freudian flavor:

> *Repression* is an unconscious exclusion from . . . consciousness of objectionable impulses, memories and ideas. The ego . . . acts as if the objectionable material were nonexistent (p. 292). *Resistance* is a continuation of repression which interferes, often actively, with the progress of the analysis. It is an

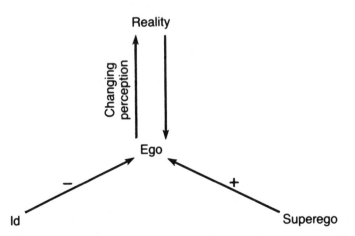

Figure 8.1. Diagram showing interaction among reality, ego, id, and superego. The ego's perception of reality changes during life. (From J. M. Notterman, *Forms of Psychological Inquiry* (1985). Copyright 1985 by Columbia University Press. Reprinted by permission of Columbia University Press.)

> expression of the wish to maintain the repression of the unconscious desires.
> The analysis of the resistances, along with the analysis of the transference,
> forms the basic task of psychoanalysis (p. 293). In *transference*, the patient
> generalizes his past emotional attachments to the analyst. . . . The analyst is
> a substitute for the parental figure. . . . In positive transference the patient
> loves the analyst and wishes to obtain love and emotional satisfaction from
> him. In negative transference the patient views the analyst as an unfair,
> unloving, rejecting parental figure and accuses him of all his parents' past
> injustices (p. 352). (after Wolman, 1989)

The analyst working together with the patient interprets the patient's dreams and associations, to make clear the source of his or her
often conflicting feelings toward the parental object, as well as other
unconscious conflicts. Reeducation then becomes possible.

PSYCHOTHERAPY AND TEACHING: THE TEACHER
AS PARTICIPANT OBSERVER

We have been hinting that psychoanalysis—more broadly, psychotherapy—involves an unlearning of maladaptive behavior and the acquisition of attitudes and actions more conducive to personal satisfaction. The teacher often is willy-nilly placed in the position of being a
therapeutic participant–observer. Students will ask for the teacher's advice, one way or another; for the teacher's caring. He or she needs to be
alert to their plea for help. He or she cannot compensate (nor should the
attempt be made) for an absent or hostile or overdemanding parental
figure. (Indeed, the teacher may be placed in the position of absorbing
anger directed toward an absent parent.) However, the teacher can lend
a sympathetic ear. He or she can lead students to trained advisors as
skillfully as possible, and continue taking up the slack if they are not
available. In short, the instructor can make the difference between hope
and despair—who does not remember the teacher who filled that need?

Relations of Freudian Psychoanalysis to Conventional Variables
and Thereby to Education

Psychoanalysis developed independently of but parallel with conventional psychology. Although the approaches were parallel, there are
points of contact between the two. Such instances appear, however, to
be almost coincidental. Certainly some psychologists are concerned with
psychoanalytic research, but by and large the working psychologist in
the laboratory or in the field has little interest in the testing of analytic

hypotheses. Despite this lack of interest there are several striking resemblances between the analytic and the research approaches to understanding behavior. Perhaps these resemblances stem from the fact that both approaches are grounded in the belief that only a deterministic view of behavior will eventually lend itself to an accurate description of behavior (we include cognition and affect as parts of behavior).

One way in which the analytical approach and the research approach seem to have a common direction is in the attachment of importance to past experience. In the Freudian instance, it takes the form of emphasis upon child-rearing and the anxieties of the infant. In the case of learning theorists, it takes the form of asserting more generally that the previous reinforcement history of the organism must be known if we are to understand the organism's current behavior. It is especially important to know the past reinforcement history of the subject because the same peripheral behavior may be established and shaped by quite different circumstances. Both the analyst and the experimentalist emphasize this point, one which has meaning for the educator. For example, looking the teacher in the eye may demonstrate either respect or disrespect on the part of the student, depending upon his or her particular cultural background, and what interpersonal actions were reinforced in that society.

A second way in which the analyst and the researcher appear to have a common outlook concerns the autoregulatory nature of drive reduction. Freud put it this way:

> In the theory of psychoanalysis we have no hesitation in assuming that the course taken by mental events is automatically regulated by the pleasure principle. We believe, that is to say, that the course of those events is invariably set in motion by an unpleasurable tension, and that it takes a direction such that its final outcome coincides with the lowering of that tension—that is, with an avoidance of unpleasure or a production of pleasure. (Hilgard, 1956, p. 291)

The essence of the foregoing quotation of Freud is quite similar in concept to the researcher's view that drive and reinforcement are defined as part of a loop system. Reinforcement does not have any empirical meaning independent of some prior operation which establishes a "tension" or drive. In short, corresponding to the pleasure principle are the experimental concepts of reinforcement through drive reduction, and of adaptation models in general.

The primary process affords still another instance in which there is a point of contact between analytic theory and conventional psychology. The primary process refers to the phase in which the human infant acquires those patterns of behavior which are based upon immediate bodily satisfaction. There is, however, no infant-originating interaction with the environment. The individual is incapable at that stage of life of doing anything to influence the environment through action originating particularly with him or her. He or she cannot walk, and cannot talk; pleasures are brought to the infant, so to speak. The circumstances just described, those in which no action is taken by the organism upon the environment, are reminiscent of the situation that exists during Pavlovian conditioning. One stimulus (the reinforcing or unconditioned stimulus) follows another stimulus (the initiating or conditioned stimulus) regardless of what the organism does. The learning that takes place is at the gut level, in that it involves autonomic modes of responding. The fact that much of our learning takes place in a classical sense, that is, autonomically, and takes place without *words* being tagged on as either stimuli or responses, has significant implications for problems of education and of therapy.

However, even as Freud found it necessary to distinguish between two psychoanalytic processes, the primary and the secondary, so the conventional psychologist distinguishes between two types of conditioning; classical and instrumental. The primary process, the functional arm of the pleasure principle, is probably related to classical conditioning; the secondary process (more broadly, the reality principle) is related to instrumental conditioning. Recall that according to the reality principle, reinforcement is obtained by the organism as a consequence of his action upon the environment. To the modern-day psychologist, this is a simple statement of instrumental behavior.

Perhaps more relevant to the concerns of the educator is the comment made earlier regarding the persistence of the primary process into adulthood. The fact of this persistence cannot be overemphasized. For example, the arational, amoral demands of the id include drives that can be satisfied temporarily by drugs, thereby leading to a "production of pleasure," and to addiction. The drug user does not want to cope with reality, to distinguish "between things in the mind and things in the external world." The consequences are evident throughout the educational scene.

Still another example of a relation between psychoanalytic theory and conventional psychology consists of the concepts of repression on the one hand and avoidance behavior on the other. One of the tenets of psychoanalysis is the belief that the potentials of behavior can exist in an unaware state, known as the unconscious. The closest operational analog to this in ordinary psychology lies in unaware, avoidance behavior. Some research has suggested that avoidance behavior can be induced in the laboratory with or *without* the subject's awareness (Hefferline, Keenan, & Harford, 1959). The triggering event can be either external or internal. In the latter case, it may be a symbolic representation—a thought, an ideation, or a feeling. These instances of avoidance extend into the educational and posteducational years—usually without the knowledge of the individuals concerned or their mentors; that is, in a state of repression or of laissez-faire. Even attributes ordinarily considered entirely rational are now being examined as evidence for "the cognitive unconscious" (Kihlstrom, 1987).

Finally, we noted in connection with Figure 8.1 that one's perception of reality is subject to change. Jones (1986) has drawn attention to the fact that: "To an important extent we create our own social reality by influencing the behavior we observe in others" (p. 41). We do so because of the expectancies we have of other persons, including students. One major consequence is that "though what we observe [in other persons] is often a reflection of what we have asked for [consciously or unconsciously], we tend to treat it as useful information that provides *independent* confirmation of our expectancies" (Jones, 1986, p. 46, emphasis added). The implications for education of this self-fulfilling prophecy phenomenon were first reported by Rosenthal and Jacobson in *Pygmalion in the Classroom* (1968). As the title implies, students tend to perform academically in a manner that confirms teacher expectations, even though the teacher is unaware of having created the necessary interactive reality (cf. Jones, 1986, pp. 41–42). Thus, Freud's notion of the flux between the ego and its perception of reality is currently relevant to research on self-fulfilling prophecies in the field of education.

Correspondence between psychoanalytic and research theories has not been deliberately sought by either the research psychologist or the psychoanalyst. Their agreement can, however, be exaggerated. The central difference between the analytic and conventional theories still remains; the former is a conceptual system in which the principal ideas—particularly those pertaining to unconscious dynamics—are not readily amenable to controlled laboratory or statistical research. The research psychologist, on the other hand, attends to the need for an operational or statistical definition of his or her variables, so that he or she may work with these variables in the laboratory or in the field. Additionally, analytic doctrine is certainly oriented much more toward therapeutic needs than is the research of most psychology. In recent years, however, there has been marked progress toward acceptance of what is therapeutically best for the patient, regardless of the source of the technique. We consider this reassessment by examining the neo-Freudians in the next chapter.

SUMMARY

The chapter begins by quoting Freud to the effect that he considered psychoanalysis to be a reeducational process. It would seem to follow, therefore, that at least some of his theorizing should be of value to teachers, if only to encourage a forming of a sharper image of the student, and broader view of education.

The fundamentals of Freudian psychoanalysis are reviewed in the usual terms of levels of consciousness, and functional components of personality. Emphasis is given to the fact that the primary process (the asocial, amoral pleasure principle) operates during adolescence and adulthood, and not only (as is commonly supposed) during infancy and childhood. Extensions appear as warranted to educational matters, especially when the secondary process (contending with reality) is developmentally influential. Along the way, we cite Freud to the effect that teachers contribute to the fiction that children are "pure"; that is, devoid of psychosexual stages, interests, and fixations. Finally to seek some balance, we discuss the relations between psychoanalytic theory and conventional psychological variables.

Throughout, the chapter tries to encourage understanding and to discourage "therapeutic" ventures.

9

Criticisms of Psychoanalysis by Jung, Adler, and Sullivan
Implications for Education

The main objective of this chapter is to consider representative challenges brought to Freudian psychoanalysis from within the movement itself. We do so in the context of their general implications for the school-age population. In order to obtain a proper perspective, a secondary objective is to describe briefly the behavioristic criticisms of psychoanalysis.

Depending upon the prospective teacher's background and tastes, one or another or even a combination of these theoretical avenues will lead to a firmer grasp of human psychology. We reiterate that we seek to encourage enlightenment, not amateur attempts at therapy.

PSYCHOANALYTIC PROTEST

The neo-Freudian psychoanalytic movement is not a unified reaction to classical psychoanalysis, as—for instance—Skinner's behaviorism was to functionalism. However, although it is diverse, the neo-Freudian protest does possess one general view: the rejection of Freud's emphasis upon the overriding importance of infantile sexuality. Thereby, psychoanalysis became more accessible to educators. The downgrading of the idea that neurosis had its roots in the arrestment of sexual development was expressed in theoretical departures from Freud's conception of the structure (levels of consciousness) and of the functional components (id, ego, and superego) of personality. We will consider representative dissent, beginning with two of Freud's original disciples, Jung and Adler. As we shall see, they criticized classical psychoanalysis for quite different reasons, and developed their own conceptual systems. In quickly reviewing the departures from Freudian conceptions, bear in mind that we do so more with the eye of the educator than with that of the clinician. Keep before you generalizations to the effects of peer pressure, intergroup tensions, drugs, self-contempt, and violence.

Carl Gustav Jung and Analytical Psychology: His Disenchantment with Science Education

Jung expanded on Freud's view of the nature and function of the unconscious. He theorized that human beings possess a collective, racially inherited unconscious, in addition to a personal one. Specifically, the collective unconscious is defined as follows:

> The part of the unconscious composed of acquired traits and cultural patterns transmitted by heredity that is the foundation of the whole personality structure. It is universal, all men being essentially the same, is almost totally divorced from anything personal or individual, and is continuously accumulating memory traces as a result of man's repeated experiences. Archetypes are its structural components. (Wolman, 1989, p. 357)

The major archetypes are so pronounced as to transcend races and to be present in the entire human species; others are specific to a given race.

More about archetypes in a moment, but first we have to confront the assumption that—because an unconscious representation of experience is present across races, or within a race—consideration *must* be given to biological inheritance. In point of fact, it is impossible from any anthropological viewpoint to counter successfully the direct, alternative explanation, namely, that the coexistent *customs* rather than the *genetics* of a race (however defined) are responsible for the presence of archetypes. In a word, we are dealing with a variation of the insoluble nature versus nurture dispute, in that customs and genetics of a race often go together. Since neither *extreme* position can be defended, we are better off setting aside the matter of whether the collective unconscious is indeed genetically determined. The issue is of no great moment in the larger context of Jung's intriguing ideas.

The Concept of the Archetype. There can be little doubt that all cultures have in common certain experiences that are repeated from generation to generation. Jung's idea of the "archetype" asserts that these repeated experiences gradually become incorporated and lead to specific psychological tendencies that we all possess. "For example, since human beings have always had mothers, every infant is born with the predisposition to perceive and to react to a mother" (Hall & Lindzey, 1957, p. 80). This particular predisposition can be utilized to reify natural phenomena into the spirit known as "mother nature." For Jung, the development of spirits and animism is but a special case of the more general manifestation of archetypes. The chief archetypes, those that are of crucial psychological importance to the entire human species, are the persona, the anima–animus, and the shadow. He identified these three after considerable research into mythology. We shall return to the salience of the myth after considering the major archetypes.

Persona. The persona is the social mask worn by people. Its function is to hide the true person (the Jungian "self") from others. The persona is the role we play, one that is acted to create in others the opinion we wish them to have of us. Sometimes we change our persona to accommodate a particular group. We all find it necessary to hide ourselves to greater or lesser extent. We cannot, so to speak, bare our hearts as a way of life. We might be ashamed or victimized. The major risk presented by the persona, however, is that the ego (in Jungian psychology, "the conscious mind") may become so identified with the mask that we lose contact with our true selves. Figure 9.1 shows how the self is influenced by the collective unconscious, the personal unconscious, and the ego. The "self" is deliberately depicted as a circle, a universal symbol known as "mandala," and believed to represent the striving for unity or oneness achieved through self-actualization. The persona is represented by the arrow going from the self to the ego.

The figure also helps us to understand the tension between the demands of an individual's ego (the conscious mind), and the demands of the social group of which he is a member (or the collective aspects of the unconscious). As Floden, Buchman, and Schwille (1987) pointed out:

> Just as it seems that one's individual perspective gets at the nature of things, it also appears that one's special or ethnic group has the proper view of how things are and should be. These sociocentric and ethnocentric natural attitudes are even more powerful and pervasive. Sociocentrism can affect scientists just as it affects garment workers; ethnocentrism can affect whites as much as Hispanics. (p. 487)

Clearly, the passage quoted is a concise description of the pressures brought to bear upon school-age children. Parental or pedagogical attempts to inculcate socially approved values are often on a collision course with the need for peer approval, especially when the latter makes

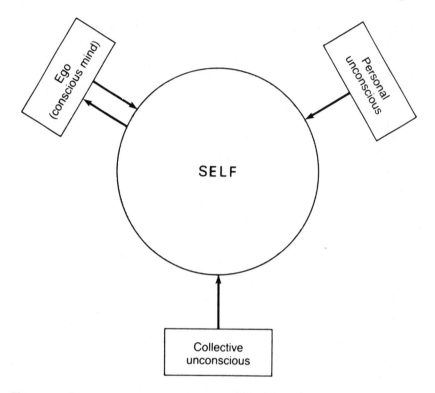

Figure 9.1. Representation of Jungian personality dynamics. (From J. M. Notterman, *Forms of Psychological Inquiry* (1985). Copyright 1985 by Columbia University Press. Reprinted by permission of Columbia University Press.)

a virtue of defiance. A proper balance must be struck, before one can break with the limits both of personal experience and of collective views or bias.

Anima–Animus. It is well known that the human being possesses both male and female biopsychological propensities. Of course, the one or the other ordinarily dominates. Jung held that there is enough of the male in the female, and vice versa, to form over generations an *idealized* conception (or archetype) in the human being of what to expect in the general behavior of a member of the opposite sex. For the man, the anima is the female archetype of his personality; for the woman, the animus is the male archetype. Misfortune befalls sexual relationships if the archetypical expectancies held by either of the parties are seriously distorted, as sometimes may be the case among adolescent school-age groups, both underprivileged and affluent. If the adolescent expects his girlfriend to be wanton, then there will be a self-fulfilling aspect to his or her behavior. If the adolescent expects her boyfriend to be aggressive, regardless of risks, then the same tendencies toward self-fulfillment will prevail.

The Shadow. This archetype includes the residual of instinctual urges, originating from the human being's evolutionary descent from primitive ancestors. The shadow is quite asocial and is given to aggression and gratification. When it infiltrates the ego (conscious mind), it can make one feel guilty about oneself, or, alternatively, cause one to perceive evil in others and act with "justifiable" aggression and selfishness.

Myth, Metaphor, and Imagery. Jung read Freud's *The Interpretation of Dreams* while he was experimenting with his word association test (see Chapter 4). He gradually became convinced that the patterns (or *complexes*) of thought–feeling disruption which he detected by means of his test indicated a pervasive narrowness in Freud's conception of wish fulfillment. Although Jung found that pleasure-related, psychosexual issues were indeed evidenced in the results of his test, and in his patients' dreams, they were quite subordinate to much deeper expressions of wishes, so deep as to transcend individual gratification, and to be indigenous to the human species as a whole. Accordingly, he formulated two hypotheses: first, that a culture's myths or legends should serve the same general purpose as that of an individual's dreams, namely, wish-fulfillment; second, myths of different cultures should possess in common the same symbolic representations of the major, fundamental wishes. Thus, it is important to recognize that issues of educational multiculturism should take into account both the uniqueness and the communality of folk myths. If the communality is sought, explained, and shown to transcend uniqueness while still respecting it, then schools can more readily and peacefully deal with diverse ethnic or racial groups.

Self-Realization, Individuation, and Midlife Crisis. Unlike Freud, Jung postponed psychological maturity until about the age of 40. He maintained that by that time, *self-realization* (or self-actualization, the fulfillment of one's potentials) should be well on its way. However, self-realization cannot take place unless the influence of the archetypes and complexes is first recognized, understood, and reconciled. He called this process *individuation.* The term is hardly equivalent to exclusive concern for one's conscious ambitions, because Jung held that one cannot *become* one's self independently of a genuine regard for others, and a genuine acceptance of unconscious dynamics. It is probable that prospective teachers would quarrel less with the notion of regard for others than with the acceptance of unconscious dynamics. Jung argued that both were necessary.

Jung drew attention to what is now called *midlife* crisis. (It occurs earlier among teachers, as Chapter 1 suggests!) He found that

> in the second half of life . . . many people are oppressed by a sense of futility and emptiness, and the need for something deeper and more significant. Jung's theory and practice were largely directed toward such people. . . . [H]e encouraged them to immerse themselves in mythology and to express themselves in some form of artistic activity. . . . [T]heir dreams also . . . were analyzed for indications of disturbing features, and for evidence of constructive stirrings of the unconscious pointing toward a degree of self-actualization. . . . Jung believed that the process of individuation was a slow one and that self-actualization was never completely achieved. (Woodworth & Sheehan, 1964, p. 311)

Overall, Jung was disenchanted with education. He felt that it was entirely too constraining, too "rational." He wrote:

> Scientific education is based in the main on statistical truths and abstract knowledge and therefore imparts an unrealistic, rational picture of the world, in which the individual, as a merely marginal phenomenon, plays no role. The individual, however, as an irrational datum, is the true and authentic carrier of reality, the *concrete* man as opposed to the unreal ideal or "normal" man to whom the scientific statements refer. What is more, most of the natural sciences try to represent the results of their investigations as though these had come into existence without man's intervention, in such a way that the collaboration of the psyche—an indispensable factor—remains invisible. (An exception to this is modern physics, which recognizes that the observed is not independent of the observer.) [In the parenthetical comment, Jung is referring to the Heisenberg or Uncertainty Principle.] So, in this respect as well, science conveys a picture of the world from which a real human psyche appears to be excluded—the very antithesis of the "humanities." (Jung, 1970, p. 252)

Alfred Adler and Individual Psychology: His Experimental School for Children

Like Jung, Adler was one of Freud's original disciples. But over a ten-year period, he contested Freud's ideas to the point where reconciliation became impossible. He resigned from the Psychoanalytic Society, which he had helped Freud to establish, and started another organization. Within a year, this group had the title it bears today: The Society for Individual Psychology.

What was the fundamental nature of Adler's dispute with Freud? The answer is given in the very concept of the "individual." For Freud, the individual was a single entity, whose ego was determined by the id, the superego, and reality. For Jung, the individual was more of a social being, but at the expense of the self being influenced by a collective, in addition to a personal, unconscious. For Adler, the individual was more autonomous as a person—he or she could more *consciously* (or cognitively) determine his or her own fate (hence, a critical distinction from Jung's idea of individuation and the influence of the personal unconscious); but concurrently (and as with Jung), the person was obliged to extend his or her interest in social matters.

Thus, the term *individual psychology* can be misleading if it is taken to connote an emphasis upon the separateness of one person from another. The interdependence among people must also be included in the concept and given equal weight. If we realize Adler's position at the onset, that "one has to learn to feel so much part of other people that egoism becomes altruism and altruism contains also egoism" (Adler, 1977, p. 238), then we can begin to understand why he is known jointly for being both the father of ego psychology and a founder of social psychology.

Adler's Model. Adler's model for the development of personality has the following steps, some of which interact with each other. They are elucidated here only as considered necessary. (1) *Experiences of infantile helplessness.* (2) *Subsequent feelings of inferiority.* (3) *Striving for superiority.* Here the child endeavors to overcome inferiority by striving toward goals that permit feelings of superiority. These goals include, but are by no means limited to, sexual attachments. (4) *Existence of guiding fictions.* This concept implies both goal-directedness as well as unrealistic aspirations. It is analogous to but goes beyond Freud's later notion of the ego-ideal, "that part of the superego which carries the child's admiration for idealized parental figures . . . [i.e., not necessarily the parent, but a hero] [and] results in the individual striving toward perfection by attempting to live up to the expectations or standards of the idealized parental figures" (Wolman, 1989, p. 107). The concept of guiding fiction is broader than that of ego-ideal, because it is not limited to the exclusive influence of idealized parental figures, but extends to the influence of powerful figures in the culture. (5) *Creative self.* The creative self begins emerging at about 5 years of age. It derives its name from how a person creates the world around him or her, including guiding fictions. One function of the creative self is similar to that indicated by the "perceptual" arrow in Figure 9.1. However, this function alone is quite insufficient to convey Adler's notion of the self taking responsibility for its own destiny. The creative self becomes capable of controlling its own future, to the extent that it is formulated both through a growing awareness of personal autonomy and through an increasing manifestation of social interest. (6) *Style of life*. The start of a person's life-style ("characteristic mode of living . . . of the way . . . he pursues his goals"; Wolman, 1989, p. 201) coincides with the emergence of the creative self. It is a critical stage, for if a child is either *pampered* or *neglected* too much, he will not develop social interests in a normal fashion. The tendency is for such people subsequently to withdraw from social interaction "into a world of pretense and illusion" (Wolman, 1989, p. 201). They do so at the eventual expense of their own self-esteem, and the esteem with which others hold them. In an ironic (but still timely) comment, Adler (1923/1964) wrote:

> Life is so diverse that it compensates for the errors of the educator. Nevertheless, a man whose childhood has been spent in a loveless atmosphere shows, even in old age, indications of this bringing-up. He will always suspect that people desire to be unkind to him and he will shut himself off from others, lose touch with them. Frequently such people appeal to their loveless childhood, as if that exercised some compelling force. Naturally enough a child does not necessarily develop mistrust because parents have been severe, to be as cold to others as they have been to him, or to distrust his own powers for that reason. It is, however, in such soil that neuroses and psychoses are prone to develop. It is always possible to disclose in such, a child's environment, *some disturbing individual* who, either through lack of understanding or evil intention, poisons the child's soul. (p. 321)

But Adler held out the possibility of change. Whereas Freudian psychoanalysis seemingly dooms the adult on the basis of how his fate was determined during infancy and early childhood, Adlerian individual psychology appears to offer more hope. The joint needs of expressing one's self and of meeting social responsibilities can only be satisfied if a person keeps looking forward toward his goals, and not backward toward circumstances over which he had little if any control.

The social point of view was actively applied by Adler to the school situation. Grunwald observed in her contributed chapter "Group Procedures in the Classroom":

> Beginning with the assumption that all problems are social problems, Adler . . . introduced group discussion with children, parents and teacher. Later, Spiel introduced the group discussion in the classroom in his Individual Psychology Experimental School in Vienna. . . . Group discussion . . . is different from a conversation in that it has direction; it examines problem areas; it deals with feelings; it analyzes cause and effect of behavior; and it faces unpleasant facts which normally are ignored or sidetracked. . . . Through group discussion children develop better interpersonal relationships. (Grunwald, 1973, p. 175)

Adler identified the three major goals which he held we all strive for: effective community living (interactions with groups), occupational fulfillment (as determined by the person himself or herself), and contented love and marriage (again, as determined by the people involved).

Harry Stack Sullivan and Interpersonal Theory: His Modes of Organizing Experience

Harry Stack Sullivan was probably the most influential of the founders of interpersonal theory. His position is that the concept of the "individual"—if taken as a singular, isolated entity—is a meaningless abstraction in theory and in therapy. An individual exists only on an interpersonal basis. Even one's perception of who he is as an individual (what Sullivan called the *self-system*) is based upon interpersonal relations. The self-system consists of habits that are acquired through interpersonal reinforcement contingencies, starting with the mother—infant relationship. These habits cultivate self-perceptions of a "good-me" (follows rules), "bad-me" (breaks rules), and "not-me" (dissociation because of infantile terror or disgust; after Woodworth & Sheehan, 1964, p. 329). The different "me's" originate as ways of coping with anxiety resulting from threats to one's interpersonal security.

Sullivan was also concerned with impressions or attributions of causality. He held that there are three successively developed modes of organizing experience. The first is *prototaxic*, and operates during early infancy. In this stage there is no notion of causality because there is no structuring of experience in space or time. All is a welter of sensory confusion, both inside and outside the organism. The second mode is *parataxic*, and emerges later in infancy. Here, events tend to become associated in time and space, but only with regard to impressions of their serial order. Hence, the individual cannot draw any logical inference of causality. All the person can "deduce" is that one event precedes another with a high degree of regularity, and even the sequence is often erroneously perceived. However, this limitation does not stop the person from behaving as if the first event were the "cause" of the second— the "reason" for its existence. Sullivan held that *parataxis is fairly characteristic of the typical adult's thinking; it is not abandoned with childhood.*

Sullivan's ideas are in accord with the treatment given to associations and to logical inference in Chapter 4. We noted then that seriality by itself can be deceiving, and that even the rules for drawing logical inferences of causality (e.g., J.S. Mill's methods of agreement and of difference) are fallible. Sullivan introduced the same canons through what he termed the *syntaxic*, or mature way of organizing experience. In this mode, the person attends to more than seriality in drawing conclusions concerning causality. One does this in an interpersonal, not a philosophical or laboratory context. Instead of depending upon logic, or laboratory replication and sampling procedures to establish that *A* is the cause of *B*, that the two are more than casually or wishfully connected, the individual depends upon what Sullivan called *consensual validation*. By falling back upon group opinion for reassurance, the individual avoids what might be misperceptions, personal biases, or ordinary superstitions. However, he or she does so at the risk of possibly accepting a false group opinion, while abandoning his or her own, correct one (Woodworth & Sheehan, 1964, pp. 330–331).

Sullivan argued that parataxic thinking is characteristic of dreams and of disordered behavior. More importantly, he held that we are all occasionally prone to drawing parataxic inferences, regardless of our best efforts to the contrary. The role of the friend, or teacher, or clergyman is to observe and to question both our assumptions and our conclusions. In a word, they participate in our customary interactions with the world, and with the people in it (Sullivan's participant observer). A professional therapist is trained to be an astute and exceptional participant observer. We cannot qualify without proper training.

Finally, the importance of interpersonal dynamics in general, and of the relation between perception and causality in particular, are currently receiving increased attention in the social psychologist's research. See, for example, Jones (1986) which comments on data obtained in the classroom and in the laboratory, and which was briefly discussed in the previous chapter.

Brief Critique of Psychoanalytic Approaches

Although the various psychoanalytic schools utilize different metaphors, they possess in common the following tendencies: (1) To reify psychological phenomena. Examples are Freud's id, Jung's shadow, Adler's creative self, and Sullivan's self-system. (2) To describe psychological processes in terms of oppositional polarities. Examples are: id versus superego, anima versus animus, inferiority versus superiority, good-me versus bad-me. (3) To assert claims for an exclusive understanding of human behavior, and to reject the approach of every other. (4) To accept the premise that all behavior is determined, while rejecting the researcher's demand that the entering variables be operationally or statistically isolatable. Perhaps this inconsistency accounts for the following episode involving Freud. The incident was related by Roy Grinker, past president of the American Psychoanalytic Association: "I can remember full well when studying with him in Vienna that he angrily threw to the

floor a letter he had received from Sol Rosenzweig, who was then studying at Harvard. Rosenzweig wanted to utilize psychoanalytic concepts
experimentally in order to test the theory of repression. Freud angrily
threw this letter away, saying, 'Psychoanalysis needs no experimental
proof'" (Grinker, 1958). Freud may have felt that even if psychoanalysis
is mainly a metaphorical model, it nonetheless is founded upon determinism. The one does not preclude the other. He therefore held that
psychoanalysis follows the laws of causation, regardless of whether the
model did or did not contain features that were amenable to the rules of
empirical research. Indeed, Jung went so far as to assert that by its very
nature, the unconscious was inaccessible to experimental analysis, "for
the unconscious cannot be represented in terms of thinking or reasoning." (See our discussion of rationality in Chapter 10.)

While the psychoanalysts were taking each other to task, the main
challenge to their collective viewpoint quite naturally came from the
behaviorists. While the aspiring teacher can learn much from the neo-
Freudians, he or she should not neglect the behaviorists. Their ideas of
behavior modification led not only to programmed instruction (Chapter
6), but also to behavior therapy.

BEHAVIORISTIC PROTEST

Behavior therapy has its roots in the animal laboratory, which—in
turn—owed its existence to Darwin's theory of evolution. The reasoning
underlying behavior therapy is roughly as follows: (1) much of human
behavior can be simulated in the laboratory by means of conditioning
procedures in which lower forms of animal life are used as subjects; (2)
conditioning procedures can be employed to produce in animals the
kind of behavior that we call "neurotic" when observed in human
beings.

In 1927, Pavlov did not hesitate to use the words "acute neurosis" in
describing the behavior of a dog which had been required to make too
keen a discrimination between circles and nearly circular ellipses. Selection of the former was followed by food; choice of the latter went unrein-
forced (method of contrasts). "After awhile, [the dog] became violent,
bit the apparatus, whined, and barked" (Keller & Schoenfeld, 1950, p.
138). The implication is that human beings, just as dogs, develop neuro-
ses when natural or social reinforcement contingencies require them to
make too many fine discriminations.

In 1941, W. Estes and Skinner used the word "anxiety" with similar
boldness in describing the decrease in rate of bar pressing for food

attendant upon a rat's being exposed to presentations of a 5-minute tone signaling the impending arrival of a momentary, unavoidable shock to the paws. During the anxiety period, the rats defecated and became aggressive. The generalization was made to human behavior as follows: "psychological clinics are filled with cases of morbid and obsessive anxieties which are clearly the outcome of disciplinary and social training overburdened with threats of punishments" (Keller & Schoenfeld, 1950, p. 310).

When we add to the foregoing the propositions that the occurrence of neurosis can often be ascribed to the acquisition of poor habits of adjustment, and that these detrimental habits can be diminished in strength and replaced with more adaptive habits, we have the essence of the behaviorist's approach to therapy (Wolpe, 1958). Essentially, behavior therapy—as do various forms of psychoanalysis—argues for the reeducation of the patient.

Of course, the behavioristic approach was grounded in the philosophical conviction that the therapist should not get involved in the patient's cognitive, purposive, or affective attributes, since the existence of these attributes could only be inferred from outward behavior. The therapist was to avoid taking explanatory recourse to all unobservable qualities, because they were epiphenomena. He was to rely only upon directly observable behavior. That mandate precluded the explanatory utility of any notion of the unconscious.

The Trend toward Eclecticism, or Nouns Need Not Be Demons

A central theoretical issue that has divided psychoanalysts and behavior theorists in the past is the charge that psychoanalysis (especially Freudian) is a modern version of demonology. The purported demon is the unconscious, with its active intrusion upon the behavior of the individual. Is the charge valid? Not when it comes down to general consideration of therapeutic practice. What the analyst perceives as active intrusion by the unconscious, the behaviorist perceives as counter control or behavioral nonresponsiveness by the patient. Neither kind of therapist falls back upon devils, whether of the unconscious, conscious, or behavioristic variety, but both *necessarily* engage in the ancient practice of reification. For purposes of communication with the patient, both find it convenient to use nouns rather than verbs to describe patterns of thought, feeling, and action (Moore, 1974). The one talks of the "unconscious"; the other, of "behavior occurring outside of awareness." Thus, the analyst presents his notion of repression in terms of the action of the unconscious; the behaviorist, in terms of unaware avoidance behaviors.

For the one, resistance is a sophisticated extension of repression; for the other, a sophisticated extension of undetected, unaware avoidance behaviors.

By now, behavior therapists, too, have encountered the occurrence of patient defiance, and have endeavored to develop strategies to cope with it.

> It is easy to offer various post hoc explanations according to learning principles, but it is obviously useless to do so in terms of their predictive value. When examining therapeutic failures, to insist that target behaviors did not shift in a desired direction because the maintaining conditions and requisite reinforcements were inadequately manipulated, may be true in many instances, but this reasoning becomes tautological when consistently invoked as an explanatory principle. (Wilson & Lazarus, 1983, p. 140)

CONCLUSION

And here we must halt, for to continue leads us into issues of psychopathology and psychotherapy that are well beyond the scope of this work. Fortunately, we can conclude on a note of optimism: psychoanalysts and learning theorists are becoming increasingly receptive to the use of each other's concepts and practices. (The interested reader is referred to Marmor & Woods, 1980, and Wolman, 1983.) The major reason is that each group (and those falling in between the two extremes) has had to acknowledge both its own failures as well as the other group's successes, and to search out the causes. Constructive reevaluation is in the air. These reassessments are fostering an eclecticism that draws upon the strengths of each approach. Even though the pace may not be constant, there is every indication that this forward movement will be maintained.

If we are to select a single professional idea which should remain with the reader, it is this: The teacher may come to serve as a point around which the student's need for expression of love and/or anger focuses—regardless of what the teacher may or may not do. Willy-nilly, the teacher can be thrust into the role of participant observer. He or she must not only understand what is taking place, but must also recognize the obligations and the limits of his or her responsibilities. An experienced colleague or principal can help make the discriminations.

Cognitive Psychology
An Emphasis on the Mind

The principal purpose of this chapter is to discuss cognitive psychology and to make contact as appropriate with the field of education. More specifically, the objectives are (1) to provide an overview of cognitive psychology's response to behaviorism, and (2) to consider the meaning and implication of using the computer as a metaphor for the mind.

Since cognitive psychology is the most recent form of psychological inquiry, and still actively developing, it deserves close scrutiny. Thus, we tend in this chapter more than in the others to be especially detailed in describing representative research, giving opposing points of view, and in suggesting possible resolutions.

THE NATURE OF COGNITIVE PSYCHOLOGY

Within the past two decades, American psychology has witnessed a renewal of interest in cognition. The accompanying surge of theory and research was mainly in reaction to behaviorism, which had set aside the common-sense notion that an entity called "mind" was the initiator of human behavior (Chapter 6). Cognitive psychology rejected behaviorism's claim that stimulus–response associationism was sufficient for an explanation of human learning, thought, and perception. The mind had to be included as a necessary explanatory component. The ensuing debate became sufficiently vehement as to lead to the emphasis being designated a "revolution." Perhaps the term "revolution" came into popular usage because of the influence of Kuhn's seminal work, *The Structure of Scientific Revolutions* (Kuhn, 1962/1970).

Strong argument is good for a discipline, but it can be viewed as leading to evolution rather than revolution. Evolution is the position we prefer maintaining, and we do so throughout the chapter. It is consonant with our belief that although there are tensions among different approaches within psychology and education, constructive engagement rather than confrontation extracts whatever is meritorious among the different views. Indeed, Flavell (1977) goes even further. He argues that cognitive psychology is an inherent part of general psychology. He wrote: "Depending only upon the state of existing theory and empirical evidence, a longer or shorter cognitive story could be told about virtually any phenomenon mentioned in an introductory textbook. We only have a single head, after all, and it is firmly attached to the rest of the body" (pp. 2–3).

A fundamental characteristic of the modern cognitive approach is its use of the computer as an analogy of how the mind works, how the mind detects, transforms, stores, and retrieves information. Is there not more to cognitive psychology than its relation to computer basics? Of course, but the computer remains the perch from which cognitive psychology pushes its viewpoint. It is in part because of the use of the computer as a metaphor for the mind, and thereby as a means of accounting for the brain's "information processing," that cognitive psychology is readily distinguishable from gestalt psychology, which also protested S-R associationism, and which also did not exclude the mind. Interestingly, whereas Kohler was mainly concerned with insight, a phenomenon that involves sudden solutions to problems (see Chapter 7), the use of computers to study cognition requires the step-by-step logic characteristic of programming. Programming, in turn, gives us a view of reasoning which is more lock-step than break-through. We shall have more to say about these matters when we briefly discuss metacognition.

The Computer as a Metaphor for the Mind

There are two general ways of using the computer as a model or analogy or metaphor for the mind. One concerns the problem of how the mind works or *operates* in computer fashion upon information of various types, such as stems from motor action, language, maturational factors, rule learning, and from the very transfer of information through networks. The other concerns the character of memory. Memory is important because without recollection of what we have experienced, learned, and done in the past, we lose continuity with the events that have created our unique identity. The computer serves as a means whereby we can simulate and study problems concerning the encoding, storage, retrieval, and basic nature of mental information. The two ways of employing the computer as a model for the mind overlap with each other; *they are not sharply dichotomized*. Although our development of the underlying rationale within each model is more-or-less historical, we have felt free to go back-and-forth in time, as technical exposition requires.

HOW THE MIND OPERATES UPON VARIOUS KINDS OF INFORMATION

Information Stemming from Motor Action

Psychologists and physiologists have long been interested in motor learning and performance, at least in part because their properties are free of cultural and linguistic bias. A portion of cognitive psychology originated in reaction to century-old, peripheralist (i.e., sensation-dominated) interpretations of motor behavior in which central processes involving cognition were downgraded (cf. Hrapsky, 1981). For example, we have already commented on William James's strictly associationist view of motor learning and performance. Specifically, James asserted that kinesthetic, closed-loop *sensory* feedback was essential to the learning and performance of purposive movement. "He suggested that the peripheral stimulation (kinesthesis) from one movement served to 'trigger' the next; thus, discrete phases of a movement sequence were thought to be linked by chained reflexes" (Hrapsky, 1981, p. 2). The mind was little involved. Further support for this peripheralist position was ostensibly supplied by Mott and Sherrington (1895). Their research described the virtual immobilization of a monkey's limb following deafferentation of nerves leading from muscle receptors to the central nervous system.

The peripheralist view of motor control was challenged by Woodworth (1899), whose position insofar as motor behavior is concerned is eminently of a central nature. He argued that although the presence of closed-loop feedback could satisfactorily account in his laboratory for the accuracy of *slow* movements (response duration greater than 500 milliseconds), which were made by his subjects using a pencil against a straightedge to match one or another standard distance, it could not explain the accuracy of similar, but *fast* movements (less than 500 milliseconds). There just was not enough time available to utilize continuous (i.e., concurrent) feedback. "He postulated that 'rapid movements have to be made as wholes . . . the first impulse of a movement contains, in some way, the entire movement' (Woodworth, 1899, pp. 54–55). This second type of control has formed the basis for what is called the 'centralist' [brain-directed] position, since peripheral stimulation from the ongoing movement is not seen to be necessary for accurate performance" (Hrapsky, 1981, p. 3).

By asserting that an entire skilled *purposive* movement could be emitted as a whole, without concurrent feedback, without the links provided by stimulus–response successions, Woodworth not only anticipated an extensive research literature on what is now called "motor programs" (well-practiced movements that unfold without thought), but also anticipated certain gestaltist (in the sense of brain-directed) aspects of present-day cognitive psychology. Note, however, that practice is essential before concurrent feedback can be disregarded. When things go wrong, the subject returns briefly to attend again to peripheral feedback.

John Dewey, one of the first educational psychologists (see Chapter 3), seems to have held neither a strict centralist nor peripheralist position with regard to motor action. Dewey held that the reciprocal flow of input–output information in a system turned sensation into action, and vice versa. Thereby he diminished expository reliance upon the stimulus–response reflex arc as a link in a chain of behavior. In other words, while arcs were necessary to account for motor learning and performance, they were not sufficient. It is also tempting to conjecture that Dewey (along with Woodworth) might also have been reaching toward the notion of motor programs. Thereby a distinction could be drawn between permanent *reflexes* (which fall into the open-loop category), and acquired *programs*—well-practiced purposive movements which come to be made without concurrent feedback, and which therefore superficially resemble reflexes. The vocational student was of special interest to Dewey. His philosophy of "learn by doing," the creed of the urban worker and farm laborer, is based upon the foregoing analysis. The same exposition provides a reason for the admonishment to "practice, practice, practice" so familiar to the school athlete.

We have already seen how Thorndike carried further the idea of stimulus–response associations through his connectionism and the Law of Effect. He laid the groundwork for Watsonian and Skinnerian reinforcement-associationist contributions to American behaviorism, the fundamentals of which are covered in Chapter 6.

We mention in passing, that the peripheralist position was further contested by E.C. Tolman, who is viewed as a harbinger of today's cognitive psychology. Tolman's latent learning experiments with rats in mazes showed that rats could learn in the *absence* of reinforcement procedures. Rats which are placed in a maze and allowed to explore freely without *food* reinforcement for correct turns, quickly catch-up in performance with rats which have been regularly reinforced with food on each trial. Tolman hypothesized that the rats were capable of organizing spatial relations because of their sensitivity to signs and gestalts. The rats formed and utilized "cognitive maps." A cognitive map is "a perceptual representation of a maze which an organism develops based on environmental cues and the organism's expectancies" (Wolman, 1989, p. 64).

By way of recapitulation of what we have said so far about motor action, and to show how cognitive psychology reinterprets and puts to use the material we have discussed in the preceding, we quote extensively from Flavell's passage concerning Infant Cognition as Sensory-Motor Intelligence (1977, p. 16):

> If the five month old infant can be said to "think" and "know" at all, he certainly does not appear to do so in the usual sense of these terms. In what sense, then? What *does* the infant have or do that permits us to talk meaningfully about the nature and development of "infant cognition"?
>
> What he or she demonstrates, in an increasingly clear and unambiguous manner as he grows older, is the capacity for organized, "intelligent-looking" sensory and motor *actions*. That is, he exhibits a wholly practical, perceiving-and-doing, action-bound kind of intellectual functioning; he does not exhibit the more contemplative, reflective, symbol-manipulating kind we usually think of in connection with cognition. The infant "knows" in the sense of recognizing or anticipating familiar, recurring objects and happenings, and "thinks" in the sense of behaving towards them with mouth, hand, eye, and other sensory-motor instruments in predictable, organized, and often adaptive ways. His is an entirely unconscious and self-unaware, nonsymbolic and nonsymbolizable (by the infant), knowledge-in-action or know-how type of cognition. It is the kind of noncontemplative intelligence that your dog relies on to make its way in the world. It is also the kind that you yourself exhibit when performing many actions which are characteristically nonsymbolic and unthinking by virtue of being so overlearned and automatized—e.g., brushing your teeth, starting the car, mowing the lawn, visually monitoring the grass in front of you for obstacles while doing so, etc. It is, to repeat, intelligence as inherent and manifest in organized patterns of sensory and motor action, and hence Piaget's description of infant cognition as presymbolic, prerepresentational, and prereflective "sensory-motor intelligence."

Information Stemming from Language

H. Ebbinghaus's connectionist approach to the study of verbal behavior conformed to the "links-in-a-chain" or "mental mechanics" model

(Chapter 4). On the other extreme, L.S. Vygotsky and A.R. Luria's social-cognitive approach carried the study of verbal learning further by describing the qualitative leap in mentation afforded by man's ability to use language (Chapter 5). The intellectual extension could not be explained on the basis of more and more "mechanical" connections. In typical two-way dialectical-materialist fashion, Luria asserted the following:

> From the very beginning of his development, the child lives and acts in close association with an adult. . . . The task is to trace how the forms of association connecting the child with surrounding adults are changed; how the elementary, direct forms of association which initially have an emotional-active character gradually become conditioned by speech; how this verbal behavior becomes separated from overall behavior into a special activity depending on a system of language; and how on the basis of these complex forms of verbal associations new forms of mental activity, which are social in their origin and speech-conditioned in their structure, begin. (Luria, 1969, p. 128)

We have already remarked on the importance of symbols and language to mentation, and how mentation—as influenced by societal values—develops its own singular reality (cf. Chapter 2 and Chapter 5). It is a reality that includes, but goes beyond, pure forms of either empiricism or idealism. It is also a reality that is not fixed. It is not immutable (so it can be argued), precisely for the very reason of its autonomy. Thus, mentation can be turned inwardly upon itself, and to varying degrees, expose inconsistencies in inferences and in values. The fact that one can presumably examine one's own thoughts has led Flavell (1977) to observe in regard to "metacognition":

> There is a sense in which interpropositional, "second degree" thinking is automatically social-cognitive in nature: propositions are stated thoughts rather than physical objects, and hence thinking about such thoughts represents a kind of social cognition. During the adolescent years, especially, people are likely to develop a heightened consciousness of their own and other people's psychological processes (metacognition). These processes gradually become "objects of contemplation"—things to think about rather than merely things to do. Accordingly, the individual becomes more introspective, much given to scrutinizing his own thoughts, feelings, and values. He also spends more time wondering about those of significant others. In particular, he may wonder what they think of his outer appearance and behavior (self-consciousness), and also what they might know or guess about his inner world. (p. 123)

But all is not so trouble-free. In commenting broadly on consciousness and the mind, Ernest G. Hilgard has pointed out that

> The new interest in consciousness has produced a wave of writing on the mind-body problem, with each of the classical proposals favored by individu-

al writers, even though every writer believes that new arguments or aspects
have been contributed to the discussion. . . . My reaction is that psychologists and physiologists have to be modest in the face of this problem that has
baffled the best philosophical minds for centuries. (Hilgard, 1980, p. 15)

To keep the topics of consciousness, thought, and mind within
psychology in the future, and to prevent another rejection, Stanford's
Hilgard has urged that we adopt a "spirit of critical realism," an attitude
of inquiry that employs two different types of scientific discourse. The
position is described as follows:

> There are conscious facts and events that can be shared through communica-
> tion with others like ourselves, and there are physical events that can be
> observed or recorded on instruments, and the records then observed and
> reflected upon. Neither of these sets of facts produces infallible data, for
> data, if accurate, may be incomplete, and inferences, regardless of how the
> data are obtained, may be faulty. It is the task of the scientist to use the most
> available techniques for verification of the data base and for validation of the
> inferences from these data. The position here recommended is sometimes
> called a double-language theory that need not commit itself regarding ulti-
> mates. (Hilgard, 1980, p. 15)

Information Depending upon Biological Maturation

Among developmental psychologists, Jean Piaget is especially recognized for his one-on-one research concerning changing patterns of
cognition in the human. He took his Ph.D. in biology, and became
interested in understanding how the developing (i.e., maturing) person
changes his ways of acquiring knowledge. He termed his program of
theorizing and research "genetic epistemology," the development of
knowledge. His work is sympathetic to and to some extent was built
upon that of Marie Montessori, an Italian educator who helped young
children in Rome's slums. She held that self-education is promoted by
familiarity with tools, toy-objects, and other physical entities, by means
of feedback from the senses. As with Piaget, critical stages of sensory
maturation were involved (Montessori, 1984).

Returning to Piaget, it is difficult to place him into a routine disciplinary slot. For example, he held views that are a mix of rationalist–
empiricist approaches. He may be considered a rationalist in that he
held that *reason* was essential to the acquisition of knowledge. He may
be considered an empiricist because he held that *experience* (and resulting action) was essential to the generation of knowledge. His basic position is that the way we reason and the kinds of experience we have
interact, and that the mode of this interaction depends upon the stage of
biological maturation.

The stages or periods of genetic epistemology (or intellectual development) are sensorimotor (birth to approximately 2 years), preoperational (about 2–7 years), concrete operational (about 7–11 years), and formal operational (about 11–15 years). The first stage is characterized by the acquisition of the idea of object permanence—the realization that covering a face (as in peekaboo) does not remove the face, or the person to whom it belongs. The person (face) is still there, even though unseen. During the preoperational stage, the child does not comprehend the principle of conservation, that although a given amount of matter can take various forms (a ball of clay can be rolled into a cylinder), the amount (volume, mass) remains the same. In the concrete operational stage, conservation is understood. But as implied by the title of this phase, logic or reasoning is directly related to physical material. For example, numerosity as such does not have meaning independently of physical entities. Addition or subtraction can be understood only in terms of the presence of physical objects entering a computational action. Symbols as such (mathematical or otherwise) are without logical meaning. In the subsequent formal operational stage, thought becomes independent of physical entities. Cognition can make use of symbols, language, and other nonmaterial abstract ways of describing the physical world, or even affective states, goals, logical inferences, and so on.

Of course all is not so neat. The intelligent adult occasionally requires the concrete in order to solve a problem, even to counting on his or her fingers! Also, knowledge of the principle of conservation does not prevent illusions of the gestalt and other varieties—illusions which may bend physical reality into apparent violations of actual size or shape.

Piaget was aware of these limitations, and tried to account for them through the processes of assimilation, accommodation, and equilibrium. These are processes which keep his theory from being rigid (some would say too much so, in the sense of preventing disconfirmation). When a child acquires a new kind of understanding, it needs to be absorbed by existing knowledge (*assimilation*). If it cannot be so amalgamated, the earlier knowledge must be modified (*accommodation*). *Equilibrium* is the resolution of the tension between assimilation and accommodation. Interestingly, Piaget believed that play facilitated the occurrence of assimilation, in that the more encounters with new experiences (even fantasies), the richer the newer understandings. "The outcome is greater flexibility, creativity, and optimism. It seems that in human evolution these characteristics have been associated with the need for versatility in novel environments and that play has potentiated the organism for such versatility. In biological terms play is a form of adaptive potentiation" (Sutton-Smith, 1977, p. 417). (Of course, one need not be a Piagetian to agree with the underlying propositions concerning the utility of play.)

In sum, Jean Piaget was a good inquirer. He did much to maintain interest in human cognition when other scientists found it more convenient to avoid the problems inherent in a description of reasoning. He defined an area of cognitive developmental psychology which continues to excite the potential educator.

What can the prospective teacher learn from Piaget? Mainly the importance of keeping a sharp eye on what you—as the teacher—are doing, on what the student does in response, and how the cognitive basis for the response may be objectively inferred. Always keep before you the fact that even if the student is in the formal operational stage (approximately junior and senior high school), it cannot be assumed that his or her language, thought, or action will be logical (recall Sullivan's description of parataxic cognition in Chapter 9). Cognizance of Piagetian genetic epistemology—especially the concepts of assimilation, accommodation, and equilibrium—helps the teacher comprehend the student's manner of intellection.

Information Stemming from Rule Learning and Connectionist Networks

Of importance to the educator is the realization that so fundamental a matter as the interrelation between language and thought has a long background. Despite the well-known Chomsky–Skinner dispute (see Chapter 6), it is hardly a new interest. For example, a review article in *Science* bears the interrogative title "Association or Rules in Learning Language?" (Kolata, 1987):

> The language debate is actually an old one in a new guise. It is, says Prince [note: one of the researchers whose work is cited] "a classical issue that keeps popping up in studies of philosophy and psychology whenever people try to understand what it is that underlies cognitive behavior and regulates thought." More than two centuries ago, for example, classical empiricists, led by philosophers George Berkeley and David Hume, argued for associations as a basis for knowledge whereas rationalists, led by philosopher René Descartes, argued for rules. (p. 133) (See also Chapter 4.)

One recent view is that children learn language not through grammatical rules, but by using associations based upon analogies. Thus, if the child learns that the past tense of "walk" is "walked," then—by analogy—he comes to say "pulled" to describe his past action ("pull") upon a wagon. The point is that the child learns to add "-ed" to verbs in order to indicate the past tense, and that he may do so because of comparison (i.e., analogy) with instances where such usage is correct.

According to this view, the child does not learn a formal rule for verbalizing the past tense; he just conforms to common usage.

The dispute between associationists and rationalists has broader implications, because adding "-ed" does not always work. To take but one example, before returning to the use of the past tense:

> The argument over rules versus analogies touches on fundamental issues in computer science and linguistics. It is part of a larger dispute within the artificial intelligence community over the meaning of a new form of ruleless systems and it bears on the question of the very nature of language. (Kolata, 1987, p. 133)

The wider dispute is based upon programs developed by artificial intelligence experts, in part aiming to provide a model of the brain. They discovered that they could program computers to "learn," and that this could be accomplished without the program containing operations for following rules in dealing with symbols.

The computers could be programmed by means of connectionist networks to simulate the way children characteristically deal with irregularities in the use of past tense (e.g., "brought" instead of "bringed"). Children first tend to use the irregular forms *correctly*; that is, before being exposed to formal rules. Then they overregularize—they go through the intermediate stage of saying "bringed" for "brought." *They infer and apply a rule that has too many exceptions.* Finally, they relearn the correct irregular usage. Connectionist networks can be programmed to go through the same stages as children do in dealing with past-tense irregularities; that is, learning, overregulation, and relearning.

Proponents of the rule learning theory have carefully examined the connectionist networks and have concluded that the program does indeed simulate the verbal behavior of children, but it does so because of a statistical artifact, and not genuinely. Of course, neither side has surrendered to the other. Kolata summarized, "In the meantime, the question of how children learn language is still open to debate." She went on to remark that the truth does not necessarily exist somewhere in the middle. "It evades the question" to assume so. As an independent scientific writer perhaps she implied that the truth is *outside* the range of inquiry limited by the dichotomous choice between associationistic versus rationalist or rule-learning interpretations of verbal behavior.

NOTE ON THE TENSION BETWEEN ASSOCIATIONISM AND REASON OR RATIONALITY

In the continuing endeavor to improve education in the United States, various philosophical and technological considerations have been introduced. For example, David Moshman's (1990) article on "Rationality as a Goal of Education" sought to bring together two points of view that are usually argued separately. The one urges concentration upon developmental or internally generated, maturational stages. The other advocates the importance of inculcating thinking skills. Of the latter, Moshman remarks: "Most (although not all) thinking skills advocates appear to see the mind in mechanical terms, as a very sophisticated computer. Thinking is construed as the processing of information. Good thinking, it is assumed, can be understood reductionistically by dissecting it into the specific processes or thinking skills that comprise it" (p. 340). He presses a compromise under the rubric of "rationality." He defines rationality as "the self-reflective, intentional, and appropriate coordination of genuine reasons in generating and justifying beliefs and behavior" (p. 342).

We have already quoted Hilgard's cautionary remarks concerning consciousness and the mind. We believe that he would extend these remarks to rationality (see his comments concerning the need for critical realism in this chapter). Without detracting at all from Moshman's laudable effort, we should remind ourselves that some 200 years ago, Immanuel Kant's *Critique of Pure Reason* also cautioned the educated of his time about the dangers involved in drawing conclusions from intentional self-reflection; that is, metacognition. As Daniel N. Robinson (1981) so strikingly puts it: "Such a view, in Kant's understanding, was akin to believing that we can increase the number of persons in a room by hanging mirrors on the wall!" (p. 285). Moshman himself is appreciative of the same dangers. In his conclusion to the cited article, he wrote: "Anyone who quickly and easily endorses rationality as an educational goal has not understood its implications. . . . Genuine rationality is unpredictable, open-ended, and potentially subversive. To educate for rationality is to facilitate processes of reflection and reconstruction from which nothing—not even rationality itself—is secure" (pp. 359–360; see also Kihlstrom, 1987).

MEMORY AND THE ANALYSIS OF MENTAL INFORMATION

Further discussion of language and thought requires that we concurrently include consideration of memory and information processing.

Episodic and Semantic Memory

Memory has two broad connotations. It refers to the ability to preserve both past *events* (episodes) that an individual has personally experienced, and *concepts* (meanings) that one has acquired (after Lachman, Lachman, & Butterfield, 1979). These two connotations of memory are convenient extremes along a continuum of which, in fact, neither endpoint is totally without some relevance to the other. However, the dichotomy helps theoretically to distinguish recollection of memories that are based mainly upon spatial and temporal associations, from semantic memories that are established through utilization of symbols, language, and the rules for combining them. The significance of the distinction may be illustrated as follows: One soon observes as a child that dogs run, and that fish swim. However, the idea of "mammal" is acquired mainly through education. It usually takes formal schooling before the developing person readdresses the earlier associations and categories, and learns that even though whales swim, they are not considered fish, and that in biological aspects they are conceptually closer to the dog.

A Change in Terminology and Concepts Describing Memory

A noteworthy aspect of current theory and research in memory is its use of ideas drawn from the structures and functions of computers. These notions ostensibly can describe the continuum between the associationistic and semantic extremes and can do so more parsimoniously than previous theoretical ventures. What was once exclusively termed in standard textbooks "acquisition, retention, and recall or recognition" is now also called "encoding, storage, and retrieval."

A reasonable scientific question is whether more than a difference in nomenclature is involved. With some qualification, the answer is more often than not given in the affirmative. A general consensus has been reached—not because the human being's mind is nothing more than a computer, but because the translation from older formulations into the programs and equations of information processing, artificial intelligence, and computer metaphors has rejuvenated inquiry and sharpened debate in a field that has long lain fallow. (A thorough, readable account of how and why the information-processing paradigm rests upon contributions from neobehaviorism, verbal learning, human engineering, cybernetics, and linguistics is available in Lachman, Lachman, & Butterfield, 1979, Chapters 2 and 3.) As is usually the case in science, however, the newer theorizing and research in memory has more than occasionally fallen victim to its own abstractions and models. The current situation is no exception. Chapter 14 in Lachman *et al.* gives versions of these criticisms, unusual in that they are expressed by Neisser and Newell, leading cognitive psychologists. Still another eminent cognitivist has commented on the lack of attempts to disconfirm the information-processing approach (Watkins, 1981):

One of the weaknesses of an information-processing approach to the study of memory is that it is so successful. It is hard to think of a finding it cannot accommodate. Select any experimental finding from the memory literature and any information processor worth his salt will have no trouble in putting together a combination of mental processes and structures to serve as a theory for it. Moreover, an information-processing theory is not only easy to create but, once created, any encounter it may have with data is unlikely to prove fatal. It might seem that we should leave such a happy state of affairs well alone, but I suspect there may be room for skepticism.

A key factor in the survival of information-processing theories is the odd way they have of proving to be more subtle than they at first appear. All too often it turns out that the critic of a theory has overlooked an implicit assumption or some other subtlety. Also, in the rare case where a theory is conceded to be at variance with the data, the problem is usually resolved with only minor tuning. Another reason for the immunity of an information-processing theory to effective criticism is that it is unlikely to attract much attention. This is because the information-processing era has brought with it the luxury of personal theories, so that researchers reserve most of their attention for their own, special theory. The upshot of this state of affairs is that theories typically survive as long as, but no longer than, the active interest of their creators. (p. 331)

The tendency to describe one's own particular view of the operations of information processing and artificial intelligence, and thereby to assert that "*This* is memory," or "*This* is intelligence," is difficult to resist. It is a modern example of James' "psychologist's fallacy." Nevertheless, a more even balance between genuine contributions and untested claims is being struck.

Information Processing

The flavor of both the information-processing paradigm, as well as the reason for tension between earlier and current views of memory, is best conveyed through a specific example. Models of information-processing systems are typically presented in the form of flow charts. Their parts and functions are still much subject to debate; for example, the distinction between short-term memory and long-term memory has long been in dispute, and remains unresolved (Craik & Lockhart, 1972). The following is a verbal description of one such rudimentary, pictorial model (after Klatzky, 1980, Figure 2.1, p. 11). The environment sends out a brief stimulus, which is detected by a sensory register (see Figure 10.1). There are registers for each modality. The sensory effect decays quite rapidly, within a second. But before doing so, the information contained in the stimulus is compared with concepts previously acquired and stored in long-term memory (LTM). The comparison is made possible via a feedback loop from LTM, and occurs as a matching process (see legend, Figure 10.1). This process is known as pattern recognition, in the

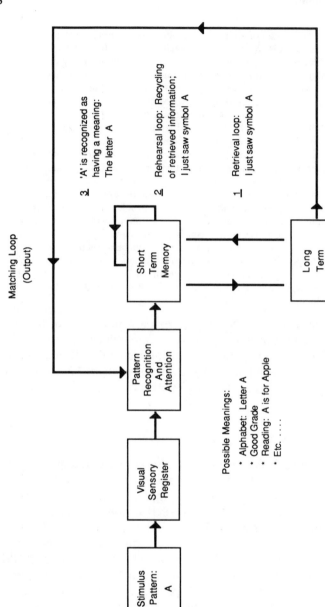

Figure 10.1. Human information-processing system. The matching loop from LTM temporally and functionally precedes the loops inter-connecting LTM and STM. (After R. L. Klatsky, *Human Memory: Structures and Processes* (1980). Copyright 1980 by W. H. Freeman. Reprinted by permission of W. H. Freeman.)

broad sense that coherent meaning (i.e., a pattern) is assigned to the input (encoding). The particular meaning attached to the stimulus depends upon perceptual, attentional, and learning variables. The encoded stimulus then enters immediate or short-term memory (STM), where—unless rehearsal takes place—the material is soon lost, within a half-minute for verbal information. With rehearsal, the information can be recycled indefinitely. The maximum number of items that can be retained in STM, with or without rehearsal, is about seven. Once the encoded stimulus has entered STM, it is concurrently passed on to LTM, where permanent storage is possible. As with pattern recognition, there is a feedback loop from LTM to STM. Thus, LTM affects not only the properties of pattern recognition, but also the character of STM. STM and LTM are the principle sources of retention and retrieval.

The following passage contains a tempered utilization of past and current language to describe information-processing's "stage analysis" of memory:

> The central problem [of memory] occurs when there is a failure of retrieval. Such a failure brings up a very fundamental ambiguity: One has no idea whether the information has been (1) acquired adequately and retained adequately but is for some reason inaccessible at the time of attempted retrieval; (2) acquired adequately but then lost (forgotten) during the time elapsing between acquisition and retrieval; or finally (3) acquired inadequately in the first place so that there is nothing there to retain or retrieve. (Crowder, 1976, p. 4)

Imaginal Information

So far, we have briefly considered memory and information processing, and have done so largely in the context of motor and verbal learning. Of course, cognitive psychology has broader interests. Of special importance is the inclusion of reasoning based upon spatial-sensory information, information that is actually present in real time, or subjectively present as images. In reviewing the U.S. Navy's Personnel and Training Program, Chipman, Davis, and Shafto (1986) remarked: "The study of the human processing of information that has a visual character—rather than a symbolic character—is a topic of high current interest in cognitive science, partially as a counterbalance to past heavy emphasis on verbal and other symbolic modes of thinking. . . . Visual thinking has high relevance to many Navy tasks, such as radar interpretation and maintenance tasks" (p. 7).

For example, the Cube Comparison Test is one of several paper-and-pencil evaluations available that help determine a subject's ability to rotate configurations mentally. Figure 10.2 gives the idea. The subject

Figure 10.2. Mental rotation as exemplified by a test item from the Cube Comparison Test. (After S. F. Chipman, C. Davis, and M. G. Shafto, *Personnel and Training Research Program: Cognitive Science at ONR* (1986), *Naval Research Reviews*, Four/1986, Vol. XXXVIII, Figure 5a. Copyright by Office of Naval Research. Reprinted by permission of ONR.)

decides whether the two cubes are the same or different. The flavor of the research is conveyed by the following:

> The research method involves collecting several kinds of data as people do the test items. A high technology computerized laboratory is used to record eye movements, showing precisely where the person is looking at each moment during the test. The total time required to answer each test item is recorded, providing the reaction times that are the most commonly used type of data in experimental psychology. Verbal reports of what the subjects are aware of doing as they perform the test items are collected also. A second step in the research is formulating computer simulation models . . . of cognitive processing that can account for the data. These experiments use subjects selected for high and low ability performance on a previously administered battery of spatial tests. Thus, separate models can be developed to simulate the performance of high and low ability subjects, and the models can be compared to identify the source of the differences in performance. (Chipman *et al.*, 1986, p. 7)

Of course, research based upon the rotation of images does not pretend to deal with image*less* thought or with insight. The previously mentioned investigations concerning the influence of planning, of programs, and of interconnecting networks are probably more relevant. The following note, however, serves primarily to extend fundamental considerations of representational information to theoretical aspects of cognitive psychology, particularly the latter's exchange with behaviorism.

NOTE ON THE EVOLUTION OF COGNITIVE PSYCHOLOGY

In an interview reported in Baars (1986), Howard Kendler commented on the dialectic between behaviorism and cognitive psychology. He remarked on *two* revolutions, the consequences of which led to evolution:

> One of the important principles enunciated in the cognitive revolution was the central role played by representational processes. . . . Because cognitive psychologists perceived themselves as participants in a great, even holy, revolution, they interpreted their emphasis on representation as a truly intellectual insurrection. I view it as an evolutionary event. . . . The behaviorists' revolution was directed against a mental psychology. They became suspicious of all introspective evidence. Cognitive psychologists reversed that trend. (p. 114)

Marvin Levine, who also was among those interviewed by Baars, had served as graduate assistant to B.F. Skinner, and then to George Miller, while he was at Harvard. He subsequently obtained his Ph.D. with Harry Harlow at the University of Wisconsin, working with monkeys on the problem of "hypothesis behavior." With such a broad exposure to different points of view, it is no surprise that Levine is tolerant. In his section entitled "An Evolutionist View of the Cognitive Shift," he expressed the cognitivist-behaviorist dialectic this way:

> An important durable influence of the behavioristic phase of American psychology [is] . . . insistence on rigor. Make your experiments as clean as possible, make your theorizing as clear and as hard-headed as possible. In doing research on cognitive concepts, have your data as tightly connected to those concepts as possible. . . . That insistence on precision, on experiment-theory tightness, I think, characterizes cognitive psychology today. In no small measure it reflects the behaviorist influence. We now talk about internal processes, but always try to find a clear behavioral manifestation. (Baar, 1986, p. 235)

To drive home Levine's point, we need but observe that metaphors are used when ideas need to be clarified. It is perhaps for this reason that the computer and cognitive psychology seem to be inseparable from each other. Major functions or properties of a computer are similar to those of a human being, and vice versa. Thus, the computer and the mind each serves as a metaphor for the other. They can be discussed in terms of "language," "memory," or "intelligence" (the human side), or of "buffer," "branches," or "hardware" (the computer side). Unless the theoretician/researcher/layman/educator can form his questions in some way that public evidence can be obtained, and that disconfirmation (as Watkins urges) is possible, a fair number of tautologies will invariably emerge.

SUMMARY

W. Printzmetal (personal communication, September 23, 1987) provided some remarks that serve to encapsulate much of the chapter as a
summary, especially from the perspective of the computer metaphor. He
wrote:

> The chapter starts off with the computer metaphor . . . [T]here are two
> domains in which the metaphor works. First, the mind might *operate* on
> information in four ways that are similar to a computer (emphasis added) . . .
> (a) One could think of the mind as operating like an information flow chart
> (e.g., Klatzky). (b) One could think of the mind operating like a computer
> program such as BASIC or Fortran in that it rapidly and ballistically executes
> a serial list of commands. Motor programs are an excellent example of this
> . . . (c) A computer could be made to operate with a series of rules ("if . . .
> then . . ."; technically these are production rules). (d) The mind might oper-
> ate like one of the connectionist machines. . . . Connectionism has some
> similarity to behavioral associationism, but it is "cognitive" in that informa-
> tion is processed with an elaborate internal network.
>
> The second domain concerns the issue of what is information, or what is
> the *internal* code for a mental computer (emphasis added). It could be verbal
> (Conrad), imaginal (Chipman *et al.*), or actually like a map (Tolman).

Overall, it is clear that behaviorism and cognitive psychology need
each other (Levin, 1987). The metaphors, research tools, and strategies
of the one challenge and sharpen those of the other. In so doing, they
enrich the broader enterprises and applications of psychology. Their
mutual enhancement is evident in educational practices, particularly in
the use of increasingly sophisticated forms of programmed instruction,
to which we referred in Chapter 6, and to which we shall briefly return
in Chapter 11.

III

Professional Aspects of Teaching

11

Instructional Methods and Nomenclature

In the best of all worlds and with a highly proficient teaching staff and limitless resources at the disposal of schools, the issue of instructional methods would revolve almost exclusively around the central questions of the goals and objectives of the lessons to be taught, and the appropriate teaching strategies on which to draw. But this is not the best of all worlds (at least we hope not), the proficiency of the teaching staff is variable and spotty, and the available resources for education are frequently well below even the modest expectations of teachers and administrators. In this "real world" situation other questions also require attention. On what teaching strategies can the teacher draw? What instructional materials are available? What logistical considerations influence strategies? To answer these questions in ways that make operational sense while maintaining the integrity of the educational goals requires a great deal of juggling and balancing. Even so, these "real world" situations occasionally take on a life of their own. In so doing, they significantly influence or even determine the goals for a class, a unit, or even a course. Stories of teachers who downplay or discard the development of writing skills as a goal because the class is too large, or who give up the idea of group work because students are less orderly than is desired, are but two typical examples.

For the purpose of this discussion, it is worthwhile to address separately each of several major issues influencing instructional strategies even as we recognize their inevitable interrelatedness.

GOALS AND OBJECTIVES

Under ideal conditions the strategies used would be based almost entirely on the goals teachers have in mind for the students in their classes. This correctly suggests the importance of identifying and articulating what it is that students need to experience, understand, appreciate, and develop. Planning and implementing a class, a unit, or a course without clarity as to the goals and objectives from the learner's point of view means that strategies and content material are selected without full appreciation of their potential for what the teacher wishes to see accomplished. As one critic of secondary education commented, "The problem is less that teachers don't know what they teach than that they don't know why they teach it." Or, as Shakespeare's Mark Antony might have commented on teaching strategies in such an approach, "You go to do you know not what." The importance of knowing what we "go to do" cannot be overestimated. Nonetheless, some educators argue that too much time is wasted in identifying and articulating educational goals. In so doing, they miss the important point of the relationship between what it is one wishes to see students accomplish, and the instructional strategies selected to facilitate the accomplishments. Selection of both appropriate content *and* appropriate strategies are vital for effective teaching and learning.

In some schools, teachers are given a course of study which includes the goals to be obtained, the content to be covered, and the approaches to be used. In these situations teacher input must take place in the curriculum development phase as opposed to the day-to-day or unit planning. Whether teachers individually develop goals, share in their development within a department, a grade level, or a school, or receive objectives from a central office administrator the necessity exists for fully understanding what it is they want to accomplish as they teach. It is equally necessary that teachers select the strategies that offer them and their students the best possibilities for obtaining the desired ends.

What do we mean by educational goals? Some examples drawn from different disciplines might be the following: understanding of basic mechanical processes, awareness of the structure of the federal government of the United States, appreciation of poetry, and application of mathematical formulas in problem solving. These appear as general statements of outcomes desired from educational experiences, and at this level have few critics. It is at the next level, when educators translate these general statements into instructional objectives, that criticism appears. Laymen, and some teachers as well, complain that this step consumes time, emphasizes minutiae, and plays with a kind of educational jargon that has little meaning. Although there may be truth to such a complaint in some instances, it is exactly at this point that the important relationship between goal and strategy is made manifest. Good instructional objectives begin with an important educational goal. To this goal, objectives add the change in student behavior which should occur, the terms to be used to observe and measure the change, the level of performance considered as an acceptable change, and the situation or condition for learning that should produce the change. The last of these additions includes the teacher's considered opinion as to the appropriate instructional strategies. Appropriate strategies or techniques go beyond mere delivery of content information. They, in fact, serve to make the content understandable in ways that would not be the case with inappropriate or less appropriate strategies. Two brief examples here might help to make the point: (1) One instructional objective for the goal of understanding basic mechanical processes might include the making and operating of physical models. However, this might not be the approach of choice if the instructional objective were the understanding of working-class sociology. (2) The writing of essays and compositions appears as a necessary situation or condition for learning, if the goal is improvement in the students' abilities to write the English language. This approach might still be used but it might be more optional, if the goal centered around the ability to apply formulas to solving algebraic problems.

Note on philosophical issues. There are, of course, larger philosophical issues that are involved, and hearken back to debates concerning the educational advantages of a rationalist (or idealist) versus an empirical (or materialist) position. Should we encourage school objectives based upon the life's experience of the student, or should we try to transcend experience and cultivate ideas? In commenting on Floden, Buchman, and Schwille (1987), Egan (1987) wrote:

> The challenge facing us in education is to find a way to give due weight to the great insights of Plato and Rousseau. Both are indispensible, but they seem to entail conflicting ideas of how to teach and how to set up a curriculum. Until we can work out a way of conceiving of education such that both their insights are honored without our becoming entrammeled in the long conflict they have generated, we can at least try to maintain a balance between them. It is to this balancing that the Floden, Buchmann, and Schwille article seems to me to contribute. They reassert the importance of the Platonic insight in an environment that seems to have gone a little too far in the direction of the Rousseauean. We *should* be able to embrace both, but embracing one, at least in the terms and categories in which educational thinking is presently framed, entails giving too little weight to the other. (p. 513)

ON WHAT TEACHING STRATEGIES CAN THE TEACHER DRAW?

At every stage of professional development, teachers are aware of a variety of different approaches. These will have been gathered from memories of their own education, reading and study, observation of colleagues, and creative imagination. It is probable that experience increases one's awareness of different approaches, although it may also be that some teachers, long in the profession, settle in with a small number of approaches and forget those once explored in a more creative youth. Beginning teachers whose active memories on the topic do not stretch back beyond college days, may have conscious recognition of fewer different teaching approaches than at the time they were midway through a high school career. Nevertheless, awareness of a variety of approaches and the length of one's experience in the profession appear to move along together.

At each stage of the professional career, teachers also have a set of operational or pragmatic teaching strategies. These form a repertory that also grows with experience in the profession, but lags well behind the number of theoretical strategies of which the teacher is concurrently aware. New working approaches and strategies are added to the repertoire for a variety of reasons. These include the desire to motivate students, efforts to deal with class management issues, and variety for its own sake, as well as the recognized need for a different approach to accomplish an educational goal. Initial efforts to use a new strategy are probably successful in proportion to their similarity to approaches already in use. For most teachers some practice is as important with a new approach as it is in sports, theatre, and many other activities. A teacher must try a technique several times before feeling comfortable that it is part of the inventory of procedural approaches. Too many young teachers have set aside efforts to mastery of a useful new strategy, because the initial attempt at its use was not as successful as was hoped.

Up to this point we have talked of teaching approaches and teaching strategies. The tendency is to use them interchangeably except that there is a need to make some distinction between a fairly discreet teaching method and the more involved combinations of methods that form the plan for addressing an instructional objective. The first we might call working approaches or pedagogical activities. The second we might call instructional strategies. Not surprisingly we often confuse pedagogical activities with teaching strategies, not realizing that different strategies might well use any number of pedagogical activities in either the same or different ways. It will help to identify some activities and some strate-

gies to clarify this. A list of pedagogical activities might include the
following:

Class discussion	Role playing
Small-group activities	Games
Individual work	Simulation
Chalkboard, handouts, etc.	Lectures
Use of overhead projector	Drills
Programmed instruction	Debates
Guest speakers	Panels
Exercises and problems	Experiments
Peer teaching	Field trips
Reading sessions	Writing sessions
Films, filmstrips, videos	Individual reports
Tapes, records, etc.	Group reports

The different strategies in which these might be used are more limited in
number. They can be categorized as either teacher-directed or student-
centered, depending on the role teachers carve out for themselves in the
overall process. Most of the pedagogical activities can be used in either
category of teaching strategies but, of course, some are more appropriate
for one than for the other. Neither category is on face value better than
the other. Only as they relate to desirable educational goals can one be
said to have greater claim on the time students spend in the classroom.
A well-structured learning experience would expose students to strategies of both types. The popular trend in education appears to be critical
of teacher-centered strategies and justifiably so because of their long
excessive use even to the exclusion of student-centered learning strategies. The remedy for this is balance—perhaps a shifting balance in
which the desire to see students take an increasing role in structuring
their own education is a determining factor in the instructional strategies
selected for use.

Teacher-Centered Strategies

Teacher-directed classroom strategies involve teachers as the continuous central actor in planning and implementing each lesson. The teacher is always center stage. Like other strategies they place a great deal of
importance on the teacher's command of the subject. More than other
strategies they consider the teacher as the medium through which information is transmitted to students. Teachers are organizers and presen-

ters. Students are listeners and learners. A successful class is one in which a body of information or a model of organization or process is transmitted from teacher to student. Teachers assume that each student should be exposed to the same learning experience, and that each can and should adjust to the common experience to which he or she is exposed. Teachers assume that they not only have clear ideas of the desirable educational goals, but also of the ways appropriate for all students to proceed toward them. The pedagogical menu for classes in which teacher-directed strategies are employed usually include individual work on reading assignments, writing assignments, drills, lectures, guest speakers (as surrogates for teachers), and teacher-dominated discussions. But the appearance of other activities does not mean that teacher direction has given way to student-centered activity. The use of audiovisual materials, small-group work, and even role playing and simulation can be so structured and dominated by teachers as to allow for their use within a teacher-directed strategy. The tendency in this direction probably relates to the background of those who enter teaching, people for whom teacher-directed strategies were typical of *their* classroom educational experiences. Observations would also suggest, not surprisingly, that the tendency away from such strategies is a result of the degree to which some teachers perceive their education as having been excessively structured and controlled.

Teacher-directed strategies can be very effective in helping students recognize the excitement and love teachers have for the subject and for the world of ideas. Students can also be provided excellent models of the approach they might take in stating a position, in establishing the basis for holding it, and in recognizing the implications of the position taken. The teacher of English whose love of poetry and whose skill as a reader is communicated to his or her listeners can serve students with a presentation effectively as an actor or an oral interpreter of literature. In like fashion, a well-delivered lecture can be a valuable part of the effort to motivate student interest. In such approaches, the passive role of the student does not automatically translate into a poor learning environment. Only when teacher direction is used excessively or becomes *the* modus operandi is there reason to question it as a teaching strategy. Unfortunately, research suggests that teacher-dominated classes are far more the rule than the exception.

Student-Centered Strategies

Student-centered strategies offer greater opportunities for students to become actively involved in the learning process, for teachers to secure continuous reactions from students, and for the teaching process to adjust to the needs of students. From the list of pedagogical activities shown earlier, it is clear that games, role playing, peer teaching, student projects and reports, and small-group activities are more likely to be part of a student-centered rather than of a teacher-directed strategy. But student-directed strategies can make good use of the entire menu of pedagogical activities. Students providing minilectures to each other as part of a jigsaw approach to a lesson, students identifying areas of their own weakness in mathematics or language study and being drilled by a peer as a review, students engaged in writing sessions as part of the maintenance of a journal or in expressing their thoughts and understandings of literature read, and a class discussion in which the teacher serves as facilitator rather than the center through which all comments must pass are but a few examples of teacher-directed type activities that can serve well within student-centered type strategies.

In the use of student-centered strategies the teacher has a more difficult job and is required to do significantly more by way of preparation and planning. The reason is that students' needs and interest are allowed to shape the direction the class takes in approaching the identified educational and instructional goals. The tidy "pregame" plan of the teacher-centered strategy gives way to a multifaceted plan which anticipates the various valuable directions the class can go. A student-centered strategy accepts that students may identify other valuable directions of which the teacher has not thought. In such situations, greater mastery of the content, greater familiarity with individual student's abilities, interests, and development, and a stronger repertoire of pedagogical activities are needed. These needs may serve to explain why teacher-directed stategies are far more common in classroom practice. Beginning teachers are generally less able to handle student-centered strategies even when they are inclined to do so. When initial efforts with more easily mastered teacher-directed strategies produce more "successful" classes, student responses reinforce the belief that the right choice has been made. The result is often the perpetuation of traditional approaches in those who intellectually are committed to child-centered learning. In instances where initial teacher-directed strategies are less successful, the same result sometimes occurs. The tendency is to assume that more structure and direction from the teacher is needed. If this scenario is correct, it suggests that widespread effective use of child-centered strategies requires careful work with and support of beginning teachers by their more experienced colleagues, since the latter are more likely to be comfortable in the role of teacher as facilitator rather than teacher as central authority.

Different Types of Student-Centered Strategies

There are several different student-centered strategies that are widely used. Marilyn Kourilsky and Lory Quaranta provide a helpful outline of some of these in their 1987 book *Effective Teaching: Principles and Practices*. Those listed include modular-learning centers, experience-based teaching, inquiry-based teaching, and advocacy learning. These are not so separate as their designations might suggest. Inquiry- and experience-based techniques overlap each other and both are likely to be a part of many modular-learning centers and advocacy-learning strategies. But each has unique features and their description can aid teachers in recognizing the possibilities of variations on the student-centered strategy theme.

In *modular-learning centers* the teacher is more the architect than the builder. Students working within this strategy are, to continue this metaphor, "do-it-yourself" builders using plans of a general nature which are developed by the teacher. Centers are largely free of continuous teacher direction. They are designed so as to provide a high level of motivation. They contain equipment and thereby provide for hands-on techniques which give students continuous knowledge of results. They place high priority on the development of independent work habits. This strategy can be used to motivate student interest, to impart knowledge, and to help students understand the intricacies of an object or a process. A center might exist as a separate section in the school or in a classroom, or it might be simply an approach which students take in seeking to reach some educational goal of the course or lesson. In all cases, centers will contain clear directions as to how the center can be used, materials which have been carefully checked by the teacher, displays of products that have resulted from students' work in the center, and information on what is to be done with student accomplishments in the center.

Experience-based teaching has its foundation in the "learning-by-doing" principle of John Dewey's progressive education. If architecture is the metaphor for understanding modular-learning centers, the metaphor for experience-based learning is the symphony orchestra. The teacher orchestrates an initial experience to involve the student, students practice (study, research, build, explore, etc.) on their own before coming together again under the skillful direction of the teacher to put together their experiences, and in so doing, to teach each other. The shared experiences include what we might call the content of the lesson, as well as the process in which each student was engaged.

We turn to the corporate boardroom as the metaphor for *inquiry-based teaching*. As chairman of the board, the teacher determines the structure of the group, outlines the procedures to be used, and identifies the bodies of content to be explored. Students, as board members, explore data in search of answers to questions posed by the teacher or questions which arise in their exploration. Recognition of important questions is as vital a part of the learning process as is answer-gathering. Classes, as board meetings, provide the opportunity for sharing information while students learn from each other and work together to establish generalizations, or to determine the most appropriate course of action. This teaching strategy is based on two assumptions: First, that group work in collecting data and generating hypotheses contributes to the development of critical thinking skills. Second, that students benefit in many ways from the individual and shared group responsibilities, not the least of which is in the area of motivation. Kourilsky and Quaranta (1987) identify two types of inquiry-based teaching; namely, discovery-oriented and policy-based. *Discovery-oriented inquiry* engages groups of students in search of answers to questions, the answers of which taken together lead students to discover meaningful information and concepts. *Policy-based inquiry* is primarily concerned with helping students decide what is appropriate action in a given situation or how to be reflective about important social issues. Thus, this strategy can be used equally well in pursuing cognitive, affective, or psychomotor educational goals.

The formal debate offers the metaphor for understanding student-centered *advocacy learning*. Students become advocates for various positions on important personal or societal issues. Analytical and communicative skills are used to locate and organize information and to defend their preassigned debating position. Those taking various positions meet in small groups to argue the issue, or the teacher determines that one or another of the debates be presented to the entire class. In this approach, the teacher serves as debate coach assigning the topics, advising and assisting students in preparation, and directing the discussion of class sessions when the structured arguments have been completed. This strategy combines explicit work on analytical skills with the gathering of information on topics about which students or society feel strongly and which have, or are likely to have, influence on individual and group value systems.

It is probable that the subject taught, the length and nature of experience in the profession, and one's personality and approach in the classroom influence the number and the choices that make up each teacher's repertoire of teaching strategies. Expansion of one's repertoire comes through the addition of new strategies and, more frequently, the addition of one or more of the almost endless variations that is possible with each. The developing teacher would do well to master several strategies appropriate for his or her situation, to refine them continuously, to realize the possibilities in their variations, and to add occasionally an existing strategy to the repertoire. Master teachers will, from time to time, develop significantly different approaches, and add them to the list of approaches to which their colleagues look for growth.

Certain strategies have far more utility to the teaching of one subject than to another, and the same strategies have different application in the teaching of science, history, language, mathematics, and so forth. For example, experience-based teaching is equally useful in physical science and in social studies. However, the predictability of results, the safety needs, the necessary materials (just to list a few) are very different in a physical science laboratory class from those in a social science class exploring issues related to self-government.

WHAT INSTRUCTIONAL MATERIALS ARE AVAILABLE?

This question has at least three levels on which it should be considered. It might be answered in terms of the materials from commercial publishers and producers for those who teach a certain grade level and subject, or the materials available in a school district, in a school, or to a teacher, or the materials seen by a teacher as having possible use in terms of the teaching strategies and activities he or she uses. In quantitative terms some districts and schools have far less than is needed, and the distribution of instructional materials within a school district and even within a school often leaves much to be desired. The same can be said about the type and quality of material. But on the other side there are also problems. Those making choices of instructional materials sometime have insufficient knowledge of what is available or, if they are not the teachers who will use the material, insufficient knowledge of the teachers' needs. Not infrequently, valuable and useful instructional materials are stored unused or receive little use because they do not fit with the strategies of teachers. The availability of audiovisual materials and simulation games in a school is of little value to students if teacher strategies focus exclusively on lecture and discussion approaches. This section approaches instructional materials in the most general way, with the recognition that identification of categories of materials say little about their usefulness to a given teacher in a given school.

Textbooks

A great deal has been written and said about textbooks during the last two decades. They have been criticized as too middle-class, too

Judeo-Christian and white male, and too oriented toward suburban standards. They have also been accused of "secular humanism" and criticized for efforts to devote space to various racial, religious, and ethnic groups, and to explore as obligatory a wide variety of points of view that are part of the culture. Groups have worked to have some purged from school libraries and discarded from classroom use. Publishers have avoided or downplayed sensitive issues, and schools have often been willing to discard one or another text rather than confront groups in the community on issues of relative merit of materials. These conflicts are likely to continue, but the textbook is likely to remain as the single piece of instructional material provided for each student for each course in elementary and secondary school. This is due in part to the very large expense of replacing textbooks with other instructional materials. It is also due to the fact that when well used by a teacher, the textbook is an excellent learning device, appropriate criticism notwithstanding. James Koerner commented on the major form of misuse in his 1963 book *The Miseducation of American Teachers*. In referring to teacher training he made the point (equally applicable to elementary and secondary schools) that "Far more reliance is placed upon them [the textbooks], and far less on the professor's teaching skill, than is consistent with the educationist's own pedagogical principles. Thus the quality of textbooks becomes a problem of some consequence in education" (p. 68). But when properly used the textbook can be a source of general information. It is a case study of the approach of an author or co-authors to the topic under consideration. It gives the broad outline of what is to be covered in the course. It indicates what will be examined and reexamined by teacher and students in a variety of activities of which the reading of the textbook is but one. Those of us who have taught secondary school courses without the use of a textbook have invariably found the need to develop or provide some other instrument to do what the text in the hands of a competent teacher does. Thus, the two most important factors applying to the textbook are the same as those applying to other instructional materials—the quality of the material and the skill of the teacher in whose course the material is put to use.

Considerations of the quality of textbooks (and other materials as well) suggest that careful attention be given to their evaluation before they are purchased. Ideally, the decisions on selection of textbooks will involve those who will teach the courses in which they are used. In such cases, as in those where a representative of the teachers or the administration will make the selections, there should be serious discussion among teachers to articulate the educational goals for the course, and the relationship between these goals and the textbook as an instructional device.

Other Print Materials

There is a wide range of other print materials available. In book form this includes reference sources, biographies, monographs, published poetry, and novels. Nonbook materials include magazines, newspapers, government documents, bibliographies, catalogs, and pamphlets. It is hard to think of any of these that do not have potential uses in a number of different teaching approaches and strategies. For instance, sections from a book of poetry might be read by students in preparation for a reading of the same poetry by the teacher. The same poetry might be identified for reading in a more student-centered strategy in which students seek to understand the interest, concern, and approach of poets by careful study of their lives, as a supplement to reading their poetry. The biography of an outstanding chemist might be read in preparation to reproduce his or her experiment in a chemistry laboratory class. Books, documents, and pamphlets containing primary and secondary source material could be assigned for reading in preparation for a teacher-directed discussion. Alternatively, the same materials might be used by individuals or by a group of students preparing a report to be presented to the class as part of an inquiry-based teaching strategy.

The librarian's responsibility for much of the nontextbook print material makes this person a good contact for the teacher. Ideally, librarians would be involved with teachers in the preparation of instructional objectives for a class. At the very least, teachers should consult with librarians before planning strategies which involve significant use of the library collection. Alert teachers have always recognized librarians as an excellent source of information in planning, and a frequent assistant in implementing an instructional plan. Failure to involve the librarian or a library staff member prior to attempting to implement a new teaching strategy, or one which necessitates the use of library materials or skills, is to court the possibility that success will be less likely than might otherwise be the case.

The sources of nontextbook materials are as varied as the materials themselves. Teachers have found the identification and gathering of such materials to be a worthwhile educational exercise. A widely used approach is the identification of several questions or problems for each of which students must identify one or several library sources that contains valuable information. Such an approach calls attention to both the information needed for the answer or solution, and the skill or technique of gathering and evaluating the usefulness of data.

Two decades ago, Charles Keller, former Professor of History at

Williams College and Director of the John Hay Fellows Program, included the use of textbooks and nontextbook materials in what he called a posthole strategy for approaching history. He described the necessity of maintaining a sense of the whole as being served by covering the sweep of history, a matter for which the textbook could be of great use. He also described the necessity of studying some matters in depth in ways which necessitated use of materials other than textbooks among which other print material figured large.

It may be that teachers depend much too heavily on print material in the educational process, but it is and will remain for some time as the major type of instructional material available to teachers and students for classroom use.

Educational Technology

In the last half century, there has been a significant increase in the development and the availability of educational technology. Until the late 1960s, most of what appeared falls under the heading of audiovisual materials. Since the mid-1960s, computers have become an established part of schools' educational technology inventory. Quality hardware has appeared in advance of quality software, and uniform accessibility to hard and software is still a problem. A second problem, that of teacher familiarity with the equipment, exists with computers. Some improvement in access to both has resulted from the expansion of traditional library services to include other media and in the development of courses and programs to serve the needs of teachers as well as students. Audiovisual materials and computers have a variety of uses in the classroom. When used as part of an instructional strategy, audiovisual materials can serve several different purposes. They can be valuable motivational devices helping to create an interest in further exploration into a topic. Their occasional use provides welcomed variety to the standard classroom approaches of teacher-talk, reading, and writing. They can be used to introduce ideas and concepts visually and orally or to provide audiovisual support for things covered in reading or discussion. These materials can also be used to set the tone or mood for a class, and— except in the hands of the most dramatic and effective users of language—they can do so more effectively than verbal description. Student reports or discussion in a history class become more effective when complemented by carefully selected visuals and by music. They both add to the understanding sought, and they significantly increase the readiness of other students to engage the material.

As for other audiovisual materials, something more needs to be said. Film, filmstrips, records, tapes, slides, television, and videocassettes have been most often associated with teacher-directed instructional strategies. These instruments, in fact, lend themselves to a wider range of uses. The teacher who assumes it impossible to alter the presentation of a film, filmstrip, or videocassette, is placing limits on his or her strategies that the materials do not require. A variety of possibilities exist for using film without the soundtrack and for stopping a film at any point that serves the instructional objectives. An excellent educational use developed for the Henry Fonda film, *Twelve Angry Men*, provides an example of this. The film describes how a jury shifts from an initial 11 to 1 vote for conviction of a person charged with a crime to a unanimous vote of "not guilty." In the process, not only is the evidence clarified, but viewers are allowed to see how factors and attitudes not related to the case influenced people's thoughts and actions. The film is shown to the point that the characters of those who form the jury have been introduced and the initial jury vote is taken. At that point the film is stopped. Viewers are told the outcome, asked who they think will be next to change positions, why they think so, and what evidence they see to suggest the change. Having viewers form small groups to discuss these questions proves very effective. After brief reports from each group and some discussion, the film is continued to the point of the next changes in position by a juror. The film is stopped again for discussion. The cycle is repeated until the end of the film. At this point, some general discussion focuses on decision-making, weighing of evidence, influences of attitudes and prejudice on rational thought, or any of a number of other issues raised in the film. It is this kind of use that can retain the control of an audiovisual class in the hands of the teacher and can make audiovisual materials useful in a variety of instructional strategies.

Teachers would be wise to have a clear idea of their purposes for using audiovisual materials in a class. Filmstrips, slides, and some videotape cassettes have a fairly clear single dimensional focus. Films, records, and most videotape cassettes are likely to involve several or many ideas and concepts. It is not necessary for a class to give equal attention to every interesting aspect of the audiovisual material used. It is wise to recognize, in passing, that a film deals with many ideas but the focus in a class should be only on those important for the immediate instructional objective.

Perhaps the visual material with the widest classroom use cannot be classified under the heading of educational technology. This is, of course, the classroom chalkboard. Although its almost universal use seems to remove it from the necessity of discussion, the simple point of its continuing value should be made in passing.

Computers represent the most recent major addition to the instruments of educational technology. They serve the same general functions as audiovisual materials, but with important additions due to their interactive possibilities. Development of computer software, especially educational software, continues to lag behind hardware development. Only recently is a reasonable quantity of quality software becoming available for the classroom.

Computers have two primary uses in the classroom—to serve as a vehicle for delivering instructional exercises, and to provide students a powerful tool that can be used to access and manipulate data and to solve problems. The first of these is commonly referred to as *computer-assisted instruction*. It includes the following: (1) drills and reviews of material previously covered, (2) programmed instruction which introduces new material and provides knowledge of results for students on their short-term mastery, and (3) simulation in which the interactive capabilities of the computer and the possibilities for widespread branching allow students to explore individually and in groups the consequences of choices and decisions they make.

The assumption that the computer is a powerful educational tool has led some educators to place it in the same category as language and mathematics. This has given rise to computer literacy programs, and to the identification of computer literacy as an important educational goal not unlike the mastery of reading, writing, and arithmetic. Proponents of this view call for introduction into the elementary school curriculum of computer instruction, including computer languages and programming. They see improved abilities in problem solving as a direct outgrowth of computer literacy.

The importance attached to computers for educational uses has reemphasized the differences between the have and the have-not schools. Districts and private schools with stronger economic support are better equipped with computers and offer more in computer instruction than do poorer school districts. Thus, the equipment needed for computer assisted instruction is least available in districts where large class size appears to make it more necessary. Similarly, computer literacy lags behind in poor districts, further widening the gap in educational progress between those who attend well-equipped schools and those less well-supported.

Simulation Games

Games have existed as a feature of every culture. In our own, the concept of "playing the game" has meaning beyond simple appearance

on the playing field. The educational value of children's games has long
been recognized, but it is only in the twentieth century that educators
have begun to design games to accomplish specific educational goals.
Simulation has no such ancient history, but neither is it new to the
educational scene. Its early uses in education were closely related to
technology when it was thought unwise to give a novice control of
complex machinery. Simulation provides a means of presenting the student with the opportunity to confront the many factors involved in a
situation under conditions where the result of error or failure is benign.
The most common exposure to simulation for those who grew up
in the 1940s and 1950s was in driver education and in pilot training.
Later generations are more likely to think of simulation in connection
with preparation for space flight, using computers. Current educational
simulation is by no means so limited. The social sciences, arts, and
humanities make ample use of this type of material as do science and
technology.

It is not surprising that educators brought games and simulation
together as an instructional approach. Games had the possibility of capitalizing on enjoyment and competition in motivating students to become engaged in the learning of factual information and in mastering
concepts, skills, and processes. Simulation had the possibility of moving
academic study closer to the reality of experience by simulating aspects
of "real life" under conditions that could be educationally managed. The
result has been the production and sale of a number of simulation games
for all ages and all subject areas, and the actions by teachers and their
students to create others. Commercially produced simulation games for
classroom use reflect a wide range of purposes, playing time, and quality. Current examples are: *Dangerous Parallel*, concerned with decision-
making, requires several days. *Star Power*, concerned with the influence
of institutional structures on individual and group attitudes, requires 1¹/₂
to 3 hours. *Paying Your Way*, designed to acquaint players with problems
of handling their own finances, requires about 40 minutes to play. *Nutrition*, with two parts, *The Energy Chain* and *Facing Famine*, requires a brief
preparation period and about 40 minutes to play for each. These are but
a few of an ever-growing list of such instructional materials available for
classroom use.

In the use of all simulation games careful attention should be given
to preparation and follow-up. Preparation ranges from short simple instruction to more lengthy familiarity with the language of the specific
game and the commands and processes for a computer-based simulation. If students' understanding of the instructions is incomplete, or if
students have not mastered language or technical requirements for suc-

cessful play, the chance is great that a simulation game will be neither enjoyable nor a successful learning experience. Equally vital to the educational value of simulation is a carefully conceived and well-conducted follow-up or debriefing. Instructions for debriefing are given with all published games, but teachers will want to improve and refine these to serve more precisely the needs and interest of their students.

Community Resources

Community resources, as used here, is a catch-all term for a host of different instructional materials. The purpose is to suggest that teachers consider carefully the human and material resources of their area which can be used as aids in instruction. Art and architecture in the community; local government and local government officials; businesses, museums, colleges and universities, plants, parks, historic areas, the local dump, and transportation lines are but a few of the possibilities. If teachers in all subjects consider that a common objective is to assist students to understand themselves and the society in which they live, the local community is a reasonable point of departure or a reasonable benchmark from which to look elsewhere. There are benefits in developing strategies which take into account the instructional materials available in the local community and the broad educational values of including them.

Tests

One might ask why tests belong in this list of instructional materials. Several reasons can be given in answer. They are, or should be, one of the major instruments helping students learn how effective they are in their study habits, in their organization of ideas, and in their approach to learning. In addition, well-designed tests can force students to examine ideas and issues in ways they have not done previously. Such tests can help students come to realize the possibility for independent learning activity as they deal with questions posed without the immediate guidance and direction of a teacher. Essay tests must obviously be seen as part of the effort to teach students to express themselves well in writing. Short-answer tests can be seen as an aid for students and to develop their abilities to identify important ideas and facts in a body of material being examined. The teacher who thinks of tests only as a means of securing grades for students makes only partial use of valuable teaching material.

WHAT LOGISTICAL CONSIDERATIONS INFLUENCE TEACHING STRATEGIES?

In the one-room school house of several generations back, teachers confronted a number of logistical problems which in recent years have been reduced or eliminated. Increased population and increased density along with school buses have alleviated the distance/time problem that limited the size of schools. Comprehensive high schools have made it possible to offer a curriculum assumed to meet the need of students with a variety of postsecondary interests. Colleges and universities produce teachers with specialties in elementary or secondary teaching, and with a variety of subject-area specialties at the secondary level. Nevertheless, the one-room school teacher had control over a number of logistical problems that are beyond the control of today's teacher. He or she controlled the bell system, determined when each course would be taught and how much time would be spent on it on any given day, probably knew each child and his or her family situation, and could with ease make individually appropriate assignments to students who occupied the same room. While on balance one must favor the multiteacher larger school divided by grades, a degree of flexibility existed in the one-room school which no longer exists, and which in the minds of some is not fully offset by other gains. The chief logistical factors that influence the instructional strategies used by teachers are the following.

Length of the Class Period

Typically the class period in secondary schools ranges from 40 to 60 minutes, with classes meeting five times each week. Teachers must structure student learning activities so as to conform to this arrangement. Strategies which require longer continuous time periods can be arranged only with some difficulty, if they can be arranged at all. Provisions for a longer period are generally arranged in one of several ways—adjustments with the several teachers with whom students study in the preceding or the following class period; adjustments to continue into a study period, activities period, or lunch period (if the class is fortunate enough to precede or follow one of these); and arrangements for a special session before the usual class schedule begins in the morning or after it in the afternoon. Colleagues are likely to be accommodating to adjustment which affect their classes only if they happen occasionally. Teachers whose strategies frequently call for longer blocks of time risk conflict with peers, especially if these peers have been thoroughly socialized to the "all-knowable-knowledge-is-divided-into-forty-minute-segments" school of thought. Requiring students to arrive at school early or stay late also presents problems. School bus schedules or the transportation arrangements made by parents cannot always be changed. Some schools have sought to deal with this logistical concern by introducing modular scheduling which provides each subject area one day each week when it has a double length period. This approach has proved helpful in allowing teachers to plan once a week to implement strategies requiring longer class sessions. It does not serve the needs of the teacher who finds the period ending as he or she is 10 minutes away from the conclusion of one of those rare and wonderful classes that was planned for a typical period, but which cannot be rushed without risk of destroying that which has made it successful. Experienced teachers become fairly adept in anticipating the bell or in picking up the pieces the next day, but the pieces are never the same. There may be no good solution to this problem in the typical school. Its statement serves to point up the importance of length of periods and schedule considerations in choosing instructional strategies.

The "Steady-State Regularity" of the Daily Schedule

In the schedule in a majority of schools, each class is assigned a time when it meets each day throughout the school year. The assumption seems to be that the learning environment that can be created is the same at each of the scheduled times Monday through Friday, even though both students and teachers recognize the peculiar problems of the last period in the day, the first period on Monday morning, the period immediately after lunch, and so forth. For history teachers faced with 10 months of "exploration of the past" at 2:15 each afternoon, the choice of strategies requires some consideration to motivation that might not be as continuously necessary if the class met in midmorning. Some schools have addressed this problem by scheduling classes at a different time each day and, in so doing, giving each class some of the most desirable and some of the less desirable schedule times. Why such scheduling is not more widely used is difficult to determine.

A compromise approach in some schools has classes meet at the same time each day until midway through the school year. At that point, the morning classes are shifted to afternoon, and afternoon classes to morning. Another approach identifies a different period as the starting point for each day's schedule while maintaining the order in which classes follow each other. In this approach a full cycle is set by the number of class periods in the day. If there are eight periods, the schedule is different on Day 1 through Day 8. The schedule on Day 9 is the same as on Day 1 as the cycle begins again. Schedules which have weekly or some other multiday rather than daily cycles are more difficult to make and cause confusion for a brief period when introduced. But these are minor considerations compared to the well-documented problems of the steady-state schedule.

The Teacher as a Person

Some attention to a point made earlier is worthwhile in concluding these comments on instructional methods. This has to do with the personality and classroom approach of the teacher. The interrelationship between the two is of vital importance. There are some teaching approaches that are appropriate or inappropriate in various subjects or grade levels and for individual students. In similar fashion there are also some approaches that are appropriate or inappropriate for individual teachers. Successful teachers are those who identify and perfect the use of teaching strategies that are compatible with who they are. This suggests that there are many different effective approaches as there are different personalities. These might well be grouped in some general categories, as Gary Fenstermacher and Jonas Soltis do in their 1986 book, *Approaches to Teaching*. They identify three categories—the executive approach, the therapist approach, and the liberationist approach after the discussion of which they address the question "How shall I teach?" In providing their answer they suggest:

> If you begin with some clear conception of what education is, as a human endeavor of body, mind, and spirit, you have the opportunity to control many of the practical forces that impinge on you, rather than fall victim to these forces. If you have some sense of the place and purpose of schooling in the education of the young, a sense developed from reflection on theory and ideal, you can shape and direct these realities in ways that support your aspirations for your learners. This activity is not always a struggle of your ideals against the powerful negative forces of the world, for there is much in schools that is already founded on good theory and high ideals. Yet you are not likely to recognize what is there, in either good form or bad, if you cannot recognize where you yourself are. (p. 55)

CONCLUDING STATEMENT

The chapter comprises a collection of diverse topics pertaining to instructional methods and the names that they go by, some of which the reader may have given prior thought to, and some of which may have come as a surprise. The topics include: goals and objectives of teaching, teacher-centered and student-centered strategies, varieties of instructional materials available, and the logistics of specific teaching situations. The chapter concludes on the note that each teacher is a unique person, whose particular characteristics constitute a parameter influencing his or her choice of instructional style. To be a good teacher, one must know one's strengths and weaknesses, as they apply to education.

Do's and Don'ts of Effective Teaching

The work of scholars in various academic fields has much to contribute to the success of those who would be effective teachers. In like fashion, the day-to-day experiences of practitioners in school classrooms have much to contribute. This chapter is a compilation of some practical suggestions gathered from the experience of many years in the classroom, from observing other beginning and experienced teachers, and from reading and talking to people who have thought seriously about teaching and for whom the quality of teaching matters a lot. Theoretical supports for some of these suggestions abound in the literature. Where they do not, the practitioner would say that existing theory needs to be reexamined or that future scholarship will provide the supports. In short, in this chapter we do not hesitate in going from the practical to the theoretical, rather than vice versa. Finally, please do not interpret our suggestions as "preachiness." They are offered as views, not dogma.

PLANNING

Teaching is a very complex operation. As practiced in the typical classroom, it simultaneously involves cognitive, affective, and psychomotor processes of 20 to 30 individuals, with different subgroup interests, and with different individual needs. In addition, it is immediately influenced by numerous institutional and organizational factors within and outside the school. The teacher's goals may or may not be accepted by students, and may be viewed differently by each individual involved. The work of the teacher is fully as complex as that of the physician, or attorney, even though the latters' may be momentarily more dramatic. The stakes in any teaching/learning situation are high, in that they involve the development of youth and thus, the future of the society. Given this importance and complexity, it is incredible that the person charged with giving direction to the teaching process could even entertain the possibility that careful and thorough planning was unnecessary. Nevertheless, there seems to be a myth that planning is a mundane activity for technicians and that "real" teachers are born, not made— they are artists, who in some intuitive way, know what is appropriate and effective at all times. This line of argument has two problems. First, it ignores rational thought and inference as a means of gaining knowledge. Second, it ignores the careful planning done by great contributors to the arts, and to other fields associated with creativity. Although "teaching is an art," it must agree with the circumscriptions of method and science. Teachers should always plan and, where time permits, plans should be constantly reviewed and revised. There is no such thing as overplanning. For every good extemporaneous lesson taught by a teacher, there are a thousand failures. What some teachers seem to object to is not the planning itself, but to requirements that plans be written and that they be made available for others to review. They seem to say that planning is necessary, but only to the extent that teachers have in mind what they plan to do. The necessity of writing and of sharing plans with others is, for these teachers, at best an annoyance and at worst a bureaucratic barrier to quality education. There may be something of merit in this argument, but it is reasonable that departments and schools should want documentation on what teachers have in mind for students. However, if written plans are indeed required with the idea of making teachers toe the line, the requirement may be more harmful than helpful. What is most important here, is the need of the individual teacher for a workable plan for his or her class. Experienced professionals can probably fare better without a written plan than can beginners, and certain lessons can be more easily conceptualized and retained without written notes than others. Nonetheless, the necessity for careful planning exists at every level of a teacher's professional development. It is problematic that anything about the necessity of recording and presenting plans for review by others can be said with the same degree of certainty.

Think carefully about the relationship of the plans for individual lessons to plans for larger units, and of unit plans to the plan for the courses. The relationship of these to the goals of the school also need attention. A good plan not only provides a structure and strategy for teaching something important in an interesting way, it considers the connection of what is to be studied and learned to the structured educational plan we call the curriculum. The planning process requires that teachers be aware of and concerned about the whole educational experience in which students are involved.

Professional educators have devised many different formats for planning. They all contain the same components, whether intended for a lesson, a unit, or a course. A good plan will answer a few important questions. How does the plan fit with what has gone before? What does it wish to accomplish? What changes in student's behavior should result if the plan is effectively implemented? What materials and techniques are to be used? How is the success of the plan to be determined? How does it relate to what comes later?

All good teachers are good planners whether they are cognizant of it or not.

FLEXIBILITY

A long-time teacher described an experience early in his career which illustrates the need to be flexible in working with any plan. He had decided to buy a set of encyclopedias and asked a salesman to meet with him to discuss the purchase. At the start of the meeting he announced that he had decided to buy the set and wanted information on the terms and the consideration to be given if and when a later edition was published. For the next half hour he was treated to the full description and sales pitch intended to convince the not-so-likely prospect that purchasing the set was a worthwhile thing to do. At the end of the "lesson," he was sorely tempted to purchase the product of a different company. He was prevented from doing so only by the realization that he had made the necessary comparisons with other products and that the set being discussed was what he wanted. Similar examples exist of teachers' inflexibility in implementing lesson plans. The American History teacher who stuck to his plan to examine the Tariff of Abomination on the day following the assassination of Martin Luther King, Jr. makes the point.

Plan carefully but do not be a slave to the plan. Insistence that every aspect of the lesson be implemented exactly as planned is to miss important opportunities to approach the objectives in terms that are more meaningful to individuals or groups of students. Sound preparation anticipates in advance possible productive directions a class might go, but other productive directions will frequently appear at any time even after a class is under way. Reasonable skill and sensitivity make it possible to respond to situations which were not anticipated. The more secure the teacher is with the structure and aims of a plan, the better he or she can incorporate other ideas and approaches that arise at any time.

The flip side is also pertinent: Do not be needlessly distracted from the plan that has been developed. Any discussion of flexibility in the implementation of plans calls to mind a technique used by some members of every generation of students—that of moving a class away from the planned activity when the students are ill-prepared, when greater enjoyment is perceived as flowing from another activity, or simply when students want to test the teacher's leadership. But what appears as deviousness might also result from the difficulty some students have with a lesson they are unable to master intellectually, or the personal discomfort experienced by some because of the direction peers are taking. It is wise for teachers to recognize the causes for such action and to address them appropriately, but giving in to them because of student preference is not what is here suggested. Flexibility does not mean allowing students to set goals and directions that are out of line with the teacher's best judgment about what is to be accomplished in a class.

It goes without saying that the need for flexibility on the part of teachers should not be limited to the implementation of lesson plans. Be flexible in dealing with other teachers, staff members, and administrators. Willingness to accommodate other teachers, and to assist when unplanned situations arise in the school, contribute enormously to the quality of the learning environment. It is difficult to imagine a successful school without teachers and administrators accepting as the modus operandi, the regular adjustment or changes of carefully thought-out plans when other educational interests require it.

ORDER

The definition of "order" includes having a prevailing mode or arrangement of things, and the idea that there is a pleasing and congruent relationship among the parts. Schools, like other institutions, have a prevailing mode or arrangements of things—that is to say—a certain order. This arrangement organizes the grade level and subject area structure for a school and assigns various roles to students and teachers, administrators, and other staff. It also provides for harmonious relations within and among each of these entities. No part of the definition of "order" is synonymous with "quiet" or with "submission." The harmonious arrangement of a learning environment may require some level of quiet for various important activities, but quiet is not a virtue in and of itself. What is unacceptable is chaos. Important activities of education need some level of order to be effective, and, by definition, education requires an organized and structured approach to ideas and processes—in other words—an ordered approach to intellectual and academic growth. Similarly, it is necessary for students to follow the directions given by teachers, but education is opposed to the idea of uncritical submission.

Assist in providing order in classes and in the school by understanding and accepting the teacher's role in the institutional structure. Teachers contribute to order in the school when they plan carefully and demonstrate mastery of their subject area. Equally important, teachers contribute to order when they act like adults, effectively manage their classes, maintain integrity, and in other ways model what it means to be mature, thoughtful, and reasonable. The professional satisfaction of the teacher goes beyond the pleasure of working with students and the joy of dealing with ideas. It includes being a surrogate for responsible adulthood.

CLASS MANAGEMENT

If an industrial plant failed to manufacture the product planned, it seems plausible to think of the person in charge as being a poor plant manager. There are some dangers in drawing analogies between education and industrial production, but this one works. The classroom teacher who fails substantially to teach the lesson planned, cannot qualify as a good class manager. Think of class management as meaning both the conduct and direction of a class, and the process of achieving one's educational objectives. With this line of thinking it is not possible to be a good class manager and a poor teacher. Neither a quiet classroom nor good rapport with students are indications of able management, unless they also serve to promote the success of worthwhile educational objectives. The teacher whose class is silent as students do worthless busy work, and the "friend" of students who entertains math classes with discussions of recent films, are both poor class managers. It is impossible to separate order and educational objectives in any discussion of class management. From this it follows that the way the class is managed, the ground rules for appropriate behavior, the level of goal achievement maintained by the teacher, and the level of self-direction encouraged in students will be determined by the educational objectives the teacher has in mind.

As a practical matter, consider the school's position on what is or is not appropriate behavior. There is an obligation on the part of each teacher to support these values. Thoughtful administrators will provide opportunities for teachers to express their views and influence decisions as to what is appropriate. Where teacher and administrative positions differ slightly, or where the issues at stake are not significant educationally, a teacher should have little difficulty in supporting a procedure even though a different one would be preferred. But for teachers whose ideas of appropriate behavior are, after a sharing of views, at great variance with those of the school, or who have major educational differences with administration on central issues of class management, there should be some serious thought about the type of school environment in which they should work.

Select teaching strategies and organize learning activities that foster a sense of the class as a small community of which each student is a comfortable part. Students' willingness to adhere to patterns of behavior is increased if they have a sense of ownership of the standards they are to follow. What one really wants from class management is self-management by students. It is not realistic to imagine that young people will develop this without assistance but neither is it realistic to imagine that it can be imposed by depending entirely on the teacher's role as the authority. Assisting students in the development of self-control—the self-management of their time, energy, and ideas—is an important intellectual and personal objective. In the process of assisting students, do not hesitate to make sagacious use of the teacher's authority to set standards when this is necessary. And in setting standards, consider that a shift from teacher direction to more student self-direction is easier than the other way around. Explain clearly to students what is expected through verbal and nonverbal statements. Both are important in communicating this information. Consistency, integrity, self-control, and sensitivity also contribute enormously to teachers' success as class managers.

DISCIPLINE

Keep at a minimum the development of situations that require you to discipline students. Make classes purposeful. Make classes interesting. Be sensitive to the needs of class members as individuals and as a group. View the need to discipline a student as a weakness of class management, rather than an instrument through which class management is facilitated. At the same time, recognize that each student is different, and that as individuals and as a group they are influenced by many factors outside the teacher's control. These factors can cause behavior which requires disciplinary action even in the most effectively managed class imaginable.

Strive to communicate to students (and to keep separate in your own mind) the distinction you draw between the student as person and the unacceptable act for which discipline is necessary. When punishment is administered, find opportunities to demonstrate this separation to the person involved. Never withhold deserved commendations, attention, affection, or courtesy from students who have been punished. Follow the old adage "let the punishment fit the crime." Do not use punishment to humiliate students. Unless the seriousness of an offense dictates otherwise, limit public actions toward a student to indications of dissatisfaction and to steps to bring the unacceptable action to an end. Assignment of specific punishment is best done away from the full class. Never give tests as punishment, or otherwise require offenders to do tasks related to the academic work of the class. Equally important, do not *appear* to be doing so. These are counterproductive to efforts to motivate interest in the academic work, and to create excitement about ideas and intellectual pursuits. The requirement that a poorly written assignment be done over should be portrayed as an opportunity to redo the work (as it is), not as a penalty for not doing well. Requiring a rewriting of a paper because of disruptive class behavior is never an acceptable approach to disciplinary action.

RELATIONS WITH STUDENTS

Much of what has already been said has to do with relations between teachers and students. But there is much more. What does one do when a student indicates a desire to talk with a teacher in confidence, and then proceeds to relate information involving illegal actions, actions that endanger the welfare of that student or others, or actions in violation of school regulations? If the student steadfastly refuses to agree that other parties can be informed, is it appropriate to violate the confidence? How does one avoid being put in such a situation?

Experience suggests a "no" answer to the initial inquiry about a confidential talk. Offer instead that the talk be based on a relationship of trust rather than confidence. In this relationship, the student trusts the teacher's judgment as to the necessity of involving others and as to what in the conversation needs to be shared and what can be kept between them. Such an approach cannot be used selectively. If one waits until the subject of such a conversation is known before setting the condition, it is often too late. The teacher has fallen into the "confidentiality trap." But if the standard practice is that trust and not confidence is the basis for the relationship, and if earlier actions have established a sense of integrity and trust, the pitfall can be avoided and the same important service given to students. Assuming that the approach to the teacher is motivated by the desire of the student to talk with someone and that the choice of the teacher is already based on some level of trust, there is little to lose by this approach. If, as rarely happens, the student is seeking protection in a situation where he or she fears that the information will become known to the teacher in some other way, no constructive interest is served by agreeing to the condition of confidentiality.

Would one place such a limitation as described above on a conversation with a friend? The answer is "No! Of course not," and there is a major difference. It is not the role of the teacher to be friends with students—to be one of the group. Be friendly with students and be open to opportunities for contact other than those that take place in the classroom, but accept that the role of teacher requires maintaining a distance from students that is not the same for peers or friends. That students might desire a relationship as friend or peer is understandable. Considering their limited day-to-day contact with interesting people who get them excited about intellectual ideas and who demonstrate concern for their overall welfare, it would be surprising if such feelings of affiliation did not develop. The most effective teacher is likely to be one who recognizes the predisposition for such relationships, but who also recognizes the need to maintain the distance that allows one to act professionally at all times.

Expect truthfulness from students and always be truthful in dealings with them. If students ask questions on an academic matter to which you do not know the answers, say so. It is acceptable, even desirable, to have students search out the answers to questions they raise, but this should never be done as part of a pretense that the answer is known if it is not. If you do not wish to respond to a question on some nonacademic matter, make clear that the area is one for privacy. Being truthful with students does not suggest the necessity of furnishing personal information about other students, discussing intimate details of one's private life, or discussing aspects of another student who is in academic difficulty or is physically ill. On matters involving these areas, it is best not to respond to questions or engage in discussions even when the information is innocuous. To do so is to provide unintended information on those situations concerning which the teacher may be unwilling to respond.

Expect students to be truthful, and to otherwise be paragons of virtue while recognizing that they will not always be so. Instances when they fail to measure up to expectations should be treated as opportunities to get back on track, not as occasions for berating a falling from grace.

When the occasion demands it, do not hesitate to say difficult things to students if they are appropriate in terms of the student's needs and the teacher's educational objectives. A student who has done miserable work on an assignment is not helped by being told that the work is not so bad. When criticism of some action or some failure to act is in order, students are, generally speaking, not well served by efforts to make them feel good or to gloss over the reality of the situation.

Consider carefully the advantages of being part of the community of which students are members. All other things being equal (they never are) there are increased possibilities for effective teaching, if students perceive that they and their teachers are part of a group having common interests and living in the same area. In small-town settings, this is so much a part of the way of life that it often passes without consideration. But in larger cities or in rural areas, school attendance districts and other factors often make it impossible for teachers and students to live in the same physical area, and thus these factors work against the sense of community which draws together teachers, parents, and students. This problem is especially acute when the majority of students and the majority of teachers in a school see themselves as being in different racial, ethnic, or economic groups. However, in all such cases, there are things teachers can do to increase the sense of shared interests. Get to know parents and to attend social and cultural activities participated in by students outside as well as inside school. Be familiar with the sports and recreational interests demanding the attention of students. Find ways to make it impossible for students to view the teacher, or for the teacher to view the student, as a stranger. If the first contact with parents comes only after a student has gotten in some difficulty, an important chance for establishing a sense of shared interest has already been missed.

RELATIONS WITH COLLEAGUES

One of the peculiarities of teaching is that, for the most part, beginners and experienced professionals are expected to perform almost identical duties. If there is a more difficult assignment to be taken by either an experienced or a beginning teacher, it is often the beginner who gets the nod. This applies not only to such logistical matters as an undesirable schedule and the assignment or different rooms for each period of the school day, but also to working with students who have the greatest difficulty in performing academic work. This is hardly the type of situation that develops collegiality.

Fortunately, there are exceptions to this. Private schools have for many years offered internships in which beginners have a reduced teaching load. Recently, public and private schools have begun to identify experienced teachers as mentors to work with newcomers to the profession. Such a program was instituted on a statewide basis in Connecticut in the early 1980s, and other programs exist in individual districts and schools in many parts of the country. But of the cadre of new teachers entering the classroom each year, only few are involved in mentor programs or any structured activity of guidance and support. What then, in the absence of structured programs, are some suggestions for beginners and experienced teachers in their contacts with each other?

Beginners: Do not assume that a recently earned college or university degree means that one is immediately and automatically more knowledgeable than people who have been out of school for 5 or 10 years or more. Be open to what can be learned from experienced colleagues about teaching and about your subject as well. At some point in the future, beginners come to recognize how much learning takes place as a result of having responsibility for organizing activities to assist others to learn. Do not let beginning status interfere with contributions that can be made to discussions and to the solution of problems. However, be alert to the widely held feeling that new teachers should become familiar with the territory before undertaking to provide advice and direction to colleagues. Seek advice from more experienced teachers as needed, and try out ideas on them in order to get a different perspective.

Experienced teachers: Do all you can to ease the transition of new colleagues from college student to effective classroom teacher. There is no virtue in a painful transition even though many able teachers had such a first-year experience. Make beginners feel a part of the school community. Listen to what they have to say. They often bring interesting new ideas along with the latest scholarship. The quality of the collegial relationship is in the hands of experienced teachers.

No teacher should ever put down colleagues in front of students, or allow students to put down colleagues in their presence. When a criticism is made of another teacher, it is a good idea to suggest that students talk out the matter with the teacher involved or with the appropriate school administrator. Should teachers pass on to colleagues comments overheard from students? Occasionally, there will be situations when the issues are sufficiently important to warrant the report. However, this is a very difficult undertaking, and must be handled with the greatest of sensitivity.

RELATIONS WITH ADMINISTRATORS

Putting down administrators is probably the subject of more faculty room talk than any other topic. New teachers often report astonishment at the level of the dissatisfaction with administrators expressed by experienced teachers. Administrators are often people about whom beginners tend to have positive feelings as a result of having been hired by them. Some teacher-educators report that they suggest that student teachers not frequent the faculty room until they have had a chance to assess the quality of their administrators through professional contacts. To avoid the faculty room is to lessen the opportunities for being socialized into an anti-administration school culture articulated by some teachers. It may or may not be that principals and other administrators are deserving of these negative attitudes, but the ways they are expressed clearly have no educational value. In making individual decisions on this question, there are several things teachers can do:

• First, assume that because of the requirements of their positions, administrators must take a broader view of school activities than individual teachers are required to take. Try to view the school from the administrator's perspective before reaching any conclusion.

• Second, assume that teachers collectively have considerable influence on administrators, and that wise use of that influence can produce changes in administrators and can help or hinder them in carrying out their jobs.

• Third, be prepared to support and carry-out administrative policies with which you disagree, as well as those with which you agree, especially those on which one's disagreement has been openly stated. Not only are administrators more likely to consider the viewpoints of such teachers, but the school cannot function as an educational unit if teachers are willing to implement only those matters with which they agree in every particular.

• Consider including administrators in some of the friendly social activities involving teachers. Communicate to administrators, as to students, that agreement or disagreement on educational policy and actions are not the bases for determining the relationship between individuals.

Other Do's and Don'ts

• Get to know people in all aspects of the school. Maintenance, secretarial, and food service people are also colleagues in a common enterprise and should be treated as such.

• Learn the sources of assistance and support that are available in the school for students and teachers. Recommend that students contact the appropriate office or individual when needs arise which you cannot or should not serve.

• Use a variety of teaching strategies. Plan some classes in which interaction among students is encouraged and in which students do most of the talking.

• Do not treat seniors the way freshmen are treated. The developmental nature of the educational process suggests that seniors should be expected and required to take greater responsibility for their own education than freshmen.

• Start class on time and end on time. Studies show that as much as a quarter or a third of the class period is typically lost, insofar as accomplishing the task identified for the day. A late start sets an undesirable tone for teachers who wish to make good use of the limited time. Furthermore, students are more likely to arrive on time if it is clear that important work begins at that point.

• Make assignments for the next day at the start or early in the class period whenever possible. To squeeze the assignment into the seconds between the ringing of the bell and the end of the period and the departure of students from the room is to risk that some will miss what they are being asked to do and that those wishing to raise questions concerning the assignment will have no time to do so.

• Share with students the objective for each lesson. In most cases there is nothing to be gained by leaving students to deduce from class activity what the teacher has as goals.

• Explain the reasons for an assignment made and how it relates to the objectives of the course.

• Correct all papers turned in by students. It is not reasonable to expect that students will take seriously homework assignments, if that work is not to receive serious attention from the teacher.

• Return all corrected papers as soon as possible. The relationship between work done on a written assignment and the classes which follow it argues strongly for promptness in this.

• Teaching necessary skills is an important part of every teacher's responsibility. If students do not have the skills needed to perform the educational task under consideration, teach the required skills. It does not aid education to diagnose correctly weaknesses in skills, but to do nothing about this because other teachers were to have helped the student develop mastery at an earlier time.

• Find some time to engage in some enjoyable activities other than school work. Even if teaching is the pivot of your life, involvement in other pursuits is necessary. To be most helpful to one's students, a teacher must be a well-rounded, comfortable, adjusted individual. The absence of any life outside of work does not contribute positively to a teacher's personal or professional life.

SUMMARY

In concluding this chapter, we remind the reader of the significance of establishing good habits in both teacher and student. William James (1958) observed in his *Talks to Teachers on Psychology*: "It is very important that teachers should realize the importance of habit, and psychology helps us greatly at this point" (p. 56) . . . "the teacher's primary concern should be to ingrain into the pupil that assortment of habits that shall be most useful to him throughout life. Education is for behavior, and habits are the stuff of which behavior consists" (p. 58). Specifically, he pointed to five maxims that assist in acquiring and maintaining good habits: (1) Begin with high motivation and broad exposure to the desired behavior. (2) Allow no exceptions until the new habit is well-established. (3) Take advantage of every opportunity to practice the desired behavior. (4) Do not substitute preaching for action. Thinking and feeling need to be *acted* upon, if they are to be of value. (5) Make it a matter of routine to do a little bit more than you have to in any given circumstance. Learn to exert yourself.

As the teacher gains experience, the do's and don'ts described in this chapter should concurrently become habits.

13

Fundamentals of Testing

Stephen L. Koffler

Psychologists and educators are called upon frequently to make decisions about individuals or groups of individuals. Those decisions require information, specifically a description about certain attributes of the individual(s). The more relevant and accurate the information—that is, the better the description—the more likely one is to arrive at sound decisions.

Measurement is the process of assigning numerical value to attributes according to defined rules and is essential to sound decision making. Attributes can be measured and described by many methods. This chapter focuses on one such method—testing, especially testing in the elementary and secondary schools.

WHAT ARE TESTS AND WHY USE THEM?

A test is *a systematic procedure for measuring a sample of behavior* (Brown, 1983). Although that definition is rather straightforward, the components and the complexities of the testing process are not.

A test is *a systematic procedure*. The test is developed, administered, and scored according to prescribed rules. Because a test is a systematic procedure, the test results are less susceptible to the influence of subjective or extraneous factors.

A test is used *for measuring*. The result of a test is the assignment of a numerical value to the test taker's performance.

A test measures *a sample of behavior*. It measures the test taker's responses to the items (i.e., the test questions). From those responses, one draws inferences about the individual's attributes that were measured. If the test adequately describes the attributes being measured, *valid* inferences can be drawn. The test contains only a sample of all the possible items that can measure the attribute. This raises the question about whether a test taker's score is *reliable*; that is, would the test taker obtain the same score by responding to a different sample of items drawn from the same domain?

Why Test?

The major function of testing in the elementary and secondary schools is to measure student achievement and, thus, to contribute to the evaluation of educational progress (Mehrens & Lehmann, 1984). Within this context, Dyer (1980) lists ten reasons for administering tests in the elementary and secondary schools. The first five reasons directly affect students and decisions about students; the last five indirectly do so:

1. *To help make placement decisions about students.* Test results are used to place students (e.g., in remedial programs) and to select students (e.g., as National Merit scholars). However, test results should never be the sole criterion for placement, selection, or, in general, any decision. Rather, decisions should be based upon multiple sources of information.

2. *To individualize instruction.* An item-by-item and skill-by-skill analysis of test results provides information about students' strengths and weaknesses in the skills measured. Using this information, teachers can (if so desired) group students with similar profiles and can better target instruction to build on the students' strengths and ameliorate weaknesses.

3. *To provide for continuity in the educational experience.* As a student progresses from kindergarten through grade twelve, a record of the student's strengths and weaknesses and level of achievement is used to effectively plan for future instruction. Annual test results contribute to this record.

4. *To help students make decisions about themselves.* Test results can be used by guidance counselors to help students and their parents understand the students' abilities, interests, attitudes, and future opportunities.

5. *To help motivate students' learning.* Sometimes tests provide an incentive to study. Although tests are commonly used for this purpose,

questions arise about long-term retention of material learned in this manner.

6. *To evaluate the results of experimental programs.* Tests are used to determine if new programs and methods contribute significantly more to student learning than do other programs or methods.

7. *To compare the effectiveness of schools.* Until the accountability movement of the 1970s, the effectiveness of schools was measured by examining the "input" of the educational process, for example, the number of books in the library or the pupil/teacher ratio. Beginning in the 1970s, primarily as a result of the continuing decline in the Scholastic Aptitude Test results and the concomitant rise in local property taxes to pay for increases in educational costs, the public began to demand that the "output" of the educational process—students' achievement as measured by certain tests—be used to judge the schools' effectiveness.

8. *To comply with the official requirements of state and federal agencies.* As a response to the accountability movement, many state legislatures and State Boards of Education mandated that students at certain grades be administered tests, typically in reading, writing, and mathematics. Consequences for failing the tests may include denial of a high school diploma for the student and withdrawal of certification for the school.

9. *To cooperate with national testing agencies in the administration of tests to be used by various institutions for the selection of students.* Schools typically cooperate with the College Board and American College Testing to provide a setting for students in which to take the Scholastic Aptitude Test (SAT) or the American College Testing Program tests (ACT).

10. *To cooperate with test publishers in trying out and norming new tests.* Test publishers periodically revise their testing programs to ensure that the programs reflect current developments in education. By testing students, the schools help the test publishers to detect technical weaknesses in the test and to establish norms. A test's norms indicate how the members of a particular reference group (norm group) scored on the test and provide a basis for comparing a test taker's score with other similar test takers. Examples of norm groups include national, regional (e.g., northeast, south), and local school (i.e., based only on the performance of a particular school or district) norms.

The same test, or type of test, cannot adequately serve all of the diverse functions cited above. Different types of tests are needed for different purposes. The next section discusses a test as *a systematic procedure*, focusing on the types of tests administered in the elementary and secondary schools and the principal item types used in those tests.

TYPES OF TESTS: APTITUDE AND ACHIEVEMENT

Tests that are administered to measure cognitive attributes can be categorized as either aptitude tests or achievement tests. Angoff (1987) provides a definition of each of those tests:

> Aptitude is by its nature prospective—indeed the word "aptitude" itself has implications for the success of future learning—and scores on an aptitude test are typically used for predicting future success in the general domain of that aptitude. Achievement is by its nature retrospective—also implied by the word—and achievement tests are typically used to evaluate the level of accomplishment in prior learning experiences. This is not to say that achievement tests cannot or have not been used to predict future success. Past achievement is always a good predictor of future achievement. (pp. 11–12)

Angoff also distinguishes between the two types of tests:

> Growth in *achievement* results from more-or-less formal exposure to a particular subject or area of content and is typically quite rapid. *Aptitude,* on the other hand, grows slowly as a consequence of ordinary living, both outside the formal learning environment as well as inside it.
>
> *Aptitude* tends to resist short-term efforts to hasten its growth. *Achievement* is much more susceptible to such efforts.
>
> *Aptitude* tests draw their items from a wide range of human experience. When aptitude tests do make use of material learned in formal course work, they typically draw on material learned several years earlier by most individuals, material that is presumably equally familiar to almost everyone. *Achievement* test items, on the other hand, are more circumscribed. They are necessarily drawn from the restricted subject-matter of a particular course of training—chemistry, European history, Latin, for example—usually a recent one. Correspondingly, aptitudes are generalizable to a wide range of endeavor, whereas the knowledge and skills represented in an achievement test normally apply to a narrower sphere of activity.
>
> Because *achievement* tests draw from a relatively narrow domain, known best by those who have been exposed to that domain, they cannot properly be used for evaluating the educational outcomes for individuals who have not been exposed to it. *Aptitude* tests, however, draw from much wider domains, not confined to the material learned in the classroom, and presumably within the actual, or accessible, experiences of all individuals. Therefore, unlike achievement tests, aptitude tests can be used to make general intellectual evaluations for everyone sharing a common culture regardless of their particular classroom experiences. On the other hand, because their coverage is not classroom-specific, aptitude tests cannot be used as achievement tests can, to evaluate the quality of particular educational programs. (pp. 11–12)

Most of the achievement tests (whether teacher-made or commercially developed) that are administered to elementary and secondary students are either norm-referenced or criterion-referenced, the focus of the next section.

Norm-Referenced and Criterion-Referenced Achievement Tests

Mehrens and Lehmann (1984) define two goals for achievement testing: (1) to discriminate among all individuals according to their degrees of achievement; (2) to discriminate between those who have and have not reached set standards (or to determine whether each person has achieved a specific set of objectives) (p. 21).

How these goals are met provides the basis for discussing the major types of achievement tests: tests that yield *norm-referenced* interpretations (and satisfy Mehrens & Lehmann's first goal) and tests that yield *criterion-referenced* interpretations (and satisfy their second goal). Mehrens and Ebel (1979) provide a clear distinction between these two types of tests:

> If we interpret a score on an individual by comparing that score with those of other individuals (called a norm group) this would be norm referencing. If we interpret a person's performance by comparing it with some specified behavioral criterion of proficiency, this would be criterion referencing. To polarize the distinction, we could say that the focus of a normative score is how many of Johnny's peers do not perform (score) as well as he does; the focus of a criterion-referenced score is on what it is that Johnny can do. (p. 49)

The terms *norm-referenced* and *criterion-referenced* refer to the type of score interpretations that achievement tests most readily yield. However, they are used frequently to refer to categories of tests. That is, a criterion-referenced test is one that provides a criterion-referenced interpretation of scores and a norm-referenced test provides a norm-referenced interpretation of the scores. It is possible to apply both types of interpretation to the scores from a single test. However, Ebel and Frisbie (1986) argue that doing so is inappropriate:

> It is seldom advantageous to interpret a set of scores in more than one way; good tests tend to be built to optimize the user's ability to make a single type of interpretation. Hence, there are important variations in the procedures adopted for constructing tests that will yield one type of score interpretation rather than another. (pp. 24–25)

Historically, most commercially developed achievement tests have been norm-referenced because the primary purpose of the testing was to compare students with their peers to distinguish among students having varying degrees of proficiency (e.g., for selection). Thus, items for norm-referenced tests are selected because they measure important outcomes and by their ability to differentiate among students of varying levels.

Commercially developed norm-referenced tests are the most widely used achievement test. However, they are not without controversy. In

1988, John J. Cannell, a physician in West Virginia, presented evidence indicating that most states and schools were scoring above average on nationally normed, commercially developed achievement tests—a phenomenon which, according to Cannell, was not plausible. Cannell's findings which were corroborated to an extent by researchers (see, for example, Linn, Graue, & Sanders, 1990) were primarily the result of outdated or inadequate norms and teaching to the test. For a discussion of this controversy, see Cannell (1987) and a special issue of *Educational Measurement: Issues and Practices* (1990).

Norm-referenced scores compare students; they do not identify what students know and can do. Yet the latter information is critical for planning instruction to build on students' strengths and ameliorate weaknesses. Such information is provided by criterion-referenced tests.

The primary emphasis of criterion-referenced tests is to determine an individual's level of proficiency of the material tested and not to provide a comparison among test takers. Thus, items for criterion-referenced tests are selected to measure important instructional outcomes regardless of their ability to discriminate among test takers. And, rather than expressing a person's score in comparison with scores of other students, scores are interpreted in relation to a criterion associated with the subject matter to indicate whether the outcomes have been attained. Typically, most teacher-made tests are criterion referenced. There are also many commercially developed achievement tests that are criterion referenced.

TYPES OF ITEMS

An important decision concerning tests is to determine the item type(s) to use, regardless of whether the test is teacher-made or prepared by a testing company. An item's purpose is to elicit information about an attribute of the test taker, and the amount and type of information obtained depend on the category of item used. Items can be divided into two major categories: *selected-response* items and *constructed-response* items. The next section describes these two types of items. In addition, there is a discussion of *performance tests* which are alternatives to the typical paper-and-pencil tests.

Selected-Response Items

Selected-response items are the most widely used type of item and include primarily multiple-choice, true–false, and matching items (see

Carlson, 1985, for a discussion of other selected-response items). A selected-response item provides a completely structured situation for the test taker. The test taker selects a response from a series of potential responses. Each item has only one correct response, and scores are not affected by the scorers' biases.

The multiple-choice item is the most frequently used selected-response item. It has two parts: the stem, which can be a question, problem, or incomplete statement, and typically four or five options consisting of potential responses to the stem.

Multiple-choice items are the most widely criticized item type (see Frederiksen, 1984, and Feinberg, 1990, for a discussion of the relative merits and criticisms of multiple-choice items compared to constructed-response items). Critics argue that multiple-choice items encourage guessing, penalize creativity, and neglect the measurement of writing skills. Further, unless multiple-choice items are carefully constructed, individuals can be coached to correctly answer these items based on approaches that consider the characteristics of the item rather than knowledge of the measured skill.

Multiple-choice items are also criticized because they typically are used to measure recall of knowledge and are considered by some to be simplistic. Yet, they can also measure higher-order skills, such as understanding, synthesis, and problem solving. Although critics argue to the contrary, almost any skill that can be tested by means of any other item type can also be tested by multiple-choice items. Further, as Feinberg (1990) notes, the measurement of knowledge is important:

> There are two problems with this accusation [that multiple-choice items are simplistic and measure recall of knowledge rather than the ability to think and solve problems]. First, a test of knowledge is not necessarily simplistic. For good reasons it is a major part of the sophisticated multiple-choice licensing exams for physicians and engineers, as well as of tests of fifth-grade science. Even though knowledge may be in disrepute among some education theorists (although not among the public), no amount of reasoning about a subject can make much sense unless students first know something about it. Even the critics concede that multiple-choice tests are an excellent way to test what students know, a consideration not to be lightly disregarded.
>
> Secondly, many multiple-choice tests are more than just tests of knowledge. In fact, the most widely known multiple-choice exam, the Scholastic Aptitude Test (SAT), tests very little knowledge; it is almost completely a test of analytical thinking and reasoning ability at quite complex and sophisticated levels. The multiple-choice questions on Advanced Placement exams— about half of each test—often require sharp analysis with a command of facts. Many other standardized tests, particularly at the high school level, also probe the ability to draw fair inferences and reach tenable conclusions. (pp. 7–8)

Multiple-choice items have significant strengths as well as weaknesses, including the speed with which items can be answered and the speed and objectivity of scoring. Thus, many multiple-choice items can be answered within a limited time period permitting a broad sample of behavior to be obtained. Further, compared to the time-consuming and judgmental scoring of constructed-response items, scoring of multiple-choice items can be inexpensive and objective.

Constructed-Response Items

The two major categories of constructed-response items are essays (extended constructed-response) and short answer, fill-in-the-blank, or sentence completion (restricted constructed-response). The characteristics of a constructed-response item are the opposite of those of a selected-response item: The test taker constructs a written answer in his or her own words and writing style rather than selects one, typically answers a small number of questions given the time limits, and produces answers with different degrees of accuracy.

The essay item is the most frequently used constructed-response item. Essay questions permit the test taker to demonstrate his or her ability to recall and evaluate factual knowledge and organize and present ideas in a logical and coherent fashion, among other things. Although multiple-choice items can be used to measure higher-order skills, essay items are better suited to solve problems, to organize, integrate, or synthesize information, and to measure originality or creativity. The response to an essay also can provide clues to the nature and quality of the test taker's thought processes—something that multiple-choice items cannot.

Serious limitations of tests composed of essays include the limited sampling of the content covered by the test and the potential ambiguity of the essay questions. Coaching is difficult but "bluffing" (capitalizing on good verbal skills and writing style when one knows little about the subject matter) is not. Finally, scoring essays is time consuming and, to an extent, subjective. Methods of scoring essays include analytic, holistic, and primary traits. For a discussion of these methods, and of scoring essays in general, see Quellmalz (1986).

Ebel (1979) summarized the differences between tests composed of selected-response items (called objective tests by Ebel) and constructed-response items (specifically tests composed solely of essays):

1. Essay tests require an individual to organize and express his answer in his own words. In the essay, the student is not restricted to a

list of responses from which he is to select his answer. Objective tests, on the other hand, require that the individual choose the correct answer from among several alternatives.

2. An essay test consists of fewer questions but calls for more lengthy answers. An objective test has more questions but ones taking less time to answer. Adequacy of sampling, efficiency, and reliability are therefore likely to be superior in objective tests.

3. Different skills and processes are involved in taking the test. In the essay test, the student spends most of his time thinking and writing. In the objective test most of the student's time is spent on reading and thinking.

4. Essay tests afford both the student and scorer the opportunity to be individualistic. Objective tests afford this freedom of expression only to the test-maker (pp. 100–101).

Performance Tests

In the 1990s, achievement is being measured increasingly by methods called *performance tests*. Frechtling (1991) defines performance tests as follows:

> Almost anything that is not multiple-choice paper and pencil test can, and has, been considered a performance assessment. Included are constructed-response, short-answer, open-ended, and essay questions. At more of an extreme are performance tasks that may include demonstrations, portfolios, research projects and dramatizations, among others. (p. 24)

Since constructed-response items have already been discussed, we will define performance item as any non-paper-and-pencil task (i.e., Frechtling's extreme case). Performance tests can be teacher-made or commercially developed. They can occur as part of classroom activities or as a response to a carefully structured condition presented by a trained test administrator. They can include individual or group activities and may require special apparatus. Student responses may be in many modes—paper-and-pencil, verbal, athletic performance, singing, dancing, and so forth. The student's performance may be observed and scored immediately or audio- or videotape-recorded and scored later. Stiggins (1987) elaborates further about performance tests:

> All performance assessments are composed of four basic components: a reason for assessment, a particular performance to be evaluated, exercises to elicit that performance, and systematic rating procedures. The reason for assessment is defined in terms of decisions to be made, decisionmakers, and examinees to be evaluated. Performance to be evaluated is defined in terms of content and/or skills, type of behavior or product to be observed, and

performance criteria. Exercises are structured or natural, preannounced or
unannounced, and variable in number. Finally, rating procedures are defined
in terms of the type of data needed, identity of the rater, and nature of the
recording method. Those who design and develop performance assessments
must consider all of these factors. (p. 34)

The primary advantage of performance tasks is that they provide a direct
means of assessing certain skills, rather than the indirect means provided by most paper-and-pencil tests (especially tests composed of
selected-response items). They can be used to examine both product and
process and, because they resemble instructional tasks, can be more
readily incorporated into programs for the improvement of instruction.
The chief disadvantages of performance tests include that test administration is costly and time-consuming and scoring is also costly, time-
consuming, and somewhat subjective.

There are many issues concerning performance tests that still must
be settled. There is currently little information available to evaluate the
effectiveness of performance tasks to improve instruction. It is also
somewhat unclear how one confirms validity, establishes reliability, or
assures standardization of test administration. However, just as these
issues were resolved for selected-response items and for constructed-
response items, they likewise will be resolved for performance tests.

In general, the test method that provides for the most valid measure
of assessing a skill should be used. To determine whether students
taking a cooking class can bake a cake, they should be asked to bake a
cake rather than describe the process via a paper-and-pencil test. Stiggins (1987) provides a comprehensive discussion of performance tests.

The next section of the chapter addresses the primary issue related
to a *test as a measuring device*—types of test scores.

TYPES OF TEST SCORES

There are two general types of test scores—raw scores and transformed scores. Raw scores are obtained directly from the test—for example, the number of percentage of items correctly answered on an
achievement test. Most teacher-made tests report raw scores. The raw
score has meaning in a criterion-referenced sense because it indicates
the test taker's proficiency level with respect to material taught. However, the raw score has no meaning in a norm-referenced sense—
knowing that a student correctly answered 82% of the items does not by
itself compare the students' performance with others.

Raw scores can be transformed into other scores that do provide normative information. Percentile ranks, standard scores, and age/grade equivalents are transformed scores most frequently used in reporting students' test results, especially on commercially developed achievement tests. The transformed scores provide norm-referenced interpretations and are determined by the relationship between a test taker's score and the scores of other test takers.

The *percentile rank* is defined as the percentage of people in a particular norm group who obtained scores lower than the test taker. Thus, if a test taker's raw score on a test is equivalent to a percentile rank of 95 compared to a certain norm group, the student scored equal to or better than 95% of the people in that norm group. Percentile ranks are typically reported in whole numbers and range from 0 to 99 regardless of whether the norm group as a whole performed well or poorly on the test.

When interpreting percentile ranks it is critical to explain the score relative to a particular norm group. For example, a student's raw score on a test may translate to a percentile rank of 88 when compared to a national norm group, but to a percentile rank of 60 when compared to a private school norm group. Thus, the student performed relatively better when compared to his or her peers nationally (regardless of whether the students attend public or private schools) than only to the students in private schools.

Percentile ranks have two major advantages and two major limitations. The advantages are the ease with which they can be computed and the clarity of their meaning. The first limitation is that they cannot be added, subtracted, multiplied, or divided because they are not equal-interval measures. This is a limitation for statistical analysis, not for interpretation. However, the second limitation is one of interpretation—the difference between two percentile ranks does not represent the same amount of raw score difference in the middle of the distribution as it does at the extremes. For example, the raw score difference between the 90th and 99th percentiles is much greater than the raw score difference between the 50th and 59th percentiles. Thus, the same increase in the number of items correctly answered will result in a larger percentile rank increase at the middle of the distribution than at the extremes.

Standard scores (or Z scores) are defined as the deviation of a raw score from the mean of the distribution of scores in standard deviation units. For example, a standard (Z) score of -0.5 indicates that the test taker's raw score was one-half standard deviation below the mean score for the group. A standard score of 1.0 signifies that the raw score was one standard deviation above the mean.

The relationship between standard scores and raw scores is identical at all points on the score scale and standard scores can be added, subtracted, multiplied, or divided. As a result, standard scores overcome the limitations of percentile ranks and are preferable to percentile ranks for most statistical analyses. However, because of their greater statistical complexity, standard scores lack the clarity of meaning that percentile ranks have.

Since standard scores can be negative and have decimal numbers, they are usually transformed to a different scale to avoid reporting negative or decimal numbers. Frequently cited examples of transformed standard scores are the SAT score scale in which scores are reported on a scale of 200 to 800 with a mean of 500 and a standard deviation of 100 and the ACT scores scale that has a mean of 20 and a standard deviation of 5. The stanine (short for standard nine) is another standard score scale that consists of 9 elements (1 to 9) with a mean of 5 and a standard deviation of 2.

Standard scores are linear transformations of raw scores and follow the same distribution as the raw scores. However, when raw scores are not normally distributed, one can transform them into normalized standard scores, that is, standard scores that are distributed according to a normal distribution. To normalize scores, there must be some basis for assuming that scores on the characteristic being measured are normally distributed. The SAT and ACT standard scores are normalized standard scores. Stanines are also normalized standard scores.

Age and grade equivalent scores are the third major type of transformed score. These scores compare a test taker's performance with that of the "average" person at various developmental (age or grade) levels.

Grade equivalent scores are used widely in schools. However, although they seem to be an appropriate and easily understood method of describing achievement, they have certain properties that make them easy to misinterpret and, as such, have limited utility. The following example illustrates the major limitation of grade and age equivalent scores.

Suppose a fifth-grade student takes a test in October and scores a 5.2 grade equivalent (signifying second month of fifth grade). That student's performance is considered to be "on-grade-level" compared to other fifth graders—the student's performance is comparable to that of the average student in the second month (October) of the fifth grade. Suppose another fifth-grade student scored an 8.2 grade equivalent on the same test (eighth grade, second month). That score is easily and frequently misinterpreted as meaning that the fifth-grade student is "on-an-eighth-grade-level," when in fact, it is not known whether the student could do eighth-grade work. The test did not measure eighth-grade work; it measured fifth-grade work. The student simply scored very high compared to other fifth-grade students on a test measuring fifth-grade material.

Similarly, were another fifth-grade student to score a 2.2 grade equivalent on the fifth-grade test, the student would not be on a second-grade level. That fifth grader would probably score high on a test covering second-grade material. Rather, the 2.2 grade equivalent indicates that compared to other fifth-grade students, this student scored poorly on the test that measures achievement of fifth-grade objectives.

Because of these and other problems associated with interpreting grade equivalent scores, many measurement experts suggest avoiding their use. Echternacht (1977) provides a discussion of the problems and advantages of grade or age equivalent scores.

VALIDITY AND RELIABILITY

The next section discusses validity and reliability, the two most critical issues related to a *test as a sample of behavior*, regardless of whether the test is commercially developed or teacher-made.

Validity

The *Standards for Educational and Psychological Testing* (1985) is published jointly by three organizations providing national leadership in measurement and testing—the American Educational Research Association, the American Psychological Association, and the National Council on Measurement in Education. The *Standards* guides the development and use of tests and provides criteria for the evaluation of tests, testing practices, and the effects of test use. (The three organizations also sponsored the development of The *Code* of Fair Testing Practices in Education, a 1988 publication that focuses primarily on issues that affect the proper use of tests in education. The *Code* addresses the roles of test developers and test users separately and should be read by everyone who develops or uses tests.)

According to the *Standards for Educational and Psychological Testing*, validity is the single most important consideration in test evaluation. It defines *validity* as

> the appropriateness, meaningfulness, and usefulness of the specific inferences made from test scores. Test validation is the process of accumulating evidence to support such inferences. A variety of inferences may be made from scores produced by a given test, and there are many ways of accumulating evidence to support any particular inference. Validity, however, is a

unitary concept. Although evidence may be accumulated in many ways, validity always refers to the degree to which that evidence supports the inferences that are made from the scores. The inferences regarding specific uses of a test are validated, not the test itself. (p. 9)

Messick (1986) provides additional details about validity:

> The key validity issues are the interpretability, relevance, and utility of scores, the import or value implications of scores as a basis for action, and the functional worth of scores in terms of social consequences of their use. These manifold aspects or thrusts of validity have been integrated in the following unified view: Validity is an overall evaluative judgment, founded on empirical evidence and theoretical rationales, of the adequacy, and appropriateness of inferences and actions based on test scores. As such, validity is an inductive summary of both the adequacy of existing evidence for and the appropriateness of potential consequences of test interpretation and use. (p. 2)

Evidence of validity can be categorized into three areas: construct-related evidence, content-related evidence, and criterion-related evidence.

Construct-related validity evidence focuses on the test score as a measure of a psychological construct (e.g., reading comprehension, endurance, leadership) and on the degree to which a relationship exists between the test scores and the theory underlying the construct. Messick (1986) argues that construct-related evidence is the essence of validity:

> The heart of the unified view of validity is that appropriateness, meaningfulness, and usefulness of score-based inferences are inseparable and that the unifying force is *empirically-grounded* construct interpretation. Thus from the perspective of validity as a unified concept, all educational and psychological measurement should be construct-referenced because construct interpretation undergirds all score-based inferences—not just those related to interpretive meaningfulness but also the content- and criterion-related inferences specific to applied decisions and actions based on test scores. As a consequence, although construct-related evidence may not be the whole of validity, there can be no validity without it. That is, there is not a way to judge responsibly the appropriateness, meaningfulness, and usefulness of score inferences in the absence of evidence as to what the scores mean. (pp. 4–5; emphasis added)

Content-related validity evidence is defined by Wolman (1989) as follows: "A measure of how well items of a test correspond to the behavior which the test attempts to assess or predict" (p. 359). Lennon (1956) provides a definition of *content-related* validity evidence:

> the extent to which a subject's responses to the items of a test may be considered to be a representative sample of his responses to a real or hypothetical universe of situations which together constitute the area of concern to the person interpreting the test. (p. 294)

Brown (1983) argues that content-related validity evidence is related to how adequately the content of a test samples the domain about which inferences are to be made:

> In these situations the variable of interest is students' knowledge of the subject matter domain. The test serves as a sample, or representation, of the content domain. Scores on the test are not ends in themselves; rather they are used to make inferences about performance in the wide domain. Because he cannot ask every possible question, the teacher selects a sample of the possible items to serve as the test. On the basis of the student's performance on this sample of items, the teacher makes inferences about the student's knowledge of (all) the material in the unit. To the extent that the items are a good sample of the total pool of potential items, the inferences will be valid; to the extent that any bias is introduced into the item selection, the inferences will be invalid. (pp. 132–133)

Human judgment is usually the primary means of obtaining content-related validity evidence. The evidence is typically determined by inspecting the items to determine whether or not each represents the specified domain of behavior.

Criterion-related validity evidence refers to the relationship between the test scores and some independent external measure(s) (criteria). For situations in which criterion-referenced validity evidence is needed (e.g., to determine if the SAT predicts how successful a high school student will be in a particular college, where success is represented by the criterion of freshman grade point average), the individual's performance on the criterion variable is of foremost importance. The value of the test score lies in how accurately it predicts the criterion.

Criterion-related evidence is usually divided into *predictive* and *concurrent* evidence of validity. The only real distinction between predictive and concurrent evidence is the time period when the criterion data are collected. Predictive evidence is evidence about the usefulness of the test data to estimate the performance on a criterion that will be obtained in the future (as in the above example about the SAT). Concurrent evidence obtains test scores and criterion information simultaneously—the test score is used in place of less efficient criterion data.

Criterion-related validity evidence is usually amassed by empirical means, based on correlational studies (e.g., identifying college freshmen who took the SAT in high school, obtaining their college freshman grade point average, and correlating the two scores). The higher the correlation, the greater the evidence of the test's criterion-referenced validity.

In summary, it is important to note that no single validation strategy is uniformly best for every inference or test use. A test must be valid for its intended purpose regardless of whether it is a classroom test or a commercially developed test; otherwise, the inferences drawn from its results will be meaningless. Further, a test that is valid for one purpose is not necessarily valid for other purposes. See Messick (1989) for a comprehensive discussion of validity.

Reliability is discussed next. The discussion of reliability is limited to tests designed to yield norm-referenced interpretations. For a discussion of reliability for tests that yield criterion-referenced interpretations, see Berk (1984).

Reliability

Once a test's validity has been established, the next important question focuses on its reliability or dependability. In order for inferences to be reliable, a test taker's score needs to be similar under different conditions—for example, with different administrators, with similar but not identical items, or during different times in a day. The greater the reliability of a test, the more confident one can be that test takers would obtain similar scores if they retake the test and the more confident one can be that the inferences drawn will be dependable.

Why do students receive different scores on the same test? Brown (1983) provides three possible explanations:

1. Differences among test takers in the attribute measured.

2. Differences among test takers on attributes that are irrelevant to the purposes of the testing but that have systematic effects on the test scores.

3. Differences among test takers on factors that cause a person's score to differ from the score the test taker would obtain if he or she took a different sample of items or took the test at another time or under different conditions.

Variation in test scores based on *differences among test takers* (Brown's first explanation) is to be expected. However, differences based on the other two explanations cause less accurate measurement and are sources of errors in test takers' scores.

Errors based on the second reason are called *systematic errors*. As an example, if mathematics test items contain complex wording and have a heavy reading load, differences among the test takers' reading ability could influence the scores even though reading ability should be irrelevant to the purpose of the test. These errors will have a negligible effect on a test's reliability but will affect its validity because the test may measure irrelevant factors in addition to what it was designed to measure.

Errors based on the third reason are called *measurement errors*. There are three categories of factors that contribute to measurement error: (1) the test (e.g., the particular sample of items on a specific form of the test), (2) the test administration (e.g., distracting factors or errors in timing), and (3) the test taker (e.g., fatigue or anxiety).

Reliability can best be defined in terms of the relationship among true scores, observed scores, and measurement errors. *A true score* is the score that a test taker would obtain if the test measured without error. *An observed score* is the score that a test taker actually obtains on a test. *Measurement errors* represent the difference between the test taker's observed score and hypothetical true score.

If there were no measurement error, a test taker's observed score would be a perfect representation of his or her true score and the differences among test takers' scores would be solely due to their differences in the attribute measured. A test taker would always obtain exactly the same score regardless of the sample of items administered, when the test was taken, and so forth. Test results would be completely reliable. However, tests are never free from measurement errors. Measurement errors affect the observed score and thus reduce the reliability (i.e., dependability) of that observed test score as a representation of the true score.

Reliability measures range from zero to one. When the reliability is near one, the variability in the test takers' observed scores is due to their differences in the attribute that the test measures. Conversely, when the reliability is near zero, measurement errors, rather than true differences, are the major reasons why test takers obtain different scores. The greater the reliability measure, the greater the likelihood that the scores are dependable and reproducible under different conditions because the test taker's score represents his or her true ability, not extraneous factors.

Mehrens and Lehmann (1984) define four different approaches to estimating reliability. The methods differ in the sources of measurement error that each address.

1. *Measures of stability* (test–retest reliability) are derived from comparing the performance of the same test at two administrations of it. This comparison provides a measure of the consistency over time of the test taker's performance on the test. Thus, one can determine how confidently a test taker's score obtained at one point in time can be generalized if the same test had been given at a different time. Typically this type of reliability estimate is used when one is measuring attributes presumed to be relatively stable over time (p. 272).

2. *Measures of equivalence* (parallel forms, alternate forms, or equivalent forms reliability) are derived from comparing the performance on two parallel forms of the same test at the same time. This type of reliability estimate is used when there are two forms of the same test and provides a measure of the consistency of the scores on the two forms. Thus, one can determine how confidently test taker's scores on a test can be generalized to scores obtained by taking a test composed of similar but different items (p. 273).

3. *Measures of equivalence and stability* are a combination of the above two measures and are derived from measuring the stability over time and the changes due to the specific items on each test. One form of the test is administered and then after a period of time has elapsed, a parallel form is administered. This estimate of reliability is typically lower than either the test–retest or parallel forms reliability estimate because it is affected by the error prevalent in both types of reliability estimates (p. 274).

4. *Measures of internal consistency* are used when there is only one form of a test and only one testing session, since neither test–retest nor parallel forms reliability estimates can be obtained. For this situation, there are two options:

> a. *Split-half reliability* requires dividing the test into two parts (e.g., the even numbered items as one part and the odd numbered items as the other part) and correlating the scores on the two parts. Split-half reliability can be considered a special case of parallel forms reliability. A problem with split-half reliability estimates is that each score is based on only half of the items in the original test. Reliability is affected by test length; hence, the reliability estimated from the odd and even items will be lower than the reliability expected from the overall test. To estimate the reliability of the overall test from the split-half estimate, the Spearman-Brown Prophecy formula is used. (Mehrens & Lehmann, 1984, p. 275)
>
> b. *Internal consistency reliability* examines the consistency of performance across all the items in the test and determines whether all of the items measure the same attribute. Formulas such as Coefficient Alpha (Cronbach, 1951) and Kuder-Richardson formula 20 (Kuder & Richardson, 1937) are the most frequently used internal consistency reliability formulas. (Mehrens & Lehmann, 1984, pp. 276–277)

The reliability of a test is related to a number of characteristics of the test and of the group tested. Typically the reliability will be greater for scores from (1) a longer test than a shorter test, (2) a test composed of more heterogeneous than of more homogeneous items, (3) a test composed of more discriminating rather than less discriminating items, (4) a test with middle difficulty items rather than very difficult or very easy items, (5) a heterogeneous rather than a homogeneous group, and (6) a test that all test takers are not expected to complete in the time available (speeded test) rather than one all test takers do complete in the time available (power test).

Thorndike and Hagen (1974) succinctly explain the relationship between validity and reliability:

> Validity, insofar as we can appraise it, is the crucial test of a measurement procedure. Reliability is important only as a necessary condition for a measure to have validity. The ceiling for the possible validity of a test is set by its reliability. A test must measure something before it can measure what we want it to measure . . . [However,] the converse of the relationship we have just presented does not follow. A test may measure with the greatest precision and still have no validity for our purposes. (p. 189)

TESTING IN THE CLASSROOM

The most widely used type of classroom test is the achievement test that teachers develop themselves. Classroom tests are very similar to commercially developed achievement tests. Validity and reliability are the most critical concerns of both types of tests. Both types are standardized to the extent that a common set of items is administered to all students in a class under similar conditions. Finally, classroom tests can use the same types of items as commercially developed tests and can provide a norm-referenced interpretation (i.e., where the class is the norm group) or a criterion-referenced interpretation (based on the teacher's determination of a proficiency standard).

Although the most frequent use of classroom tests is for grading, another important use is to assist in the learning process. Brown (1983) outlines *three points in the learning sequence* where tests (or other assessment methods) may provide useful information:

> 1. The first is at the beginning of a course or unit, prior to the start of instruction. Here we might administer a pretest to measure students' knowledge of prerequisite material and/or the material to be taught. If students have not mastered the prerequisite knowledge and skills, we will have to teach them; if they have already mastered some of the material to be taught, we can spend time on other topics. Pretests can also direct learning by pointing out important concepts and materials so that students can focus their attention on these areas. And, of course, pretests can provide baseline data to be used when evaluating the effectiveness of learning and instruction.
>
> 2. Tests can also be administered during the course of instruction. While these tests may be used for grading, a more important use is to facilitate learning. By providing students with feedback as to what material they have mastered and what material is still to be learned, tests can direct studying.

Analysis of students' performance, particularly the errors they make, can be used by the teacher to diagnose problem areas and suggest remedial action. Tests given during instruction can also motivate students, either by showing them they need to work harder (if they do not do well) or by increasing their confidence (if they have been able to master difficult material). They can also be used to check whether students have understood the main point of a reading assignment or as a basis for discussion. The teacher can use the results to determine whether her instruction has been effective and to suggest what material should be reviewed or retaught using a different approach. Evaluation of learning made during the course of instruction are called formative evaluations (Bloom, Hastings, & Madaus, 1971; Scriven, 1967).

3. The third point to measure achievement is at the end of a unit or course. These assessments are called summative evaluations and are designed to determine whether students have mastered the course objectives. Although summative evaluations are most frequently used as a basis for grading, they also indicate whether students have mastered the material and indicate whether the instruction has been effective. Since these assessments are collected at the end of instruction, and measure the results of learning, they are of less value for directing instruction and learning. (pp. 233–234)

One of the chief problems with classroom tests is that they are created without adequate planning. Mehrens and Lehmann (1984) suggest that the teacher consider two general questions in planning the tests: (1) What is the purpose of the test? (2) What is the best means to achieve the purpose? Mehrens and Lehmann (1984, p. 65) provide a checklist to assist the classroom test developer:

- Specify the course or unit content
- List the major course or unit objectives
- Define each objective in terms of student behavior
- Discard unrealistic objectives
- Prepare a table of specifications
- Decide upon the type of item format to be used
- Prepare test items that match the instructional objectives.

By first deciding on the objectives (purpose) for the classroom test, the teacher can determine the optimal design (table of specifications) for the test—for example, when the test will be administered; what material will be covered and in what relative emphasis; how many items there should be in total and for each content area measured; and what types of items to use.

Classroom tests have certain limitations when compared to commercially developed tests. Since they are usually constructed by only one teacher, that teacher may overemphasize his or her preferences. In addition, many teachers have not been trained in item writing, have difficulty writing good items, and only write items measuring knowledge. Furthermore, the reliability of classroom tests is often lower than desired.

Compared to commercially developed tests, classroom tests also have several advantages. They can be adapted to the goals of a particular class. They have great flexibility in terms of length, types of items, time of administration, and coverage. And the results can be used to improve learning and instruction in a variety of ways. As Mehrens and Lehmann (1984) note:

> Classroom tests, because they can be tailored to fit a teacher's particular instructional objectives, are essential if we wish to provide for optimal learning on the part of the pupil and optimal teaching on the part of the teacher. Without classroom tests, those objectives that are unique to a particular school or teacher might never be evaluated. (p. 58)

A FINAL NOTE

There are legitimate concerns about tests, the use of tests, and the consequences associated with those uses. Particularly today because testing is so prevalent in the schools and accountability measures have been imposed by forces external to the school, the controversies about the use of tests and test results have been intensified. Dyer (1980) and Ebel and Frisbie (1986) outline some of the major issues of debate:

1. Whether tests are biased against any student because of the student's racial/ethnic, gender, or linguistic background. Eliminating bias in tests is of utmost importance. A student's test score must be solely a function of his or her achievement or ability, not influenced by extraneous factors. See Berk (1982) for a discussion about bias in testing.

2. Whether tests freeze the curriculum or "drive" the curriculum.

3. Whether passing tests should be required for promotion or high school graduation.

4. Whether students' test results should be used to evaluate a teacher.

5. Whether external testing programs impose external controls on the curriculum and lead teachers to "teach to the test." This issue is becoming increasingly important given the country's education goals established in 1989 by President George Bush and the governors from the fifty states and the notion of an American Achievement Test proposed by U.S. Secretary of Education Lamar Alexander in his 1991 education plan *American 2000: An Education Strategy*.

Testing will not be eliminated simply because there are concerns or problems associated with tests. Rather, as Mehrens and Lehmann (1984) argue, the problems need to be corrected:

> Psychologists and educators have an obligation to inform the public as to how tests should be used and as to how they are being used. However, much of the negative affect toward tests is precisely because tests are used as they should be, to help make decisions. The decisions are not always pleasant to the people involved. Since tests help make decisions, they have been attacked. Unfortunately, there are some people who assume that by doing away with tests we could avoid making decisions. That is not the case. Decisions must be made. Information helps us make decisions. Tests provide information. As professionals, we must ensure that valid tests are used for making appropriate decisions. (p. 591)

14

Fundamentals of Reading

Leonore Itzkowitz

The teaching of reading has many approaches, but in the end, it always entails helping a child or an adult learn how to figure out what the words say (decoding), and what the words mean (comprehension). No matter how many euphemisms are used, the teaching of reading always comes down to decoding and comprehension.

HISTORICAL OVERVIEW

Among the first instructional materials for teaching reading in the seventeenth century was the Hornbook (N.B. Smith, 1974, p. 16). On a printed page attached to a small paddle of wood that fit into a child's hand was printed the alphabet. Under the alphabet were printed some syllables and the Lord's Prayer. The child was expected to recite the alphabet, not only forwards, but backwards as well. The popular eighteenth-century New England Primer (N.B. Smith, 1974, p. 21) continued this mechanical approach to reading, using columns of two-letter syllables which progressed to words of five syllables.

This serial approach to reading continued to be used almost exclusively until the latter part of the nineteenth century when it was condemned by Horace Mann. Then secretary of the Board of Education in Massachusetts, Mann was convinced that something was terribly wrong with this method of teaching children to read. In a famous lecture on education entitled "On the Best Mode of Preparing and Using the Spelling Books" (Mathews, 1966), he wrote: "There stands in silence and death the stiff perpendicular row of characters, lank, stark, immovable without form or comeliness, and as to signification wholly void" (p. 77).

Expressive an indictment as Horace Mann's statement was about the teaching of reading in a letter-by-letter manner, it fell to James McKeen Cattell, William Wundt's first assistant in the world's first laboratory of experimental psychology at the University of Leipzig, to do something about it. He took the hatchet to the idea that learning to read serially is the way one learns to read (cf. comments on serial associations and memory in Chapter 6). Cattell's (1886) later-nineteenth-century finding that words take less time to identify (process) than single letters was a revolutionary one. It led to the popularization of the whole-word approach (the look-say method) that had been advocated by Horace Mann.

Readers

Concretization of Horace Mann's ideas came in the form of the McGuffey Eclectic Readers. Appearing in the third decade of the 1800s (Smith, 1974), and ubiquitously on the scene for at least 40 years and even used today, the McGuffey Eclectic Readers brought fame and fortune to William H. McGuffey, then president of Ohio University.

McGuffey's readers featured whole words, pictures, sentences, stories, poems, and classic literature. Sexist and moralistic as the stories were, they related to children's lives. The materials for the instruction of reading had begun to have meaning.

The McGuffey readers were eventually replaced by basal readers which emerged in the 1930s, after a period of intelligence testing and measurement often referred to as the scientific era in United States education. This period of scientific emphasis upon reading and other school subjects can be said to have begun in 1910, when one of the first tools for measuring educational products in a scientific way, Edward L. Thorndike's handwriting scale, was published (Smith, 1974, p. 157). A new era characterized by tests in arithmetic, composition, speaking, and reading was launched. The parade continues today in the form of standardized achievement tests that march along with the student from kindergarten to graduate school. A child's results on standardized reading tests are frequently used today to place him or her in a particular basal reading program.

Published by every major educational publisher, and still the most widely used material to teach reading in today's schools, basal reading programs are a multimillion-dollar industry. Components of such programs are reading-readiness workbooks, preprimers and primer texts, followed by one or two hardcovered first-reader texts and accompanying workbooks on the same levels. They stretch from first- to eighth-grade levels. Teacher's manuals that instruct how the reading is to be taught are included in the package, as are supplementary materials. The latter relate to the text by way of reading charts, records, tapes, posters, and additional books. More is involved than "Look, Ted. See Sally." They provide a plan for teaching reading from the child's first year in school to the time she or he enters high school. Using illustrations, stories, poetry, content-area material, and (recently) more and more excerpts of fine children's literature, they are the most popular way of teaching children how to recognize text and understand its meaning.

Perspectives (Code-Based and/or Meaning-Based Emphases)

Much time has passed since the Hornbook's appearance with its skill-based page of ab, eb, ib, ob, ub, and that of McGuffey's readers with their pages of text that were meant to convey word recognition through meaningful stories. Nonetheless, the debate concerning the merits of a code-based emphasis versus a meaning emphasis still occasionally surfaces in the world of reading research.

Those who hold with a code-based emphasis argue that a child can learn to read by being taught the sounds of the letters and how to blend those sounds together. The populist writer who commercially exploited the code-based theory was Rudolph Flesch, whose *Why Johnny Can't Read* explosively burst on the best-seller lists in 1955. He maintained that a secure grounding in phonics (letter–sound correspondence) was the only way to teach reading.

Adherents of the meaning-based emphasis counter that reading should develop as naturally as language, and that new words should be couched in context and experience. In this regard, the writer whose work found a popular following is Sylvia Ashton Warner, author of *Teacher* (1963). This book, considered inspirational by many teachers, tells of the organic way Warner taught Maori children in New Zealand to read through what she called the Key Vocabulary. It convinced many that it is the children's own language, not phonics, through which they must learn to read.

Warner would write the words that her five-year-olds chose. This led to their writing two or three autobiographical sentences, then stories which in turn led "to all the other reading . . . to the inorganic and standard reading" (Warner, 1963, p. 57). Unlike the stories of the basal primers written by educators, Warner's students' text was the stuff of their own language. For example, "Mummie got a hiding off Dad. He was drunk. She was crying. I went to the river and I kissed Lily and I ran away. Then I kissed Philliaa. Then I ran away and went for a swim" (p. 53).

Both Flesch's book and Warner's were popular successes. Their opposing points of view concerning reading instruction were to be echoed in the field of reading research from the 1960s to the 1980s.

Flesch's commercial prophonics stance was given support (whether or not deliberately) in reading and psychology journals, by the research of those workers who maintained that reading was a "bottom-up" process. Bottom-up proponents theorized that lower levels of thought, such as recognizing letters and words, must occur before comprehension can take place. They devised graphic models which illustrated what happens from the moment the eye hits print to the moment when comprehension arrives.

Gough's model is particularly refreshing (Gough & Cosky, 1977). He assumed that reading begins with regular left-to-right progression of eye fixations in which letters are read out of the icon serially, one every 10 to 20 msec. These are deposited into a character register, and coded into phonological form. This "phonemic tape" locates the meaning of the word in a mental lexicon, and it is then deposited in primary memory. At this point "a gifted homunculus" takes over. This inner person applies his knowledge of syntax and semantics, and deposits the meaning in a depository which Gough whimsically labeled TPWSGWTAU (The Place Where Sentences Go When They Are Understood).

Warner's work with Maori children, which led her to argue vehemently that the child's first words must have an intense meaning, would find support from those scholars who regard reading as a "top-down" process. Top-down adherents (Goodman, 1967) hypothesize that it is comprehension that dictates whether one must even recognize certain words at all. They too have their models, but meaning, not decoding plays the main role. Frank Smith (1988) prefers the terms "outside-in" which he describes as roughly equivalent to skill-based, or bottom-up perspectives; and "inside-out," as roughly equivalent to meaning-based or "top-down" perspectives. For Smith, the reader plays the main role in approaching the text, handling it, and interpreting it.

Despite the two schools of thought being heavily argued in many of the thousand-plus articles on reading written in journals since 1980 (F. Smith, 1988), there is probably no one today who is rigidly either bottom-up or top-down. The "great debate," as Jeanne Chall (1967) has called the dispute between code-based and meaning-based instruction, seems to be nearing an end with the tacit acceptance that both decoding and meaning are imperative in reading, beginning with the earliest instruction. Though Chall recommends that a code-based emphasis be employed in the initial stages of teaching reading (up to the end of third grade), she clearly does not recommend ignoring reading-for-meaning practice.

The recognition that both bottom-up and top-down processes take place while a person is reading has led to a number of scholars espousing "interactive" models of reading (Rumelhart, 1977). Just and Carpenter (1987) maintain that the reader operates on several levels, simultaneously processing each word as far as possible on a lexical level, semantic and syntactic level, referential level, and text schema level. Kamhi and Catts agree that "simplistic serial processing models, whether bottom-up or top-down, cannot adequately capture the complex interactions that occur within and between different processing levels" (1989, p. 7). Interactive models of reading may also be seen as a combination of bottom-up and top-down theory, a compromise of sorts, and the 1990s may be the decade in which parallel processing of reading is explored.

Psycholinguistic theory, prevalent in the 1960s and 1970s, popularized the idea of interaction between the reader and the text. We are seeing the results of this kind of thinking in basals of the 1990s, which present "whole language" activities and "interactive approaches."

That psychology cannot be divorced from the reading process is also elucidated in *On Learning to Read* by Bruno Bettelheim and Karen Zelan (1982). Their thesis that children's preconscious and unconscious thought account for most of the errors they make while learning to read, is one which psychoanalytically oriented teachers will second. The substitution of the word "drunk" for "father" by a student of any age reading aloud, may be an indication of something else going on, especially if it is followed by the substitution of "bar" for "car." Reading is a complicated process and it involves many facets of the reader's being, including an unaware one (recall Locke's position on sympathies and antipathies).

Prior Knowledge and Schema

The teacher maintaining an interactive approach believes that "reading is a process in which information from the text and the knowledge possessed by the reader act together to produce meaning" (Anderson, Hiebert, Scott, & Wilkinson, 1985, p. 8). Essentially, a dialogue must go on between the words of the author and the thoughts of the reader. The one cannot do without the other, if comprehension is to take place.

Helpful in understanding this dialogue or integration are two terms that no reading teacher today can afford not to know. They are "prior knowledge" (what one knows) and "schema" (one's view of the world).

Though the term "schema" has been used in philosophy (Kant, 1781/1965) and memory research (Bartlett, 1932), it is only in the past three decades that it has changed the very nature of teaching reading. Conceptual awareness of schema may well cause institutions of higher learning to stop producing teachers like Thomas Gradgrind, who in Dickens's *Hard Times* cries out, "In this life, we want nothing but Facts, sir: nothing but Facts."

The idea that knowledge is a bunch of individual facts has been replaced by the notion that we have a schema, a knowledge of the world that helps us to organize old and new information. The reader who wishes to understand a text needs to be able to activate a schema that allows her or him to take in new information and fit it, instantiate it, into "slots" that have been set up by that schema (Schank & Abelson, 1977).

The schema depends upon what is referred to in the reading literature as *prior knowledge*. F. Smith (1988) views it as a constraint on one's thinking:

> The first constraint on thinking is *prior knowledge*. Like language, thought always has a subject. And just as we cannot talk or write competently if we do not know what we are talking about, so it is not possible to demonstrate thought in any way if we do not understand what we are expected or trying to think about. If I have difficulty understanding an article on nuclear physics, it is not because I am unable to draw conclusions, but because I do not know enough about nuclear physics. And good nuclear physicists are not necessarily good writers, chess players, or automobile mechanics. (p. 21)

The point is that what one is able or unable to understand depends a great deal upon what one already knows or does not know. The child facing a paragraph in a science text, social studies text, or any content-area text for that matter is constrained immediately by what she or he already knows about that subject.

Those people rich in schemata will bring more to what they read than those whose schemata are impoverished. That one can have a schema in almost anything is shown by studies consisting of a restaurant schema (Schank & Abelson, 1977), a baseball schema (Spilich, Vesonder, Chiesi, & Voss, 1979), and a Star Wars schema (Means & Voss, 1985). They all attest to the idea that what one learns depends upon what one knows.

DEVELOPMENTAL APPROACHES

When one considers the physiological and intellectual development necessary for first-grade performance, it is not rash to say that one's proficiency in the act of reading begins in the womb, if not before. A gene gone awry, poor nutrition during vital periods of pregnancy (Birch & Gussow, 1970), effects of disease or abuse on the embryo, and extremely premature birth may all have their effect on the fetus's later cognition.

An infant's safe arrival into the world does not preclude the occurrence of other problems. Lags in neurophysiological maturation (De-Hirsch, Jansky, & Langford, 1966), disturbances in speech development (Doehring, Trites, Patel, & Fiedorowicz, 1981), impaired hearing or vision are a few of the physiological sources that may cause a child's slow progress in the beginning or later stages of reading. Environmental effects, too, whether from individual or societal ills, can be detrimental factors in a child's academic development.

Development, whether intellectual (Ginsberg & Opper, 1969), psychological (Erikson, 1950), or linguistic (Brown & Fraser, 1963), has long been viewed as a continuous series of stages. Jeanne Chall (1983) has developed a stage model that gives a general picture of reading development. Like other theories of developmental stages, Chall's is susceptible to expansion or contraction at any particular stage.

Chall's Six Stages of Reading

Chall's developmental model provides us with an awareness of the realization that reading is a language-based skill, and that the business of decoding and reading for meaning and learning are both paramount for eventual mature reading. Inherent in her model is the traditional view that a series of subskills must be mastered so that a child can decode, but it is a broader picture in its emphasis on the goal of construction and reconstruction of meaning.

Chall's stages are:

Stage 0:	Prereading: Birth to Age 6.
Stage 1:	Initial Reading, or Decoding, Grades 1–2, Ages 6–7.
Stage 2:	Confirmation, Fluency, Ungluing from Print: Grades 2–3, Ages 7–8.
Stage 3:	Reading for Learning the New: A First Step. Grades 4–8 and/or 9, Ages 9–14.
Stage 4:	Multiple Viewpoints: High School, Ages 14–18.
Stage 5:	Construction and Reconstruction—A Word View: College, Age 18 and above.

In her elaboration of these stages (Chall, 1983, pp. 13–24), we perceive an individual's reading development from birth to adulthood. We further learn how a youngster progresses from learning to read, to reading to learn.

Reading Readiness

Reading readiness may be viewed as a series of subskills that children need in order to begin decoding, or as experiences that bring a child to reading. Aulls (1982) offers six kinds of information that he thinks are useful in deciding what kind of instruction would be most suitable for children at the beginning of the first school year:

1. The child's experience with books.
2. The child's understanding of the concept of letter, word, and sentence.
3. The child's ability to predict words from context and to recognize that language units must make sense within a larger message context.
4. The child's knowledge of the letters.
5. The child's ability to read any of the most frequent words in written language.
6. The child's readiness to benefit from sight word instruction.

Tests that assess this information have been used as a means to predict children's success in first grade (Richek, 1977–1978; Evans, Taylor, & Blum, 1979).

Reading stories to children is an important part of kindergarten and first grade (and later grades as well), and its correlation with decoding ability, vocabulary, and comprehension is well known. Recognized, too, is the fact that early readers or children who have learned to read before entering school are often read to at home (Durkin, 1966; Morrow, 1983).

Reading readiness is usually a major part of kindergarten and frequently continues into first grade. It takes the form of visual, auditory, and kinesthetic activities that help the child to distinguish first gross, then gradually more subtle differences between objects, pictures, letters, and words.

Associating the correct letters to the correct sounds, is, of course, imperative to the act of decoding. A recent technique labelled "say it and move it" is described by Kamhi and Catts (1989), who have children moving disks to represent sound.

Children were shown that three-phoneme items could be built from previously segmented sounds. For example, disks were used to represent the sound /a/, then /at/, and finally /sat/. Phonemes could be deleted in a similar fashion (e.g., /sat/ became /at/ and then /a/). The teacher goes on to model the pronunciation of the word "sat." Telling the children to "say it and move it" has them repeat the word and to move one disk for each sound in the word as it is said.

This new technique and older ones such as rhyming activities, reciting nursery rhymes, doing readiness workbook exercises, and playing visual and auditory games that enhance left-to-right eye movement and phonological awareness, are used to prepare children for the act of reading. Depending on the background of the children in the class, a greater or lesser amount of time may be expended on readiness exercises aimed at visual and auditory discrimination.

As children progress in first grade, they spend a great deal of time identifying whole words (there are many published lists of sight words that children are encouraged to recognize instantly, lists containing words such as "come," "here," "jump," "the," "in," "saw," "mother," "father," etc.), learning the letters of the alphabet, matching sounds to letters, identifying letter clusters, and blending sounds together, not necessarily in that order. More or less emphasis may be placed on any of these categories in the beginning stages of reading. The aim is one of getting youngsters automatically to recognize needed common words, letter combinations, and phonograms (ick, ell, ong, etc.) so that smooth syllabication will begin to take place.

If figuring out words takes too long a time, children may forget what they read at the beginning of the sentence by the time they get to the end of the sentence. If comprehension is not to suffer, the recognition or the "activation" of words must become automatic (LaBerge & Samuels, 1974).

Phonics. Whether we call it "phoneme–grapheme correspondence" or good old phonics (reading instruction based on decoding to the sounds the letters make), the key to deciphering most of the English language is knowing the sound that letters can make.

Still an extremely popular approach to instructing reading in the first three grades, phonics entails teaching the sounds of consonants, consonant blends (bl-, br-, cl-, cr-, dr-, gr-, pl-, pr-, sk-, spr-, st-, str-, sch-, tr-, -ft, -nd), consonant digraphs (ch, sh, wh, th, ph, ng), short and long vowels, diphthongs (ou, ow, oi, oy), vowel combinations (ay, ea, ee, ie, oa, oo, au), r-controlled vowels (ar, er, ir, or, ur), and many phonograms such as (-all-, -alk-, -ight-, -ing-, etc.).

Structural Analysis. Breaking a word into its parts (syllabication), particularly its syllables and its affixes (prefixes and suffixes), is referred to as structural analysis, word analysis, or syllable segmentation.

Syllabication. It is hoped, both in reading readiness and the teaching of consonant and vowel sounds, the child has developed a phonological awareness, an appreciation for and knowledge of the sound that the letters make, and is ready to begin to analyze unfamiliar words by breaking them into syllables.

Certain syllables are used so often in words that Fry (1977) points out the utility of teaching the most common ones. He tells us that knowing the initial syllable "ex-" means the students knows the beginning part of 141 relatively common words, that knowing the final syllable "-ing" means that the student knows the final sound of 881 relatively common words. There is no question that knowing even part of a word can be a tremendous clue to unlocking it, especially if the reader can also use context clues and additional phonic clues. Fry's practical approach is often comforting to teachers faced with the mass of educational jargon and euphemism in the reading research literature.

Affixes. Teaching children that affixes are prefixes and suffixes that have been added to base words (sometimes referred to as root words, or stems, or free morphemes) is another way of helping them to decode a polysyllabic word. They need to see that a word such as "incompletely" can be segmented into the prefix "in," the root word "complete," and the suffix "ly." Eventually, the meanings of these affixes will be taught and that leads us to the acquisition of vocabulary.

Vocabulary

As I walked into school one day with a nickel-sized open bloody wound on my face, my fellow teachers greeted me in their normal way, saying nothing about the new condition of my face. I thought to myself, "Great, it's not noticeable!"

A half-hour later, my first-period class, a group of seventh graders, marched into my reading class. They took one look and began screaming, "Oh God, Mrs. Itzkowitz, what happened to you? You've got blood all over your face."

Exposed by their honesty and elated by their interest, I began, "Well, yesterday I took my son to the *dermatologist*, the skin doctor. (As I said this, I wrote the word "dermatologist" on the chalkboard as I did every word to come that is in italics.) You know, he's 15 and he has some *acne*. You know how many teenagers get pimples on their face when they enter *adolescence*. I accompanied him to the doctor's to get a certain cream, a *salve*, an *ointment* of some kind that the doctor puts on his eruptions.

Anyway, I was sitting in the waiting room when the dermatologist came out and told me my son's acne was clearing up. Suddenly he pointed at my cheek and said, rather loudly, "What's that on your face?"

"Oh, it's just a pimple."

"How long have you had it?"

"Oh, about eight weeks, maybe nine."

"Mrs. Itzkowitz. Nobody has a pimple for nine weeks. Come into my office and I'll do a *biopsy*, just cut off a little piece of your skin, send that *epithelial tissue* to the *laboratory* at Temple University. There the pathologist, he's the doctor who determines if the tissue is *diseased* or not, will look at it under the microscope and tell me whether it's *benign*, good and healthy, or whether it's *malignant*, meaning that something is wrong or *cancerous*."

By the time I had finished my true story, I had not only a hushed and interested class, but over ten words on the board. I asked the students to try reading these words. To my surprise, this remedial class read every word perfectly. The period now almost over, I asked them to write down the words and come in tomorrow with a story of their own creation using the words. They did and the stories were charming. One began, "The veterinarian was putting salve on my dog's nose when suddenly. . . ." What amazed me even more was that the group recognized and knew the meaning of the words 6 months later.

What were the factors in this acquisition of some sophisticated vocabulary by my "poor" readers? One was interest, whether for a little blood or gore or as I prefer to think, interest in another human being with whom they had worked for 45 minutes a day for a couple of months. Another was their own prior knowledge. They were entering adolescence themselves and were well aware of what they called "zits" from their own experience, watching TV ads for Clearasil, or hearing about pimples from others. A third was the context I had given them with all the semantic clues I had parenthetically added, trying perhaps to give them a "dermatology schema." There was also some redundancy in that I used the words again as we talked. But most important, I think, was the fact that they had had an experience with those words. It was vicarious, but it was an experience. The relation of their own experience to those words is what provided the meaning. It was not so much the "what" of those words, but the "how" of them.

Vocabulary, essential for comprehension, perhaps even the predominant causal factor (Yap, 1979), is of major concern in teaching reading. Average 6-year-olds may have mastered 14,000 words by the time they arrive at the first-grade classroom (Carey, 1978). Now they must begin to recognize these words in print. Thus, reading begins with children clutching their preprimers, primers, and first-grade readers trying to learn how to recognize words whose meaning they already know. As they master these, they begin to be presented with words whose meanings they do not know. The emphasis on word recognition in the early years begins to be replaced with an emphasis on word meaning.

Not only do unfamiliar words have to be learned, but new meanings for old words also have to be mastered. First graders may know that "rushes" means "hurries," but in a fourth-grade text, they will someday have to learn that it can also mean "tall grasses with hollow stems" and by the time they get to a sixth-grade text, they may need the meaning "prints of movie scenes processed directly after the shooting for review by the director or producer." By high school they are learning an average of 3,000 words every year (Nagy, Herman, & Anderson, 1985).

How the vast repertoire of vocabulary is built from childhood to adulthood depends largely upon informal social interaction and reading (Vygotsky, 1978). Teachers try to increase vocabulary by using a number of methods.

Perhaps the most popular and possibly the most dreary is the traditional total class activity in which students write 20 or more words, define them, write a sentence using them, and get to define them again in the weekly test after which time they may or may not be used again. The fallacy of this definition-memorization method is illumined in Charles Dickens's novel, *Hard Times*. The harsh schoolmaster, Gradgrind, who reveres facts, asks Girl No. 20 for her definition of a horse. She knows what a horse is from experience, but she is so terrified by Gradgrind that she is unable to answer. The schoolmaster calls on a boy named Bitzer: "Quadruped. Graminivorous. Forty teeth, namely twenty-four grinders, four eye-teeth, and twelve incisive. Sheds coat in the spring in marshy countries, sheds hoofs too. Hoofs hard, but requiring to be shod with iron. Age known by marks in mouth."

Thus (and much more) Bitzer.

"Now girl number twenty," said Mr. Gradgrind. "You know what a horse is."

The assumption that Bitzer or Girl No. 20 know from this definition what a horse is is questionable, yet today's youngsters are still being asked to regurgitate definitions à la Gradgrind. Both the precision and the ambiguity of language can be appreciated in George Miller's statement, "The meaning of any word depends on how it works together with other words in the same lexical field to cover or represent the conceptual field. If that statement sounds vague, then it accurately captures the flavor of most writing on this subject" (1978, p. 94).

"Essentially ambiguous" is the way Estes and Vaughan (1978) describe language. Inherent in their paragraph which follows is the suggestion that the only way to bring students to vocabulary is to let them have experiences:

> What a word means to any two people must be different, for if it were exactly the same, their experiences and hence their conceptualization associated with the word, would need be the same. *Exactly* the same. And that is both impossible and undesirable if language (or anything else) is to work. Thus, the meanings which students have for words (notice that words don't have meaning; people have meaning for words) are essentially different. The purpose of vocabulary development is to allow people to share their individual experiences and to provide them opportunity to have common experiences out of which may grow a richer meaningful vocabulary for every person involved. (p. 185)

Teaching isolated words and expecting a definition of them on the typical Friday test is a mistake. Devoid of experience and context, possibly used only that week and rarely again, they are apart from meaning and quickly forgotten.

Teachers use many methods to help students both remember words and determine their meanings. From teaching the meanings of the word parts (prefixes, suffixes, and root words) to exercises of closure (filling in what is missing), teachers are always looking for ways to enrich vocabulary development. Crossword puzzles, word hunts, matching games (word to definition), creation of their own words using known roots and affixes (*pyroped*—a foot of fire), or substitution of their own words for known ones (*pyrobelcher*—a volcano), are commonly used strategies to help students acquire vocabulary.

Teaching students how to use the dictionary and thesaurus takes up a variable amount of time in schools today. They must learn how to use alphabetical order, guide words, pronunciation keys, and deal with multiple meanings and the ofttimes circularity of the dictionary. The latter was beautifully illustrated in an Ernie Bushmiller "Nancy" cartoon. Nancy comes across the word "frustrate" and says, "Frustrate—I must look up that word." Looking in the dictionary, she reads that "frustrate means to thwart." The third panel of the comic strip shows her finding that "thwart means to balk," the next has her finding, "balk—to foil," the next, "foil—to baffle," and to the last panel which has her head revolving as she reads, "baffle—to FRUSTRATE." Question marks circling her head, Nancy has arrived back at square one, but not before she has taught us how frustratingly circular using the dictionary can be for youngsters.

Vocabulary, that many-splendored thing, is built upon meaning and interest. Teachers need to convey their own joy of reading so that children, infused with the magic of words, become like a certain novelist's mother who read Dickens in the spirit in which she would have eloped with him.

READING COMPREHENSION

Comprehension and Schema Theory

Frequently heard in the teacher's lunchroom in any school is this plaint: "Then there's Leslie. That child can read the words perfectly, even reads with expression. Only trouble is that Leslie doesn't understand one word of what was read. What am I going to do with Leslie?"

Despite a large part of the basal reading programs' attention to comprehension exercises, despite a clamorous cacophony of specific comprehension skill booklets entitled "Finding the Facts," "Getting the Main Idea," "Using the Context," "Locating the Answer," and so forth, comprehension remains a challenging teaching category for teachers.

The prevailing view of reading comprehension is dominated by schema theory. It is radically different from the conventional one that perceived comprehension as a matter of determining the units (words, phrases, sentences) of a paragraph. One was supposed to progress from the meaning of a word to the meaning of a phrase, to the meaning of a sentence. Then on to a paragraph, a page, and "Eureka!" one supposedly understood what had been read. It was akin to revelation.

Today, comprehension is viewed as building meaning from text. The main ideas and inferences must still be found, but the search is easier if one has enough prior knowledge and enough of a schema with which to look for it. Those who have these prerequisites may be able to find the main idea automatically upon reading a paragraph, while others may have to use other strategies.

This was found to be the case by Afflerbach (1990), who had anthropology doctoral students and chemistry doctoral students read texts in both subject areas, one of which was familiar to them and the other unfamiliar. He found that expert readers could automatically construct the main idea significantly more often when reading texts about familiar topics. "In contrast, when the text was unfamiliar and prior knowledge was lacking, the reader might have to restructure an existing schema to accommodate the unfamiliar text or construct a new schema" (p. 42).

Advance Organizers

A device that seems to help readers construct schemata when their own are sparse is the "advance organizer." Devised by David Ausubel (1960), it is, practically speaking, a general reading selection about a subject that will be taught in a more specific way later. It is based on a study by him in which undergraduates who had read a passage on a general level about "alloys" understood more of an abstract selection about "steel," than those students who had not read the passage about "alloys." Ausubel's language of "subsuming" new material with old material is today's language of "instantiating" slots in one's schema. For a teacher, this would translate into giving students as much background as possible to prepare them for the particular work to come.

Content-Area Reading

Simultaneously helping students to understand the content of what they are reading while enhancing their reading skills has come to be called *content-area reading*. The reason for the current attachment of importance to content reading has been noted incisively by Bean and Readance (1989):

> There are at least three aspects of reading at the secondary level that strongly suggest a need for content area teachers to incorporate reading strategies into their instruction: (1) a change in instructional emphasis from learning to read to reading to learn, (2) a change in the nature of instructional texts as students advance through the grades, and (3) a recent change in curricular emphasis that corresponds to our growing use of technology. (p. 16)

Techniques such as the three-level guide (Herber, 1978) have students arrive at the literal, interpretive, and applicative levels of comprehension concerning what they have read whether it is math, science, literature, or history. A technique that enhances the understanding of text structure is the pattern guide (Estes & Vaughan, 1978). The pattern of the author (cause/effect, comparison, listing, sequence, etc.) is used to get students to understand what they have read.

Content-area textbooks also describe techniques for studying, taking notes, outlining, and preparing for exams. One of these study methods, called *SQ3R*, has been so popular that it has a number of versions, but they are all variations of *surveying* a text, converting the chapter headings to *questions*, then *reading*, *reciting*, and *reviewing* what has been read.

Other aids to help students chunk information and understand narrative or expository text have been called cognitive maps, semantic networks, structured overviews, flow charts, causal chains, and hierarchical representations. Essentially, they are diagrams that help students to see as graphically as possible the interrelationships of the concepts they have read about. Anything that teachers can do to help students learn how to organize information and ideas for themselves is to be applauded.

Matching Materials to Reading Levels

The results of standardized reading achievement tests and informal reading tests administered to students give teachers an idea of what is called a student's "reading level" (Fry, 1972). Although one cannot be certain about the meaning of any "level" of reading, these tests can help teachers match materials to students.

Material that is too difficult for the student to comprehend despite all the help a teacher may give that student should be avoided. It is considered to be on a *frustrational* level. Material is considered to be at an *instructional* level if with the teacher's help, readers can recognize more than 90% of the words correctly, and understand about 75% of the text. If readers can understand the material without any help from the teacher, it is said to be on their *independent* reading level.

Devices that measure readability (the quality of a reading selection that makes it easy or difficult to read) are called *readability formulas* or *graphs* (Bormuth, 1968; Klare, 1974). One of the most popular and easy to use is Fry's (1977) extended readability graph, shown in Figure 14.1. Fry suggests the following steps:

1. Randomly select three 100-word passages from near the beginning, middle, and end of the selection or book.
2. Count the total number of sentences in each 100-word passage (estimating to the nearest tenth of a sentence). Average these three numbers.
3. Count the total number of syllables in each 100-word sample. There is a syllable for each vowel sound. For example: cat (1), blackbird (2), continental (4). Do not be fooled by word size. For example, *polio* has three syllables, *through* has one. Endings such as -y, -ed, -el, or -le usually make a syllable. For example: ready (2), bottle (2). (A suggestion made by Fry is that you put a mark above every syllable after the first in each polysyllabic word and add 100 to your total count of marks.) Average the total number of syllables for the three 100-word samples.

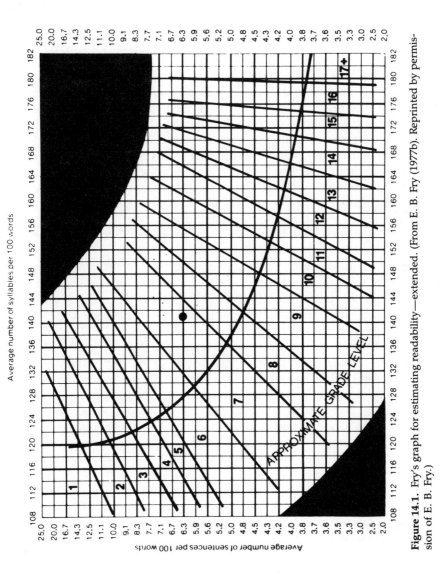

Average number of syllables per 100 words

Average number of sentences per 100 words

Figure 14.1. Fry's graph for estimating readability—extended. (From E. B. Fry (1977b). Reprinted by permission of E. B. Fry.)

4. Plot on the accompanying graph the following example from Fry (1972): Assume that the number of sentences in each of three 100-word passages is 6.6, 5.5, and 6.8. The average is 6.3. The number of syllables in each of the passages is 124, 141, and 158. The average is 141. The dot shows where the two averages converge, and falls into the seventh-grade area.
5. If a great deal of variability is found, more samples to determine an average should be used.

Readability formulas depend only on such linguistic variables as sentence length, vocabulary, and/or syllable count. They cannot measure the difficulty of the concepts that the author wishes to convey. Their usefulness comes in giving a teacher some basis for determining the difficulty of a reading selection, deciding which textbook to order without relying on the reading level that the publisher has arrived at, comparing books when given a choice in ordering texts, and comparing individual stories or chapters in a book. (In some books, middle parts or end parts are easier than the beginning ones.)

Through such a readability graph or formula, the teacher can theoretically match reading material to students' reading levels, but as George Gershwin had it, "It ain't necessarily so." What is important to remember in both testing of students and testing of text is that both assessments are imperfect. That said, one has to confess that both standardized tests and readability formulas are better than nothing.

The Reading or Content Lesson. A reading or content lesson is often viewed as having three parts. These can be called Prereading, During Reading, and After Reading (Hyde & Bizar, 1989) or Pre-reading Anticipation, Information Search, and Reflective Reaction (Estes & Vaughan, 1978). What happens in an ideal lesson is that students activate their own schemata or are given some kind of prior knowledge to handle what they are about to read, then do the reading, and then discuss and reflect upon what they have learned and decide where they can go from there to learn more.

DRTA. One strategy for helping students understand text is called DRTA (Directed Reading-Thinking Activities), devised by Stauffer (1969), whose objective was to get students to read critically. He outlined a plan that was a problem-solving approach to reading that could be used with fiction or nonfiction. Stauffer suggested that the teacher set the climate for DRTA with frequent use of the questions, "What do you think?" "Why do you think so?" and "Can you prove it?" This approach leads to a stronger interaction between student and text than the conventional passive one of reading and answering the mostly recall questions of the teacher.

It is hoped that students will continue to read on their own and learn on their own when they leave school. Seen in this light, the process of learning to read resembles the psychological journey we make from symbiosis through separation to individuation detailed by the British psychoanalyst D.W. Winnicott (1965). Critical to the manner in which this journey is accomplished is the quality of the relationship between mother (or nurturing figure) and child. If the mother is too symbiotically involved with her child, anticipating every need before it is even expressed, successful psychological development will be impaired. If the mother is not attentive enough, the child's ego development will be hampered. Winnicott coined the term "the good-enough mother" for the mother who provides the proper facilitating environment for her child by not being too good or too bad, but just "good-enough."

So too in the process of learning to read, the "good-enough teacher" provides a facilitating environment that makes reading a warm, welcoming, nurturing, delicious affair. This teacher goes from helping children tremendously to giving them the wherewithal to separate from this help and become people who read on their own and love it.

SUMMARY

The chapter opens with the comment that all theories concerning the teaching of reading reduce to two components: learning what the words say (decoding), and what the words mean (comprehension). It continues with a historical overview beginning with the seventeenth-century emphasis upon serial associations, through "bottom-up" and "top-down" approaches, and concludes with the interactive mode which combines the two. The developmental stages of reading are then considered, always with an emphasis upon the interactive aspects of decoding and comprehension, taken as a function of age. In the process, technical matters such as phonics, syllabication, affixes, vocabulary, advance organizers, content-area reading, and readability measures are discussed.

15

Epilogue and Prologue
A Look to the Future

> When I was just a little girl
> I asked my mother, "what will I be?"
> "Will I be pretty?
> Will I be rich?"
> Here's what she said to me:
> "Que sera, sera!
> Whatever will be will be.
> The future's not ours to see.
> Que sera, sera."*

If the authors of these lyrics are correct, then this chapter and the ageless efforts of enchanters, financial advisors, fortune tellers, magicians, oracles, witch doctors, and warlocks have all been exercises in futility. More importantly, the implications of such a shoulder-shrug attitude are enormous. Such a position runs counter to past and present views of education in the United States, which included the firm belief that what takes place in the future will be determined in part by the nature and the quality of what transpires in schools. There is probably general agreement that *a* goal, if not *the* goal, of formal education is to assist students in coming to understand themselves and the society in which they live and, thereby, increase the possibility that they can play a productive and

---

satisfying part in society's—and their—future. Such understanding will not cause us to know the future, but should provide the base for reasoned thoughts about, and shaping of, what is to come.

Thomas Jefferson and other founders of this country saw a bleak future for "republican institutions" without education. Benjamin Franklin and others saw the future economic health of the nation as being shaped by the education provided in the schools. Although few laid claim to their ability to see specifics about the future, all had visions of it, and the relationship of education to it. In this regard, there is little question that Americans have differed in the past and continue to differ today on the approach they take toward determining the pertinent psychological and educational issues. With respect to psychology, the American scene has witnessed the different points of view offered by functionalism (purposivity), associationism (contiguity between events), Russian dialectical-materialist psychology (classical conditioning), behaviorism (action), gestalt psychology (insight), psychoanalysis (unconscious dynamics), and cognitive psychology (mind and the computer metaphor). Although each of these approaches has *necessary* implications for understanding what goes on during the educational process, none has been *sufficient*. Education is its own undertaking. But, as with psychology, there is no single prevailing viewpoint. (A thorough exploration of variables possibly affecting the future of educational psychology is available for the advanced research student in Wittrock & Farley, 1989.)

However, two matters are clear: First, there is unanimity among American educators that serious deficiencies exist in the country's system of education. Second, there is near unanimity on the group of important issues that will affect the structure and function of education in the future. There is, however, wide disagreement as to the way the issues will play out, and the way they should be addressed in order to be most effective in improving the education of students and reforming the system. Agreeing on the *set* of issues to be addressed, but differing broadly on *approaches* to be taken are such wide ranging groups as the U.S. Department of Education, the Malcolm Issues Management Program (supported by the Michigan Board of Education), the Holmes Group, the Consortium for Excellence in Teacher Education, the National Education Association, the United Federation of Labor, and the college undergraduates enrolled in education departments and teacher-training programs across the country, to name but a few. Before considering a portion of this set of issues, we should turn to a few of the factors that influence the way major issues are approached by different individuals and groups.

GENERAL AND INDIVIDUAL FACTORS

Focusing on teachers and teaching, the factors shaping the future of educational practices can be divided into two categories—those which apply to members of the teaching profession as a whole or to large subgroups thereof, and those which are shaped by the personality and particular experiences of individual teachers. In the first category are included such things as society's attitudes toward school teaching, the aims of schools, and school structure and control. The second category includes such matters as the personality and energy of individual teachers. Each of these categories requires brief attention.

General Factors

Society's Attitude toward Teaching. One line of thinking suggests that the enormous scale of the educational enterprise, its percentage of the gross national product, its historic place in American life, and its alleged importance in the American democratic system, would produce for teachers a strategic position in our socially differentiated society. If true, this would yield for teachers a highly desirable level of access to status, income, and power. Such is not and, in spite of nostalgia about earlier days, has never been the case. Although the profession has much to recommend it as a career choice, it does not fare well in prestige, immediate influence on the general public, or income when compared with other career pursuits requiring similar levels of academic preparation. Nor does it fare well in income and short-range influence when compared with numerous trades, the entry into which requires no postsecondary education. This observation has been made over and over again during the last century. Joseph M. Rice in his report in the late nineteenth century (reprinted in 1969); James B. Conant in three books published in the 1960s (1961, 1963, 1967); and *A Nation at Risk* (1983) all make this point. The national attention to education, of which Rice and Conant's works were earlier parts, was followed by brief flurries of activity intended to address a number of issues, including the preparation and status of teachers.

For example, much has been said about the extent to which the academic abilities of undergraduates planning teaching careers lag behind those of other students. Data necessary to make definitive statements are hard to come by; nonetheless, evidence is included in several national studies such as Feistritzer (1986), *A Nation Prepared: Teachers for the 21st Century* (1986), and *A Nation at Risk* (1983). But as noted in a subsequent section on individual characteristics of teachers, although academic ability above a reasonable level is certainly necessary, other qualities are much more important in determining "the good teacher."

The value society assigns to an activity is often shown in the remuneration participants in that activity receive. "You get what you pay for," is widely accepted axiom of the marketplace. It suggests that American society does not expect to get much from teachers. Few members of school boards would trust their luxury automobiles, or even their mid-price domestic or foreign cars, to mechanics earning what the average teacher earns. There has been improvement in teachers' salaries during the last two decades, but most careers requiring comparable education, and some requiring less, provide higher remuneration to those in them. Teachers more than anyone else are aware of this income differential. To assume that such a situation does not influence the way teachers feel about and act in their work is to assign them undeserved virtue and a giving spirit.

There will, of course, be numerous occasions when widespread admiration and respect is directed toward a teacher, a department, or a school. But if one thinks in terms of the profession itself, then the student interested in teaching must look within himself or herself, to others in the profession, and to the success of his or her students for affirmation of career choice. For those who can do this, the satisfaction is enormously gratifying—perhaps unmatched by other professions.

Aims of Schools. Changing patterns in American family and social life are among the factors influencing educational practices and, in the process of change, the schools are being severely strained. Schools are expected to transmit the cultural heritage, inculcate moral and ethical values, teach the basic academic skills, prepare students for meaningful employment, address difficult and perplexing social problems, and provide stability in a culture in which the family is but one of a wide range of individual/institutional relationships that are undergoing change. In this period of flux, there is no clear set of priorities to guide what is expected of schools and teachers. Increasingly, outspoken parents and community groups press for one or another objective as do employers, policymakers, and the students themselves. In attempting to respond to so wide a range of pressures, practices in schools mirror the uncertainty of the policymakers and the public at large concerning both the priorities to be followed and the values that undergird them. In part, the confusion is inherent in the age-old questions: Is morality relative to specific experience within cultures and situations? Does morality rest upon universal principles of right and wrong, rules that are appreciated in maturational stages? Is morality essentially a biological trait that functions in terms of what is life-sustaining for most people? In a democracy, is morality the school's business at all? (A brief, useful statement on moral development is available in Robert Hogan's description, 1977.)

School Structure and Control. Research suggests that the quality of leadership in a school is a key factor in determining the degree to which it is a successful place for learning (Bennett, 1988; Rutter, Maughan, Mortimer, & Smith, 1979). The school head sets the tone and determines what discipline and order is necessary to provide an environment in which students and teachers can most efficiently pursue the acquisition of knowledge and the development of intellect and character. A wide range of styles exists among those who would qualify as good leaders. Unfortunately, the measure by which school administrators are frequently judged is often less concerned with the quality of the learning that takes place within the environment than it is with structure and order. Appointments and promotions may instead go to those whose schools have orderly classrooms, clean halls, and timely done paperwork. The more important matter of learning is less easily evaluated and therefore may receive less attention. Perhaps these administrators are aware of the suggestion made in Bagley, 1907, pp. 96–97. Principals and teachers are advised that "your success in your life's work depends upon your success in . . . [getting order] more than it depends on anything else." Some school personnel sense and object to this short-sighted view of leadership. When combined with and exacerbated by insufficient financial resources, crowded classrooms, and differences related to negotiations between school districts and teachers' organizations, low morale and internal conflicts result.

At an earlier time, school structure was perceived as contributing to the sense of community among teachers and administrators. This was reflected in the use of the terms *principal* or *headmaster* and *headmistress* (the latter two, while still in use in independent schools, are increasingly giving way to the gender-neutral term "head") to imply that the administrator was the "principal" or foremost teacher or the headmaster or headmistress among the other masters and mistresses responsible for instruction. The declining use of "master" and "mistress" is probably due to their autocratic sounds and the implied conflict they suggest for an educational system charged with training students for a democratic society. Their passing is not to be mourned, but the relationship symbolized by them and by the original use of "principal" is a more serious loss. Because of the size of schools, because administrators are seen as management in the negotiation process, because teachers have little to say in decision-making of the day-to-day operation of schools, and because administrators are often not permitted to take regular teaching responsibilities, the sense of collegiality between teachers and administrators has declined. This trend must be reversed.

Individual Factors

The factors mentioned so far influence educational practice in ways that are indirect but nevertheless powerful. Much more direct in influence are factors that are shaped by teachers' individual personalities and experiences. Two of these which are of special importance—personality and energy—deserve our attention.

Personality and Energy. Care should be taken not to place undue emphasis on the highest intellectual and academic abilities as a prerequisite for successful teaching. *If we accept a quite high minimum standard*, the factors influencing educational practice (and determining success in teaching) relate more to personality and energy than to IQ and to course grades. Most university students have encountered brilliant scholars who were poor teachers and, perhaps more common, the well-educated person who lacks practical, operational wisdom and those required abilities necessary to convey information to others, and to stimulate intellectual growth. Published works on great teachers indicate that a profile of the successful personality would be difficult to put together. Nevertheless, there are some things that can safely be said. Persons with considerable energy who feel strongly about that which they teach, who have a rational or intuitive grasp of what is involved in the teaching/learning process, and who like what they are doing and the youth with whom they work have a high likelihood of success.

SIX ISSUES IN THE FUTURE

Having examined several general and individual factors that will determine the future of education in this country, we can now turn with some confidence to consideration of the issues they helped to bring into existence.

1. *Society's needs.* The perception of education as failing to meet the needs of society is seen as a continuing issue, the reform efforts now underway not withstanding. Several reasons for this exist. One is the significant developments in public education that have occurred in quite a few foreign countries, compared to which the United States consid-

ered itself to be far more advanced only a short time ago. A second is the variability of quality of educational opportunities available to students in the United States from state to state, from district to district, and from school to school within a district. These factors include financial resources available in the state and in the district, educational background and income of students' families, the influence of issues related to race and ethnicity, the quality of school leadership and faculties, and many others. The broad range of individual student needs further complicates the matter. A third reason for the perception of a failing educational system is the absence of consensus as to what society wishes of education. This results, in part, from slowness to build a new consensus to replace that which gave way to movements designed to correct prior and current serious problems. Current conditions witness very different views of education among the many identifiable groups in society. The "establishment" desires that education continue to be an instrument for cultural transmission and conformity. Those perceiving themselves as outside the establishment want education to be an instrument for further change. People in various groups want it to produce patriotic citizens, but differ as to the appropriate expressions of patriotism. Some want schools to stress good citizenship and moral values. Others want them to produce productive citizens for an industrial or postindustrial society. The combinations of views about what *should* form the consensus are quite varied.

Differences have long existed over what society wants of its schools, but the present situation presents an added difficulty. In the past, criticism of schools existed side by side with a widespread perception that universal education served societal needs, and that public education in "common schools" was a public good. Today there is nearly uniform feeling that society is not well served by the existing educational system. However, there is no consensus on what the Malcolm Issues Management Program (Michigan Board of Education) calls the "sense of mission"; or even that public schools as the major basis of a national system of education is a good thing.

What is the reason for this loss of consensus? By far, the most important explanation is to be found in the massive changes in many aspects of late-twentieth-century society. Urban growth, changing family structures, wide-ranging social values, efforts of oppressed groups to participate fully in life of the community, growing expectations of what the school should do, and giant leaps in technology are but a few of these. Rapid changes in socioeconomic life, coupled with the slowness of formal education to make changes, produces increased discontinuity between life inside and outside the schools. Reforms have sought to tinker with the system in an effort to make existing practices work more effectively. But reform efforts have given insufficient recognition to the degree to which existing practices are themselves part of the problem. It is our expectation, supported by the views of students and skilled observers, that a decade from now, a wide variety of (sometimes conflicting) educational policies and practices will still be distinguishable to those persons who devote their attention to them today, and that the issue of consensus will still be part of the educational debate.

2. *Educational reform.* The sense that systemic problems exist is seen as likely to produce more talk about educational reform itself. There is likely to be an increase in the frequency with which one hears the terms *education governor* applied to chief executives in various states and the *education decade* applied to the 1990s. Presidential campaigns are likely to devote great quantities of rhetoric to the need for reform in education. There are some indications that parents and educators are joining together to move beyond talk, but such groupings have no significant history of success in providing leadership for change. Successful implementation of reform by nongovernmental agencies, desirable as it might be, is not clearly in the picture. There will, perhaps, be more involvement of individuals and institutions that have not traditionally been directly engaged with public education. Examples of this can be seen in the "Adopt a Class" program of the I Have a Dream Foundation (established by E.M. Lang in New York), in the takeover of the administration of a public school district by Boston University, and in the interest currently expressed in the use of educational vouchers. Whether and how well these succeed may depend more on a host of economic, social, and political issues than on the educational merits of the case.

3. *Racial, ethnic, and socioeconomic separation.* The present state of de facto separation of school districts along racial lines is likely to be viewed as less of a problem in the next 10 years than in the last decade. This appears to be due not so much to the success of education breaking through racial and class barriers, as to the tendency to accept such separate arrangements as "the way things are." This attitude exists despite information from the U.S. Bureau of the Census (1991) which shows that 31.9% of black households and 17.9% of Hispanic households are headed by a single person who is parent to at least one child under 18 years of age. For the whole population, the percentage is 11.5. To the degree that class status is determined by income, it is discouraging to learn that the growth of the black and Hispanic middle class has been actively flat in the two decades from 1970 to 1989. In 1989, 40.9% of black families and 33.9% of Hispanic families had incomes under $15,000. Middle-class black and Hispanic parents appear increasingly to respond,

like other middle-class parents, by moving to suburban or other areas where schools are perceived as "better," or to send their children to nonpublic schools (*Statistical Abstract of the United States*, 1991). Inasmuch as class divisions tend to follow race and ethnic lines, urban public schools are becoming increasingly black and Hispanic. Conversely, because of the smaller percentages of blacks and Hispanics in the middle class, whites are in considerably higher proportions in suburban public schools than in the population. This produces the alarming prospect that even greater distance will exist between have and have-not schools with the division being largely along race/ethnic lines. The result will be a continuation of the decline in the number of able, highly motivated students from public schools, and of able lay leadership from among parents living in urban districts. Schools will have to adjust increasingly to situations in which urban minority parents have not themselves had many of the experiences that their children need to encounter, in order to attain academic success. This will include situations in which the parents' inability to aid their children in dealing constructively with subtle prejudice and discrimination may interfere with the student's academic achievement, unless schools can begin to address issues with which they have not dealt well in the past. (Implicit discrimination is a more insidious matter than dealing with the blatant expressions of segregation that preceded the court-ordered end in the 1960s to de jure segregation and de facto segregation based on race.)

4. *Professionalization of teaching*. The preparation of teachers will continue to draw national attention. Increased efforts will be made to attract able college graduates into the teaching profession, to make teacher training more relevant to the demands placed on teachers in today's schools, and to further professionalize education. As one looks at differences between current reform efforts and those of earlier periods, the present level of involvement of teachers in efforts to further professionalize the profession is an encouraging sign.

5. *Relations among teachers, administrators, and parents*. Alongside the positive efforts of school administrators and teachers to work together on matters of teacher preparation, there continues to be widespread tension and conflict in the area of collective bargaining for salary and working conditions. College undergraduates perceive this as one of their important concerns. The Malcolm Issues Management Program admonishes teachers, administrators, and board members to reverse the trend of disagreement and conflict. Our personal observations in schools reveal too many examples of arbitrary actions on both sides that are detrimental to quality education. Groups of parents and citizens will increasingly call for lessening this conflict over the next few years. In

this, the quality of leadership in teacher organizations and in school boards will be of primary importance.

6. *Education of younger and older populations.* A final important issue for the next decade is the expansion of services of organized education to a larger group of clients, mainly to people older and younger than the traditional school-age student. This is by no means new. Early childhood education and adult education have been around for some time. What is new is that the changes taking place in society make it both mandatory and desirable that we address the educational needs of "preschool" children and of senior citizens with a new urgency.

Growth in the number of single-parent homes and families in which both parents work outside the home raises questions about the welfare of children in the first four or five years of life. This is much more than a problem of a caretaker while the parent(s) works. These are crucial years during which children traditionally learn much about society from interaction with their parents, and the interaction of their parents with others in the community. Simple security and comfort during the parents' working hours, provided by even the best monitor, is not sufficient. The experiences of young children of working parents need to become part of our overall program of education. At the other end of the age continuum, the expansion in available years has not been matched by improvement in the quality of life. The same kind of serious attention to the needs of this group is necessary to produce a comprehensive program of education that matches our concept of health care, prenatal to old age.

The Tension between Prediction and Unfolding

Two and a half centuries ago, the English philosopher John Stuart Mill addressed the same issue of seeing and influencing the future, but from a very different view. He wrote:

> However universal the laws of social development may be, they cannot be more universal or more rigorous than those of the physical agencies of nature; yet human will can convert these into instruments of its design. . . . Human and social facts, from their more complicated nature, are not less, but more, modifiable than mechanical and chemical facts; human agency, therefore, has still greater power over time. . . . [T]hose who maintain that evolution of society depends exclusively, or almost exclusively, on general causes, always include among these the collective knowledge and intellectual development of the race. (Mill, 1843/1962, p. 149)

This is a far cry from the predestination of the lyricist quoted at the start of this chapter. It suggests that the human can foresee the future and, through the shaping of institutions and the molding of people's thinking, can collectively determine what changes should take place. Mill used collective knowledge as providing insight about the future and placed importance on the need to develop ideas to conform with the future as best it can be perceived. The temptation for many in education is to lean too strongly toward Mill. Indeed, much of the curriculum used in schools today suggests that curriculum builders believe not only that the future can be clearly foreseen, but that they uniquely possess the vision which dictates what specific knowledge students should have. But such a view of Mill has the problem of assigning undue directness to the relationship between education and knowledge of the future, in the same way the lyricist has the problem of ignoring completely such a relationship. Perhaps a different view, one which combines elements of both positions, is more useful in finding a rationale for a closing chapter on the future of education. Advancements in knowledge have greatly improved man's ability to "foresee" coming events, to predict with reasonable accuracy some things about the physical world, and—though considerably less successfully—how large groups of people are likely to act under certain circumstances. These improvements are a result of careful study of the relationship between present and past, and of important advancements in the tools for recording and measurement. Since our present relationships to the future is comparable to the past's relationship to the present, such study increases the possibility of "foreseeing" what will take place. Furthermore, study of past–present relationships make clear that the present is shaped to greater or lesser degree by what has preceded it. And since from the perspective of the future, the present is part of the past, decisions we make and actions we take today play a part in determining what the future will be.

CONCLUDING STATEMENT

It seems fairly simple to say that the future is determined by what has preceded it, and thus knowledge of the past and present can provide what we need to know to foretell and influence the future. That such is not the case has been commented upon or reflected in the works of an endless number of writers over the centuries. Edward Bellamy, in an early-twentieth-century book, *Looking Backward*, pointed out that the seeds of change can be identified when one looks back in time. He saw in his time the seeds for the utopian changes he predicted for the world some years hence. That that utopia has not arrived does not mean that the clues Bellamy thought he saw did not exist. In hindsight, man has always had great vision. And the same clues to change are visible when one looks ahead, but they are scattered among a massive collection of false clues and random events in such a way as to make crystal-ball gazing a very imperfect science at best. What crystal ball to use or what clues to consider is our question when we think of the future of education.

One final remark of a general nature before bringing this chapter to a close. We have stated that past and present events shape the future, at least retrospectively. To the degree that our actions today are determined by the way we perceive the future, it might also be said that the future shapes the present. It is this line of reasoning that makes it an important exercise to consider even in cursory fashion, the future of education in the United States. We need also to remind ourselves of John W. Gardner's cautionary statement to a class of high school graduates: "as the French say, be sure you want the consequences of what you want" (Commencement Address, Sidwell Friends School, June, 1986). Or, as the same idea has been expressed with a slightly different arrangement of the words, "Be careful of the things you say you want in the future. You may get them."

References

Adler, A. (1964). *The practice and theory of individual psychology* (P. Radin, Trans.). London: Routledge & Kegan Paul. (Original work published 1923)

Adler, K. A. (1977). Alfred, Adler (1870–1937). In B. B. Wolman (Ed.), *International encyclopedia of psychiatry, psychology, psychoanalysis, and neurology* (Vol. 1, pp. 235–240). New York: Van Nostrand Reinhold.

Afflerbach, P. P. (1990). The influence of prior knowledge on expert reader's main idea constructing strategies. *Reading Research Quarterly, 25*(1), 31–45.

Alexander, L. (1991). *American 2000: An education strategy.* Washington, DC: U.S. Department of Education.

American Educational Research Association, American Psychological Association, & National Council on Measurement in Education. (1985). *Standards for educational and psychological testing.* Washington, DC.

American Educational Research Association, American Psychological Association, & National Council on Measurement in Education. (1988). *The code of fair testing practices in education.* Washington, DC.

A nation at risk: The imperative for educational reform. (1983). National Commission on Excellence in Education. Washington, DC: U.S. Department of Education.

A nation prepared: Teachers for the 21st century. (1986). New York: Carnegie Forum on Education and the Economy.

Anderson, R. C., Hiebert, E. H., Scott, J. A., & Wilkinson, I. A. G. (Eds.). (1985). *Becoming a nation of readers: The report of the commission on reading.* Washington, DC: National Institute of Education.

Angoff, W. H. (1987). *Philosophical issues of current interest to measurement theorists.* Princeton, NJ: Educational Testing Service.

Astin, A. W., & Green, K. C. (1987). The American freshman: An overview of the data. In A. W. Astin, K. C. Green, & W. S. Korn (Eds.), *The American freshman: Twenty year trends, 1966–1985.* Los Angeles: Higher Education Research Institute, UCLA.

Aulls, M. W. (1982). *Developing readers in today's elementary school.* Boston: Allyn & Bacon.

Ausubel, D. (1960). The use of advance organizers in learning and retention of meaningful verbal material. *Journal of Educational Psychology, 51,* 267–272.

Baars, B. J. (1986). *The cognitive revolution in psychology.* New York: Guilford Press.

Bagley, W. (1907). *Classroom management: Its principles and techniques.* New York: Macmillan.

Bain, A. (1891). *Education as a science.* New York: D. Appleton.

Bangert, R. L., Kulik, J. A., & Kulik, C.-L. C. (1983). Individualized systems of instruction in secondary schools. *Review of Educational Research, 53*(2), 142–158.

Bartlett, F. (1932). *Remembering: A study in experimental social psychology.* Cambridge, MA: Cambridge University Press.

Bean, T. W., & Readance, J. (1989). Content area reading: Current state of the art. In D. Lapp, J. Flood, & N. Farnan (Eds.), *Content area reading and learning: Instructional strategies* (pp. 14–19). Englewood Cliffs, NJ: Prentice-Hall.

Bennett, W. (1988). *American education: Making it work.* Washington, DC: U.S. Government Printing Office.

Berk, R. A. (Ed.). (1982). *Handbook of methods for detecting item bias.* Baltimore: Johns Hopkins University Press.

Berk, R. A. (Ed.). (1984). *A guide to criterion-referenced test construction.* Baltimore: Johns Hopkins University Press.

Bettleheim, B., & Zelan, K. (1982). *On learning to read: The child's fascination with meaning.* New York: Knopf.

Biniaminov, I., & Glasman, N. S. (1982). Possible determinants of holding power in Israeli secondary schools. *Journal of Educational Research, 76,* 81–88.

Birch, H. B., & Gussow, J. D. (1970). *Disadvantaged children: Health, nutrition and school failure.* New York: Harcourt Brace & World.

Bloom, B. S., Hastings, J. T., & Madaus, G. F. (1971). *Handbook on formative and summative evaluation of student learning.* New York: McGraw-Hill.

Bormuth, J. (1968). *Readability in 1968.* New York: National Conference on Research in English.

Brown, F. G. (1983). *Principles of educational and psychological testing.* New York: Holt, Rinehart & Winston.

Brown, R., & Fraser, C. (1963). The acquisition of syntax. In C. N. Cofer & B. Musgrave (Eds.), *Verbal behavior and learning* (pp. 158–197). New York: McGraw-Hill.

Cannell, J. J. (1987). *Nationally normed elementary achievement testing in America's public schools: How all 50 states are above the national average* (2nd ed.). Daniels, WV: Friends for Education.

Carlson, S. B. (1985). *Creative classroom testing.* Princeton, NJ: Educational Testing Service.

Cattell, J. M. (1886). The time it takes to see and name objects. *Mind, 11,* 63–65.

Chall, J. (1967). *Learning to read: The great debate.* New York: McGraw-Hill.

Chall, J. S. (1983). *Stages of reading development.* New York: McGraw-Hill.

Chipman, S. F., Davis, C., & Shafto, M. G. (1986). Personnel and training research program: Cognitive science at ONR. *Naval research reviews,* Vol. XXXVIII. Washington, DC: Office of Naval Research.

Chomsky, N. (1971). Review of B. F. Skinner, *Beyond freedom and dignity. The New York Review of Books, 17,* 18–24.

Chronicle of Higher Education, December 3, 1986, p. 1.

Conant, J. B. (1961). *Slums and suburbs.* New York: McGraw-Hill.

Conant, J. B. (1963). *The education of American teachers.* New York: McGraw-Hill.

Conant, J. B. (1967). *The comprehensive high school.* New York: McGraw-Hill.

Craik, F. I. M., & Lockhart, R. S. (1972). Levels of processing. *Journal of Verbal Learning and Verbal Behavior, 11,* 671–684.

Cronbach, L. J. (1951). Coefficient alpha and the internal structure of tests. *Psychometrika, 16,* 297–334.

Crowder, R. G. (1976). *Principles of learning and memory*. Hillsdale, NJ: Erlbaum.

DeHirsch, K., Jansky, J. J., & Langford, W. S. (1966). *Predicting reading failure*. New York: Harper & Row.

Dewey, J. (1940). *My pedagogic creed*. In *Education today by John Dewey*, J. Ratner (Ed.). New York: Putnam's Sons. (Original work published 1897)

Dewey, J. (1968). The reflex arc concept in psychology (excerpt). In R. J. Herrnstein and E. G. Boring (Eds.). *A source book in the history of psychology* (pp. 321–325). Cambridge, MA: Harvard University Press. (Original work published 1896)

Dey, E. L., Astin, A. W., & Korn, W. S. (1991). *The American freshman: Twenty-five year trends, 1966–1990*. Los Angeles: Higher Education Research Institute, UCLA.

Doehring, D., Trites, R., Patel, P., & Fiedorowicz, C. (1981). *Reading disabilities: The interaction of reading, language, and neuropsychological deficits*. New York: Academic Press.

Dunkin, M. J., & Barnes, J. (1986). Research on teaching in higher education. In M. C. Wittrock (Ed.), *Handbook of research on teaching* (pp. 754–777). New York: Macmillan.

Durkin, D. (1966). *Children who read early*. New York: Teachers College Press.

Dyer, H. S. (1980). *Parents can understand testing*. Columbia, MD: National Committee for Citizens in Education.

Ebel, R. L. (1979). *Essentials of educational measurement*. Englewood Cliffs, NJ: Prentice-Hall.

Ebel, R. L., & Frisbie, D. A. (1986). *Essentials of educational measurement*. Englewood Cliffs, NJ: Prentice-Hall.

Echternacht, G. (1977). Grade equivalent scores, *Measurement in Education, 8*(2). Washington, DC: National Council on Measurement in Education.

Edel, L. (Winter 1977/78). Portrait of the artist as an old man. *American Scholar, 47*, 52–68.

Educational Measurement: Issues and Practices. (1990). *9*(3). Washington, DC: National Council on Measurement in Education.

Egan, K. (1987). On learning: A response to Floden, Buchman, and Schwille. *Teachers College Record, 88*(4), 507–514.

Erikson, E. H. (1950). *Childhood and society*. New York: W. W. Norton.

Estes, T. H., & Vaughan, J. L. (1978). *Reading and learning in the content classroom*. Boston: Allyn & Bacon.

Evans, M., Taylor, N., & Blum, I. (1979). Children's written language awareness and its relation to reading acquisition. *Journal of Reading Behavior, 11*(1), 1–19.

Feinberg, L. (1990). Multiple-choice and its critics. *College Board Review. 157*. New York: College Entrance Examination Board.

Feistritzer, C. E. (1986). *The condition of teaching: A state by state analysis*. Princeton, NJ: Carnegie Foundation for the Advancement of Teaching.

Fenstermacher, G., & Soltis, J. (1986). *Approaches to teaching*. New York: Teachers College Press.

Fiske, E. B. (1987, January 6). *New York Times*, p. C1.

Flavell, J. H. (1977). *Cognitive psychology*. Englewood Cliffs, NJ: Prentice-Hall.

Flesch, R. (1955). *Why Johnny can't read and what you can do about it*. New York: Harper & Brothers.

Floden, R. E., Buchman, M., & Schwille, J. R. (1987). Breaking with everyday experience. *Teachers College Record, 88*(4), 485–506.

Frechtling, J. A. (1991). Performance assessment: Moonstruck or the real thing? *Educational Measurement: Issues and Practices, 10*(4), 23–25.

Frederiksen, N. (1984). The real test bias. *American Psychologist, 39*(3), 193–202.

Freud, S. (1957). *A general introduction to psychoanalysis*. New York: Permabooks.

Fry, E. (1972). *Reading instruction for classroom and clinic*. New York: McGraw-Hill.

Fry, E. (1977a). *Elementary reading instruction*. New York: McGraw-Hill.

Fry, E. A. (1977b). Fry's readability graph: Clarifications, validity, and extension to level 17. *Journal of Reading, 21*(3), 242–252.

Fulton, J. F. (1949). *Physiology of the nervous system* (rev. 3rd ed.). New York: Oxford University Press.

Ginsberg, H., & Opper, S. (1969). *Piaget's theory of intellectual development*. Englewood Cliffs, NJ: Prentice-Hall.

Goodman, J. S. (1967). Reading: A psycholinguistic guessing game. *Journal of the Reading Specialist, 6,* 126–135.

Gough, P., & Cosky, M. J. (1977). One second of reading again. In N. J. Castellan & D. Pisoni (Eds.), *Cognitive theory* (Vol. 2, pp. 271–288). Hillsdale, NJ: Erlbaum.

Grinker, R. R. (1958). A philosophical appraisal of psychoanalysis. In J. H. Masserman (Ed.), *Science and psychoanalysis* (Vol. 1, pp. 126–142). New York: Grune & Stratton.

Grunwald, B. (1973). Group procedures in the classroom. In H. H. Mosak (Ed.), *Alfred Adler: His influence on psychology today* (pp. 175–182). Park Ridge, NJ: Noyes Press.

Hall, C. S., & Lindzey, G. (1957). *Theories of personality*. New York: Wiley.

Harnad, S. (Ed.). (1978). A special issue on cognition and consciousness in nonhuman species. *Brain and Behavioral Sciences, 1,* 515–629.

Hefferline, R. F., Keenan, B., & Harford, R. A. (1959). Escape and avoidance conditioning in human subjects without their observation of the response. *Science, 130,* 1338–1339.

Herber, H. L. (1978). *Teaching reading in content areas*. Englewood Cliffs, NJ: Prentice-Hall.

Hilgard, E. R. (1980). Consciousness in contemporary psychology. *Annual Review of Psychology, 31,* 2–23.

Hogan, R. (1977). Moral development. In B. B. Wolman (Ed.), *International encyclopedia of psychiatry, psychology, psychoanalysis, and neurology* (Vol. 7, pp. 265–269). New York: Van Nostrand Reinhold.

Holland, J. G., & Skinner, B. F. (Eds.). (1965). An analysis of the behavioral processes involved in self-instruction with teaching machines. (Final report, grant number 71–31–0370–051.3, HEW, Office of Education.)

Hrapsky, J. S. (1981). *Effects of training in visual observation upon subsequent visual-motor performance*. Unpublished doctoral dissertation, Princeton University, Princeton, NJ.

Hurn, C. H., & Burn, B. B. (1982). An analytic comparison of educational systems. (Report prepared for National Commission on Excellence in Education.) Amherst, MA: University of Massachusetts.

Hyde, A. A., & Bizar, M. (1989). *Thinking in context*. New York: Harper & Row.

James, W. (1958). *Talks to teachers on psychology*. New York: W. W. Norton. (Original work published in 1899)

James, W. (1968). Principles of psychology (excerpt). In R. J. Herrnstein & E. G. Boring (Eds.), *A source book in the history of psychology* (pp. 609–610). Cambridge, MA: Harvard University Press. (Original work published in 1890)

Jones, E. E. (1986). Interpreting interpersonal behavior: The effects of expectancies. *Science, 234,* 41–46.

Jung, C. (1970). *Civilization in transition* (2nd ed.; R. F. C. Hull, Trans.). Princeton, NJ: Princeton University Press.

Just, M., & Carpenter, P. (1987). *The psychology of reading and language comprehension*. Boston: Allyn & Bacon.

Kamhi, A. G., & Catts, H. W. (1989). *Reading disabilities: A developmental language perspective*. Boston: Little, Brown.

Kant, I. (1965). *Critique of pure reason* (N. K. Smith, Trans.). New York: St. Martin's. (Original work published 1781)

Katz, D. (1989). *The world of touch.* L. E. Kreuger (Ed. and Trans.). Hillsdale, NJ: Erlbaum. (Original work published 1925)

Keller, F. S. (1937). *The definition of psychology.* New York: Appleton-Century.

Keller, F. S. (1968). "Goodbye, Teacher." *Journal of Applied Behavior Analysis, 1,* 78–79.

Keller, F. S., & Schoenfeld, W. N. (1950). *Principles of psychology.* New York: Appleton-Century-Crofts.

Kendler, H. H. (1986). Evolution rather than revolution. In B. J. Baars (Ed.), *The cognitive revolution in psychology* (pp. 110–122). New York: Guilford Press.

Kihlstrom, J. F. (1987). The cognitive unconscious. *Science, 237,* 1445–1452.

Klare, G. (1974). Assessing readability. *Reading Research Quarterly, 10,* 62–102.

Klatzky, R. L. (1980). *Human memory: Structures and processes* (2nd ed.). San Francisco: Freeman.

Kling, J. W., & Schrier, A. M. (1971). Positive reinforcement. In J. W. Kling & L. A. Riggs (Eds.), *Experimental psychology* (pp. 615–702). New York: Holt, Rinehart & Winston.

Koerner, J. D. (1963). *The miseducation of American teachers.* Boston: Houghton Mifflin.

Kohler, W. (1929). *Gestalt psychology.* New York: Liveright.

Kohler, W. (1969). *The task of gestalt psychology.* Princeton, NJ: Princeton University Press.

Kolata, G. (1987). Associations or rules in learning language? *Science, 237,* 133–134.

Kornilov, K. N. (1930). Psychology in the light of dialectical materialism. In C. Murchison (Ed.), *Psychologies of 1930* (pp. 243–278). Worcester, MA: Clark University Press.

Kourilsky, M., & Quaranta, L. (1987). *Effective teaching: Principles and practices.* Glenview, IL: Scott, Foresman.

Kuder, G. F., & Richardson, M. W. (1937). The theory of the estimation of test reliability. *Psychometrika, 2,* 151–160.

Kuhn, T. S. (1962/1970). *The structure of scientific revolutions* (2nd ed.). Chicago: University of Chicago Press.

Kulik, C.-L. C., Schwalb, B. J., & Kulik, J. A. (1982). Programmed instruction in secondary education. *Journal of Educational Research, 75,* 133–138.

LaBerge, D., & Samuels, S. J. (1974). Toward a theory of automatic information processing in reading. *Cognitive Psychology, 6,* 293–323.

Lachman, R., Lachman, J. L., & Butterfield, E. C. (1979). *Cognitive psychology and information processing: An introduction.* Hillsdale, NJ: Erlbaum.

Ladygina-Kots, N. N., & Dembovskii, Y. N. (1969). The psychology of primates. In M. Cole & I. Maltzman (Eds.), *A handbook of contemporary Soviet society* (pp. 41–70). New York: Basic Books.

La Mettrie, J. O. de. (1968). L'homme machine (excerpt). In R. J. Herrnstein & E. G. Boring (Eds.), *A source book in the history of psychology* (pp. 272–278). Cambridge, MA: Harvard University Press. (Original work published 1748)

Lennon, R. T. (1956). Assumptions underlying the use of content validity. *Educational and Psychological Measurement, 16,* 294–304.

Levine, M. (1986). An evolutionary view of the cognitive shift. In B. J. Baars (Ed.), *The cognitive revolutions in psychology* (pp. 223–237). New York: Guilford Press.

Linn, R. L., Graue, M. E., & Sanders, N. M. (1990). Comparing state and district test results to national norms: The validity of the claims that "Everyone is above average." *Educational Measurement: Issues and Practice, 9*(3), 5–14.

Locke, J. (1968). An essay concerning human understanding (excerpt). In R. J. Herrnstein & E. G. Boring (Eds.), *A source book in the history of psychology* (pp. 334–340). Cambridge, MA: Harvard University Press. (Original work published 1700)

Lomov, B. F. (1982). Soviet psychology: Its historical origins and contemporary status. *American Psychologist, 37,* 580–586.

Luria, L. R. (1969). Speech development and the formation of mental processes. In M. Cole & I. Maltzman (Eds.), *A handbook of contemporary Soviet psychology* (pp. 121–162). New York: Basic Books.

Marmor, J., & Woods, S. M. (Eds.). (1980). *The interface between the psychodynamic and behavioral therapies*. New York: Plenum.

Marshall, E. (1986). Science in Japan: School reformers aim at creativity. *Science, 253,* 267–270.

Mason, W. A. (1976). Environmental models and mental modes: Representational processes in great apes and men. *American Psychologist, 31,* 284–294.

Mathews, M. M. (1966). *Teaching to read: Historically considered.* Chicago: University of Chicago Press.

Mathis, B. C., Menges, R. J., & McMillan, J. H. (1977). Content and boundaries of educational psychology. In D. J. Treffinger, J. K. Davis, & R. E. Ripple (Eds.), *Handbook on teaching educational psychology* (pp. 25–43). New York: Academic Press.

McDill, E. L., Natriello, G., & Pallas, A. M. (1985). Raising standards and retaining students: The impact of the reform recommendations on potential dropouts. *Review of Educational Research, 55,* 415–433.

McDougall, W. (1968). Outline of psychology (excerpt). In R. J. Herrnstein & E. G. Boring (Eds.), *A source book in the history of psychology* (pp. 615–618). Cambridge, MA: Harvard University Press. (Original work published 1923)

Means, M. L., & Voss, J. F. (1985). Star wars: A developmental study of expert and novice knowledge structures. *Journal of Memory and Languages, 24,* 746–757.

Mehrens, W. A., & Ebel, R. L. (1979). Some comments on criterion-referenced and norm-referenced achievement tests. *Measurement in Education, 10*(1). Washington, DC: National Council on Measurement in Education.

Mehrens, W. A., & Lehmann, I. J. (1984). *Measurement and evaluation in education and psychology.* New York: Holt, Rinehart & Winston.

Messick, S. (1986). *The once and future issues of validity: Assessing the meaning and consequences of measurement.* Princeton, NJ: Educational Testing Service.

Messick, S. (1989). Validity. In R. L. Linn (Ed.), *Educational measurement* (3rd ed., pp. 13–103). New York: American Council on Education and Macmillan Publishing Company.

Mill, J. (1968). Analysis of the phenomena of the human mind (excerpt). In R. J. Herrnstein & E. G. Boring (Eds.), *A source book in the history of psychology* (pp. 363–377). Cambridge, MA: Harvard University Press. (Original work published 1829)

Mill, J. S. (1962). History of determinism. In M. G. Singer & R. R. Ammerman (Eds.), *Introductory readings in philosophy* (pp. 145–154). New York: Charles Scribner's Sons. (Original work published 1843)

Mill, J. S. (1968). A system of logic (excerpt). In R. J. Herrnstein & E. G. Boring (Eds.), *A source book in the history of psychology* (pp. 377–380). Cambridge, MA: Harvard University Press. (Original work published 1843)

Miller, G. A. (1978). Semantic relations among words. In M. Halle, J. Bresnan, & G. A. Miller (Eds.), *Linguistic theory and psychological reality* (pp. 60–118). Cambridge, MA: Massachusetts Institute of Technology Press.

Montessori, M. (1984). *The secret of childhood.* India: Sangham Press. (Original publication date unknown)

Moore, R. (1974). Imprisoning abstractions. *Contemporary Psychoanalysis, 10,* 503–510.

Morrow, L. M. (1983). Home and school correlates of early interest in literature. *Journal of Educational Research, 76,* 221–230.

Moshman, D. (1990). Rationality as a goal of education. *Educational Psychology Review, 2,* 335–364.

Mott, F. W., & Sherrington, C. S. (1895). Experiments on the influence of sensory nerves upon movement and nutrition of the limbs. *Proceedings of the Royal Society*, 57, 481–488.

Murphy, G., & Kovach, J. K. (1972). *Historical introduction to modern psychology*. New York: Harcourt Brace Jovanovich.

Nagel, E. (1955). Self regulation. In D. Flanagan (Ed.), *Automatic control* (pp. 2–9). New York: Simon & Schuster.

Nagy, W. E., Herman, P. A., & Anderson, R. C. (1985). Learning words from context. *Reading Research Quarterly*, 20(2), 233–253.

New York Times, February 16, 1987, p. 11.

Notterman, J. M. (1970). *Behavior: A systematic approach*. New York: Random House.

Notterman, J. M. (1973). Discussion of on-line computers in the animal laboratory. *Behavioral Research Methods and Instrumentation*, 5, 129–131.

Notterman, J. M. (1985). *Forms of psychological inquiry*. New York: Columbia University Press.

Notterman, J. M., & Mintz, D. E. (1965). *Dynamics of response*. New York: Wiley.

Notterman, J. M., Schoenfeld, W. N., & Bersh, P. J. (1952). Conditioned heart rate response in human subjects during experimental anxiety. *Journal of Comparative and Physiological Psychology*, 45, 1–8.

Notterman, J. M., Tufano, D. R., & Hrapsky, J. S. (1982). Visual-motor organization: Differences between and within individuals. *Perceptual and Motor Skills*, 54, 723–750 (Monograph Supplement 2-V54).

Notterman, J. M. (1985, May). Opening remarks as chair, *Separation, loss, and resolution: The college population*. Panel discussion conducted at the meeting of the American Academy of Psychoanalysis, New York.

Notterman, J. M. (1987). Comments as discussion-evaluator of *The art of psychoanalysis as a technology of instruction* (J. E. Gedo, Presenter). Panel discussion conducted at the meeting of the American Academy of Psychoanalysis, New York.

Pavlov, I. P. (1902). *The work of the digestive glands* (W. H. Thompson, Trans.). Philadelphia: J. B. Lippincott.

Pavlov, I. P. (1968). Lectures on conditioned reflex (excerpt). In R. J. Herrnstein & E. G. Boring (Eds.), *A source book in the history of psychology* (pp. 564–569). Cambridge, MA: Harvard University Press. (Original work published 1928)

Poole, M. E., & Low, B. C. (1982). Who stays? Who leaves? An examination of sex differences in staying and leaving. *Journal of Youth and Adolescence*, 11, 49–63.

Pratt, C. C. (1969). Introduction. In W. Kohler, *The task of gestalt psychology* (pp. 3–29). Princeton, NJ: Princeton University Press.

Quellmalz, E. S. (1986). Writing skills assessment. In R. A. Berk (Ed.), *Performance assessment: Methods and applications* (pp. 492–508). Baltimore: Johns Hopkins University Press.

Razran, G. (1958a). Konstantin Nikolaevich Kornilov, 1879–1957: An obituary. *Science*, 128, 74–75.

Razran, G. (1958b). Soviet psychology and psychophysiology. *Science*, 128, 1187–1194.

Razran, G. (1961). The observable unconscious and the inferable conscious in current Soviet psychophysiology. *Psychological Review*, 68, 81–147.

Rice, J. M. (1969). *The public school system of the United States*. New York: Arno Press. (Original work published 1893)

Richek, M. A. (1977–1978). Readiness skills that predict initial word learning using two different methods of instruction. *Reading Research Quarterly*, 13(2), 209–221.

Ripple, R. E. (1981). Educational psychology as a liberal art. *Contemporary Educational Psychology*, 6, 28–32.

Robinson, D. N. (1981). *An intellectual history of psychology* (rev. ed.). New York: Macmillan.
Robinson, D. N. (1982). *Toward a science of human nature.* New York: Columbia University Press.
Robinson, D. N. (1986a). The Scottish enlightenment and its mixed bequest. *Journal of the History of the Behavioral Sciences, 22,* 171–177.
Robinson, D. N. (1986b). Psychology and the American ideal. Invited address marking centennial of psychology at Colgate University, Hamilton, NY.
Rohlen, T. P. (1985/1986). Japanese education: If they can do it, should we? *American Scholar, Winter,* 29–43.
Rosenblith, W. A. (1970). On cybernetics and the human brain. In J. M. Notterman (Ed.), *Readings in behavior* (pp. 229–238). New York: Random House. (Original work published 1966)
Rosenblueth, A., Weiner, N., & Bigelow, J. (1970). Behavior, purpose, and teleology. In J. M. Notterman (Ed.), *Readings in behavior* (pp. 45–54). New York: Random House. (Original work published 1943)
Rosenthal, R., & Jacobson, L. (1968). *Pygmalion in the classroom.* New York: Holt, Rinehart & Winston.
Rumelhart, D. E. (1977). Toward an interactive model of reading. In S. Dornic (Ed.), *Attention and performance VI* (pp. 573–603). Hillsdale, NJ: Erlbaum.
Russel, W. A., & Jenkins, I. J. (1954). *The Complete Minnesota Norms for Responses to Words from the Kent-Rosanoff Word Association Test.* ONR Tech. Rep. 11, Contract Number N8 ONR-66216.
Rutter, M., Maughan, B., Mortimer, P., & Smith, A. (1979). *Fifteen thousand hours.* Cambridge, MA: Harvard University Press.
Schank, R. C., & Abelson, R. P. (1977). *Scripts, plans, goals, and understanding: An inquiry into human knowledge structures.* Hillsdale, NJ: Erlbaum.
Scheibe, K. E. (1977). Values and value systems. In B. B. Wolman (Ed.), *International encyclopedia of psychiatry, psychology, psychoanalysis, and neurology* (Vol. 11, p. 356). New York: Van Nostrand Reinhold.
Schultz, D. P. (1981). *A history of modern psychology* (3rd ed.). New York: Academic Press.
Scribner, S., & Cole, M. (1981). *A history of modern psychology* (3rd ed.). New York: Academic Press.
Scriven, M. S. (1967). The methodology of evaluation. In R. Tyler, R. Gagné, & M. Scriven (Eds.), *Perspectives of curriculum evaluation.* AERA Monograph Series on Curriculum Evaluation, No. 1. Chicago: Rand-McNally.
Sechenov, I. M. (1968). Reflexes of the brain (excerpt). In R. J. Herrnstein & E. G. Boring (Eds.), *A source book in the history of psychology* (pp. 308–321). Cambridge, MA: Harvard University Press. (Original work published 1863)
Skinner, B. F. (1938). *The behavior of organisms: An experimental analysis.* New York: Appleton-Century.
Skinner, B. F. (1961). Why we need teaching machines. *Harvard Educational Review, 31,* 377–398.
Skinner, B. F. (1963). Reflections of a decade of teaching machines. *Teachers College Record, 65*(2), 183–192.
Skinner, B. F. (1968). *The technology of teaching.* New York: Appleton-Century-Crofts.
Skinner, B. F. (1971). *Beyond freedom and dignity.* New York: Knopf.
Skinner, B. F. (1975). The steep and thorny way to a science of behavior. *American Psychologist, 30,* 42–49.
Skinner, B. F. (1981). Selection by consequences. *Science, 213,* 501–504.
Skinner, B. F. (1984). The shame of American education. *American Psychologist, 39,* 947–954.

Skinner, B. F. (1990). Can psychology be a science of mind? *American Psychologist*, *45*, 1206–1210.

Sloan, D. (1980). Preface. In D. Sloan (Ed.), *Education and values* (pp. 1–6). New York: Teachers College Press.

Smith, F. (1988). *Understanding reading*. Hillsdale, NJ: Erlbaum.

Smith, N. B. (1974). *American reading instruction*. Newark, DE: International Reading Association.

Spigel, I. M. (1965). Problems in the study of visually perceived movement: An introduction. In I. M. Spigel (Ed.), *Readings in the study of visually perceived movement*. New York: Harper & Row.

Spilich, G. J., Vesonder, G. T., Chiesi, H. L., & Voss, J. F. (1979). Text processing of domain-related information for individuals with high and low domain knowledge. *Journal of Verbal Learning and Verbal Behavior*, *18*, 275–290.

Statistical Abstract of the United States. (1991). Washington, DC: U.S. Bureau of the Census.

Stauffer, R. G. (1969). *Directing reading maturity as a cognitive process*. New York: Harper & Row.

Stiggins, R. J. (1987). NCME instructional module on design and development of performance assessments. *Educational Measurement: Issues and Practices*. *6*(3). Washington: National Council on Measurement in Education.

Sulzer-Azaroff, B. (1981). Issues and trends in behavior modification in the classroom. In S. W. Bijon & R. Ruiz (Eds.), *Behavior modification: Contributions to education* (pp. 63–93). Hillsdale, NJ: Erlbaum.

Sutton-Smith, B. (1977). Play and curiosity. In B. B. Wolman (Ed.), *International encyclopedia of psychiatry, psychology, psychoanalysis, and neurology* (Vol. 8, pp. 415–417). New York: Van Nostrand Reinhold.

Terrace, H. S., Petitto, L. A., Sanders, R. J., & Bever, T. G. (1979). Can an ape create a sentence? *Science*, *206*, 891–892.

Thorndike, E. L. (1898). Animal intelligence: An experimental study of the associative process in animals. *Psychological Review Supplements*, *2*(4), Whole No. 8.

Thorndike, R. L., & Hagen, E. (1974). *Measurement and evaluation in psychology and education*. New York: Wiley.

Vygotsky, L. S. (1978). Mind in society: The development of higher psychological processes (Posthumous collection of essays). M. Cole, V. John-Steiner, S. Scribner, & E. Souberman (Eds.). Cambridge, MA: Harvard University Press.

Warner, S. A. (1963). *Teacher*. New York: Bantam Books.

Warren, H. C. (1916). Mental association from Aristotle to Hume. *Psychological Review*, *38*, 87–95.

Watkins, M. J. (1981). Human memory and the information processing metaphor. *Cognition*, *10*, 331–336.

Watson, J. B. (1913). Psychology as the behaviorist views it. *Psychological Review*, *20*, 158–177.

Wertheimer, M. (1945). *Productive thinking*. New York: Harper & Row.

Wertsch, J. V. (1988). L. S. Vygotsky's "new" theory of mind. *American Scholar*, *Winter*, 81–88.

Wiener, E. (1948). *Cybernetics*. New York: Wiley.

Wilson, G. T., & Lazarus, A. A. (1983). Behavior modification and therapy. In B. B. Wolman (Ed.), *The therapist's handbook: Treatment methods of mental disorders* (2nd ed., pp. 121–154). New York: Van Nostrand Reinhold.

Winnicott, D. W. (1965). *The maturational processes and the facilitating environment*. New York: International Universities Press.

Wittrock, M. C., & Farley, F. (Eds.). (1989). *The future of educational psychology*. Hillsdale, NJ: Erlbaum.

Wolman, B. B. (Ed.). (1983). *The therapist's handbook: Treatment methods of mental disorders* (2nd ed.). New York: Van Nostrand Reinhold.

Wolman, B. B. (1989). *Dictionary of behavioral science* (2nd ed.). New York: Academic Press.

Wolpe, I. (1958). *Psychotherapy by reciprocal inhibition*. Stanford, CA: Stanford University Press.

Woodworth, R. S. (1930). Dynamic psychology. In C. Murchison (Ed.), *Psychologies of 1930* (pp. 327–336). Worcester, MA: Clark University Press.

Woodworth, R. S., & Schlosberg, H. (1954). *Experimental psychology* (rev. ed.). New York: Henry Holt.

Woodworth, R. S., & Sheehan, M. R. (1964). *Contemporary schools of psychology* (3rd ed.). New York: Ronald Press.

Yap, K. O. (1979). Vocabulary-building, blocks of comprehension? *Journal of Reading Behavior*, *11*(1), 49–59.

Zaporozhets, A. V. (1960). Origin and development of conscious control of movements in man. In *The central nervous system and behavior: Translations from the Russian medical literature*. Bethesda, MD: NIH, U.S. Public Health Service.

About the Authors

JOSEPH M. NOTTERMAN is Professor of Psychology and past departmental chair at Princeton University, where he has taught since 1956. He served as division editor for experimental psychology in the *International Encyclopedia of Psychiatry, Psychology, Psychoanalysis, and Neurology*, which won the American Library Association award. He is author, most recently, of *Forms of Psychological Inquiry* (1985). Since the mid-1980s, he has taught educational psychology at Princeton, pursuing an interest he started as a student at Trenton State Teachers College in New Jersey. In 1986 he was awarded a senior fellowship by the Office of Educational Research and Improvement (U.S. Department of Education), where he began to work on this book.

HENRY N. DREWRY, an historian, is Program Associate at the Andrew W. Mellon Foundation in New York, New York, in which capacity he is involved in awarding grants in the field of education. Previously he taught for 14 years at Princeton High School and spent 20 years as Director for the Teacher Preparation Program at Princeton University and as a Lecturer in History with the rank of Professor. He is coauthor (with Thomas O'Connor) of *America Is* (1987). In 1964 he received Harvard University's Distinguished Secondary School Teaching Award.

Index